MARY & DAVID MACAREE

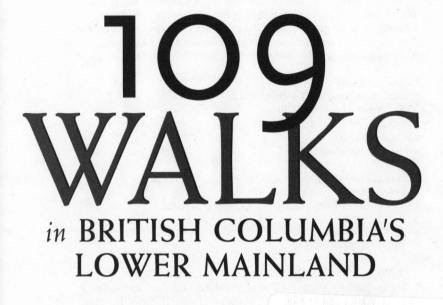

109 WALKS
in BRITISH COLUMBIA'S LOWER MAINLAND

GREY STONE BOOKS
Douglas & McIntyre Publishing Group
VANCOUVER/TORONTO

Fifth edition 2002

Greystone Books
A division of Douglas & McIntyre Ltd.
2323 Quebec Street, Suite 201
Vancouver, British Columbia
Canada V5T 4S7
www.greystonebooks.com

NATIONAL LIBRARY OF CANADA CATALOGUING IN PUBLICATION DATA
Macaree, Mary.
    109 walks in British Columbia's Lower Mainland

    Includes index.
    ISBN 1-55054-906-5

    1. Walking—British Columbia—Lower Mainland—Guidebooks.
2. Trails—British Columbia—Lower Mainland—Guidebooks. 3. Lower
Mainland (B.C.)—Guidebooks. I. Macaree, David. II. Title. III. Title:
One hundred and nine walks in British Columbia's Lower Mainland.
GV199.44.C22B746 2002   917.11'3044   C2002-910258-8

Editing by Naomi Pauls and Lucy Kenward (fifth edition)
Cover and text design by Val Speidel
Cover photograph by P&K Smith/Tony Stone Images
Typeset by Tanya Lloyd Kyi
Interior photographs by Mary Macaree
Maps by Mary Macaree and Gray Mouse Graphics
Printed and bound in Canada by Friesens

Greystone Books is committed to reducing the consumption of
old-growth forests in the books it publishes. This book is one step
toward that goal. It is printed on acid-free paper that is 100%
ancient-forest-free, and it has been processed chlorine free.

We gratefully acknowledge the financial support of the Canada
Council for the Arts, the British Columbia Ministry of Tourism,
Small Business and Culture, and the Government of Canada
through the Book Publishing Industry Development Program
(BPIDP) for our publishing activities.

CONTENTS

KEY TO MAP SYMBOLS

	highway, freeway
	paved road
	street
	unpaved road
	railroad
	described trail
	trail is parallel to road
	walk on road
	other trail
	stairway
	route
	park boundary or other boundary
	power line
	fence
	ski lift
	Trans-Canada highway
99	provincial highway
	gate
	parking area
	large parking lot
(P)	parking and starting point
(i)	information station
	navigational light
	microwave tower
	viewing tower or other tower
	tank, water tower
	lookout
	viewpoint
	large building
	school
	church
	small building, cabin or lodge
	factory
	reservoir
	sports field
	cemetery
	monument
	corral
	campground
	informal campsite
	picnic area
	boat launch ramp
	bridge, boardwalk, trestle
	marsh
	river or stream
	waterfall
	direction of stream flow
	direction of river flow
	body of water

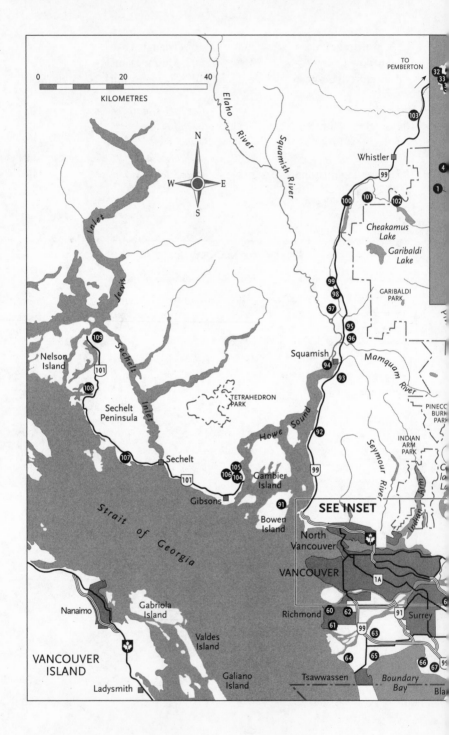

INTRODUCTION

This new edition of *109 Walks* retains, with a few exceptions, the principles established in its predecessors: the walks described are generally less than 4 hours; elevation gains, if any, are moderate, and routes are clearly established; and, with the exception of Vancouver itself and West Vancouver, in each area walks nearer the city centre precede those farther afield. Descriptions, both verbal and graphic, record the state of affairs at the time of publication. However, you should be on the alert for possible subsequent changes due to human intervention and/or natural disasters. Houses, schools and shopping malls spring up where once was freedom to roam; flash floods and washouts are all too commonplace given this area's climate and topography.

We focus on walks close to the region's population centres, Vancouver and its neighbouring municipalities, though we also provide for those of you who want to sample the trails in the vicinity of campgrounds or combine country excursions with walks. (See "Other Destinations" at the back of the book.) Many walks are accessible by public transport, especially within the metropolitan area, and study of the transit system (or a telephone call to TransLink's information line, 604-953-3333) will often suggest a one-way in preference to the out-and-back walk required of those captive to their cars. For all outings, we mention approaches, provide liberal time allotments and, in the case of the longer walks, suggest intermediate destinations. When distances of less than a kilometre are supplied in the text, they are given in metres only, as one yard is roughly equivalent to one metre. Please note that distance alone is not a sufficient guide: the state of a trail and its ups and downs are important factors in determining how long a walk will take, and thus we have included elevation gains of 150 m (490 ft) or more. Note also that the weather and seasonal variations may affect the "Best" period suggested for any walk, more particularly in rural areas. Be prepared, therefore, when hiking in forest or on mountain, to abandon any outing if you find conditions beyond your capabilities or the daylight hours too short to permit your safe return.

We are pleased to record the appearance of new walks as well as the refurbishing of some old favourites. Lately the idea of the long-distance trail has sparked popular imagination; thus the 1971 Baden-Powell Centennial Trail from Horseshoe Bay to Deep Cove has been succeeded more recently by the more ambitious Trans Canada Trail, and the distinctive TCT markers now appear along many familiar routes. Another fairly recent positive trend has been the increased involvement of public bodies in trail creation and maintenance, supplementing the activities of outdoor clubs and individuals. B.C. Parks, regional districts and the B.C. Forest Service are joined in their activities by municipal boards and even B.C. Hydro. An unexpected spin-off from SkyTrain a decade ago was the creation of B.C. Parkway, one element of which is John Molson Way, spanning the 21 km (13 mi) between Vancouver's Main Street and New Westminster Quay, with scenic features en route devised by the area's cultural communities. At the short end of the distance scale, imaginative green strips and trail systems have been designed in new residential neighbourhoods and augment facilities in municipal parks, themselves expanding opportunities for the walker.

Should you seek company on the trail, the Federation of Mountain Clubs of B.C. (604-878-7007) will provide information about outdoor clubs, and many community centres sponsor walking groups. If, on the other hand, you wish to go out informally with a few friends, you have many aids to assist you. Major provincial, regional and municipal parks often supply brochures at their entrances, as does B.C. Hydro at its recreation sites. A useful publication produced by TransLink is its *Transportation Services Guide for Greater Vancouver* (available from 7-Eleven and Safeway stores), as well as its many schedules for the various muncipalities (available in public libraries). Tourist infocentres, too, and many municipalities now produce leaflets describing opportunities for walking within their

boundaries. As well, most organizations today have Web sites with more or less up-to-date, more or less useful information.

In addition, you may wish to have a basic stock of maps, including the two *Citimaps: Vancouver also including Whistler* and *Fraser Valley also including Whistler* published by Rand McNally and free to members from the British Columbia Automobile Association. A good selection of recreation maps, as well as the federal topographic map series, is available from International Travel Maps & Books, 530 West Broadway, Vancouver, B.C. V5Z 1E9 (604-879-3621).

Part of the pleasure of walking is combining it with other pursuits: bird and animal watching, the study of rocks, flowers, fungi, trees and other natural features, plus local history as represented in various restored buildings, old roads and abandoned rights-of-way. All these, along with the health-giving effects of exercise, are yours for a minimal expenditure on books or equipment. Necessary, of course, are stout boots or shoes, well broken in, and suitable cloth-

ing for this province's changeable weather. You will want food and liquid for all but the shorter walks, and sunscreen has become a constant necessity in these days of the thinning ozone layer. You will want sunglasses and, last but not least, a first-aid kit to take care of accidents, though these are no more likely on a woodland walk than on our downtown streets.

Outdoor etiquette requires that you do not damage trails by cutting corners, and you will, of course, leave gates as you find them. In fact, please leave all property, public and private, undisturbed, and carry out any garbage, leaving the surroundings unspoiled for others to enjoy. These few injunctions aside, the freedom of the trails is yours.

To end on a personal note: a book such as this could not have come into being had not

we, the authors, received the assistance of many others, friends and casual informants, as well as representatives of numerous official bodies. To all of these I must express my sincere thanks for their patience and the hope that the resulting product will give them the sense that their time was not ill-spent. Our wish has always been that this labour of love provides pleasure to all who use it.

1 UBC GARDENS

| Round trip 9 km (5.6 mi) | Allow 3 hours |
| Paths and roads | Good all year |

At the entrance to Main Garden.

The University of British Columbia, despite its superb setting, provides a minimum of inspiring architecture. For this reason, a campus walk is best fashioned through its various gardens and along treed avenues, where, especially in spring and summer, art and nature are in harmony.

With public transport, you begin from the bus loop at the intersection of University Boulevard and East Mall, while visitors' parking is available nearby. From either arrival point, walk north on East Mall and head for the gardens in front of the Main Library before rising to Main Mall, the new plate-glass Koerner Library now before you a striking contrast to the old buildings of the original university core. Turn right along the tree-shaded avenue towards the flagpole, with its magnificent marine and mountain view, and below, the glories of a formal rose garden.

From the viewpoint, descend through the garden, veering right by the rotund Chan Performing Arts Centre before crossing S.W. Marine Drive and going left past Green College and then right into Cecil Green Park itself, with its attractive grounds and fine view. Next make your way west and south along the cliff top opposite the Museum of Anthropology, then turn left behind Haida House and its totems to arrive in front of the museum. Cross S.W. Marine Drive here onto West Mall and take a path between the C. K. Choi Building and International House leading you through tall trees to the temple-like Asian Centre with the Pacific Bell in its courtyard. A few steps more bring you to the Japanese Nitobe Memorial Garden (admission fee in season).

Next, go south along Lower Mall, passing on your left the old arboretum with the First Nations House of Learning in its midst, and on your right the

Place Vanier complex. Continuing thus, cross the end of University Boulevard, pass St. John's College and two federal research laboratories, and make your way towards Totem Park Residences where, on the far side of a little woodland, you turn right towards S.W. Marine Drive. Now going southeast, walk alongside that busy thoroughfare en route to the Main Garden (admission fee in season), which includes outstanding collections in its Asian, Alpine, B.C. Native, Physick, and Food Gardens. Do not enter if you are pressed for time, for there are many diverse attractions over which you will wish to linger.

After this happy interlude, return along Marine Drive as far as the Totem Park tennis courts, where you may cut through on residence pathways to West Mall and Agronomy Road and thus to Main Mall, on which you turn north for the last lap of your trip. Presently, on the left, you pass the Barn, rescued and restored for its role as cafeteria when the farm moved to the south campus; and, on the right, another piece of university history, Fairview Grove, a commemoration of UBC's first home.

Continuing northwards you come to the intersection with University Boulevard, with the bus terminal visible to your right. But, to delay your departure from the groves of academe, you may continue your walk along Main Mall, passing the university's simple War Memorial before returning to your starting point by going right through the library gardens to East Mall, perhaps taking refreshment in the Student Union Building (SUB) en route to bus or car.

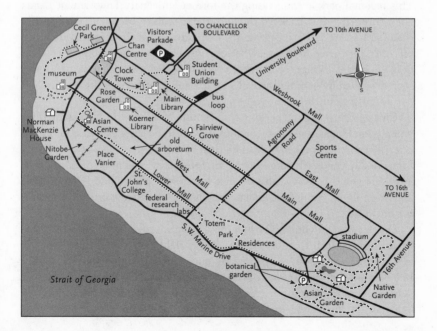

2 PACIFIC SPIRIT REGIONAL PARK

north to south:	Round trip 8 km (5 mi)	Allow 3 hours
east to west:	Round trip 5.5 km (3.4 mi)	Allow 2.5 hours
	Trails	Good all year

Imperial Trail in winter.

This regional park encompassing the former University Endowment Lands has a surprising drawback for the uninitiated walker: too many trails rather than too few. At first glance even the map provided at the information office off West 16th Avenue is somewhat overwhelming. To help you get started, here are two walks, one from north to south, the other from east to west, each described by naming the trails used, names celebrating the history and natural history of the area.

For the former, a good parking spot is on Blanca Street just north of 16th, where Vine Maple Trail takes you into the forest, meeting Newt Loop shortly after. Then Newt is taken over in its turn by Lily of the Valley after crossing Salal. Finally you reach your major trail, Salish, after one more path crossing. Turn left (south). On Salish you first intersect a power line (Heron Trail) and, beyond one more fork, must cross busy 16th Avenue prior to continuing on Salish.

On this part of your walk, you cross Zeke's Bridge over a small stream, then at a fork with Hemlock Trail you stay right and cross Council Trail to arrive at the wide clearing of Imperial, once a road but now reverting nicely to lane condition, the illusion of rusticity spoiled only by the power line that runs along it. Here you must go left for a short distance before picking up Salish again. Turn right on it, plunging once more into the forest. At last, however, the sound of traffic disturbs your sylvan idyll, the signal that you are reaching S.W. Marine Drive, and here you leave the trail that you have followed so long, going left to pick up Clinton, then, on the verge of a wide clearing, forking left again on Sasamat, your main return route. On it you recross Imperial, reach a covered reservoir and, having skirted its edge, go briefly left on Top Trail before emerging on 16th again, a short distance from where you started.

For the other outing, drive south off 16th on Imperial Road until, at a divider, it breaks back sharply to become 29th Avenue. Park here and set off along the one-time road beyond the barrier, gently descending, and perhaps noting the two segments of Salish Trail as you pass them. Where the power line you have been following goes straight ahead, you veer off left, the forest deepening around you. The disembodied voice that you may hear need not disturb you; it is merely the public-address system of TRIUMF, tri-university meson facility. But before that installation has come into sight, you have turned left on Sword Fern, to emerge unexpectedly on S.W. Marine Drive just opposite Simon Fraser's monument.

Here, at the top of the sheer drop to the North Arm of the river that bears Fraser's name, you have a view of the deltaic lowlands and the southern Gulf Islands. Now recross S.W. Marine Drive and return on Sword Fern as the start of your way back. This time, however, stay with the trail when it crosses Imperial and stay with it as it intersects two more routes, Long and Powerline, before you yourself turn right on Council Trail, which, most accommodatingly, takes you back to your starting point.

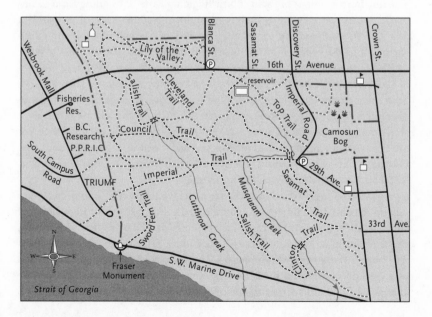

3 CHANCELLOR WOODS

shorter circuit:	Round trip 3.9 km (2.4 mi)	Allow 1 hour
longer circuit:	Round trip 6 km (3.7 mi)	Allow 2 hours
	Trails	Good all year

Sunshine-dappled forest path.

The northern segment of Pacific Spirit Regional Park—extending from Chancellor Boulevard to Spanish Banks—contains a number of trails, mostly in forest. There is, however, considerable variety of tree cover, some quite deep ravines, and the beach if you want an alternative route for part of the way.

The trail system lends itself to circular walks, so described here are two of them, starting from the same point and in part covering the same ground. Your point of departure, at the break in Chancellor Boulevard, allows you to park off a main thoroughfare; it is convenient for buses also, being only a short distance west of Blanca Loop. If driving, turn west off Blanca Street onto Chancellor Boulevard and drive to road's end at a large mound. Just beyond, Chancellor is reborn, connecting with West 4th Avenue on a considerable bend. Cross here to the north side.

Now take Spanish Trail into the forest, travelling north among tall trees, second-growth though they are, as the great stumps of the original forest show. Thus you proceed in the midst of fine cedar, Douglas-fir and hemlock, the trail dropping gently as you advance until, after some 20 minutes, you find yourself at a three-way junction. The little track beyond the stile takes you into an overgrown field, the remains of a pioneer homestead on the "Plains of Abraham." Cross to the seaward side and, if you do not wish to drop to the beach here, turn left to head west close to the edge of the bluffs on Admiralty Trail. Next comes a deep ravine, and here is the parting of the ways; the left-hand trail gives a short outing of 3.9 km (2.4 mi) that takes about an hour, while the right-hand branch descends into the depths.

The shorter route follows the ravine's eastern edge fairly closely, though it is forced away from the main canyon by washouts here and there. As you head inland, you begin to hear traffic and you find yourself back on the boulevard some distance west of where you started. To return, you may use the pedestrian sidewalk on the south side; however, an attractive alternative presents itself if you take the forest trail (Pioneer) into the woods opposite. Follow this for some 300 m to a cross trail and go left. At the next fork, go left again and you are back near your point of departure.

On the longer loop, you drop into the ravine, necessitating a climb out of it again if you wish to continue on the bluffs. You may, however, avoid this by crossing N.W. Marine Drive and walking along the beach until the road starts uphill. A little above the Acadia Beach parking lot, recross to the landward side and pick up Salish Trail heading inland past the west end of Admiralty Trail. Now you proceed above another deep gully until you emerge by University Hill Elementary School, with Chancellor Boulevard just ahead of you.

Use the pedestrian crossing and stay with Salish south to its intersection with Spanish Trail, then go left. This track goes through scrub timber and crosses a creek before entering nice open forest. Here you are joined by the short route on Pioneer Trail and henceforth the two routes coincide, with the next fork left bringing you back to houses and transportation.

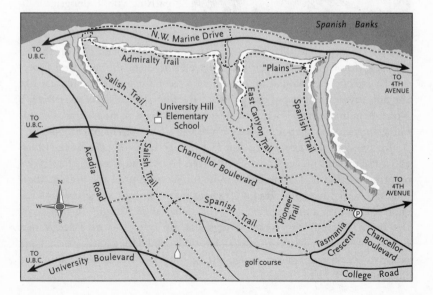

4 POINT GREY

Round trip 13 km (8 mi)   Allow 4.5 hours
Beach, paths and trails   Good all year

Steps on Trail #3.

Here is a circuit that you may shorten or lengthen according to your inclination, thanks to various trails connecting the beach with the cliff top near UBC. Your starting point is at Acadia Beach parking lot west of Spanish Banks, where N.W. Marine Drive begins its rise towards the university. (The Spanish Banks bus terminus is some 20 minutes' walk to the east.)

First you wander west along the beach, then after about 25 minutes, by an old searchlight tower, comes Trail #3, the ascent of which, with a turn left at the top onto the path downhill alongside Marine Drive, gives you a short circular tour with views of mountain and city on the return leg. If you stay on the beach, you see evidence of the sometimes spectacular effects of erosion as you make for a second wartime installation like the first tower, then round the point for the first sight of the Fraser River's North Arm breakwater. Here you have a second flight of steps, Trail #4, this one giving access to a point just south of UBC's Museum of Anthropology.

To complete this circuit of 5 km (3.1 mi), go left along the track behind the museum and proceed past Cecil Green House and Green College via a one-time section of Marine Drive to its intersection with the present thoroughfare near the top of Trail #3, whence you take the same route as the shorter walk. Yet a third option is to continue a short distance farther along the beach to Trail #6, which brings you up opposite the Place Vanier Residences. This time you turn back left on Marine Drive until, just beyond Norman Mackenzie House, you go left again to join the earlier trail behind the museum.

If you are really ambitious and are not deterred by numerous downed trees and other obstacles, make for Wreck Beach itself, working along the bottom of the treed slope on a rough route that skirts the mud flats and salt marshes to reach the next access point, Trail #7, the original Wreck Beach Trail. Ignore this, however, for it leads only to the old Marine Drive, almost as busy in summer as the new, and continue along a pleasant stretch of trail shaded by large cedar, fir, hemlock and maple trees until you come to a fork, the left branch angling gently uphill on Booming Ground Trail to emerge at the Simon Fraser Monument.

Cross S.W. Marine Drive from the east end of the parking lot and reenter forest on the Sword Fern Trail, which, with a few interruptions, goes clear across Pacific Spirit Regional Park. Stay with Sword Fern, then, as it crosses Imperial, Long, Powerline and Council Trails in succession before it is absorbed temporarily by Salish, which you follow to 16th Avenue. Now, though you might jog left here to regain Sword Fern, which continues along the margin of the forest, your best plan is to stay with Salish as it winds its way towards University Boulevard, on the far side of which it continues, to be reunited with Sword Fern a little short of Chancellor Boulevard. Cross this thoroughfare and enter the trees again beyond the primary school, a verdant ravine on your left as you near N.W. Marine Drive and the parking lot.

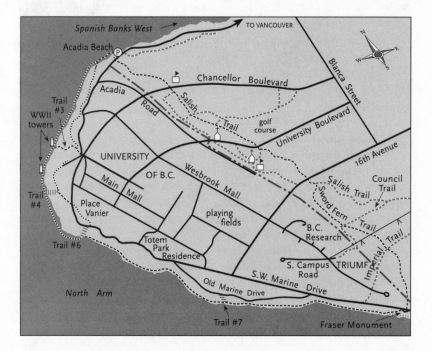

5 JERICHO PARK/ SPANISH BANKS

Round trip 6 km (3.7 mi)	Allow 2 hours
Trails and streets	Good all year

Lagoon in Jericho Park.

Spared from residential development, Jericho Park, a pocket wilderness north of West 4th Avenue between Wallace Street and N.W. Marine Drive, was opened to the public when the Department of National Defence relinquished it several decades ago. At that time, a whole stretch of parkland fronting English Bay became available to walkers. Nor are you confined to one route: walks of varying length are possible; even round trips along streets of stately Point Grey dwellings are feasible.

To make the most of what this area has to offer, begin not in Jericho Park proper but at the Hastings Mill Store Museum at the end of Alma just north of where it meets Point Grey Road. (The nearest bus stop is at 4th and Alma.) The unpretentious wooden building is a relic of Vancouver's earliest days: built in 1865 by Capt. Edward Stamp, it served as the first post office, community library and recreation centre on Burrard Inlet.

Starting here, cross little Pioneer Park and head west past the Royal Vancouver Yacht Club and Jericho Tennis Club before swinging past Brock House Senior Centre (once the Brock family home) towards the beach and a small Park Board pavilion. From now on, you have the North Shore mountains across the bay on your right and Bowen Island more or less ahead as you step, on the seaward side of a small lagoon, towards what is left of the old Jericho army base, now the Jericho Sailing Centre. Once past it, continue half left towards a grove of trees, and you come to a second pavilion, at Locarno Beach.

This landmark may serve as the destination of a short walk (round trip about one hour); however, if you wish to go farther, there is nothing to stop you. Make your way, then, to Spanish Banks East, with its refreshment counter and changing rooms. Here, too, you may turn around. An interesting alternative presents itself, though, if you do not wish to return by your outward route.

Across N.W. Marine Drive from the bus loop you will note a flight of steps ascending the steep bank on the landward side. These bring you out at the foot of Blanca Street, and a short walk uphill leads to a five-way intersection. This point you may also reach by a slightly longer route if, from Spanish Banks East, you continue westwards on the waterfront to about halfway along the parking lot, where another set of stairs ascends to emerge on Belmont Avenue. Turning left along this street of majestic homes takes you to the five-way crossing where you go half right onto Bellevue and down West 2nd, passing Aberthau, a one-time gracious home, now a community centre. From here, recross N.W. Marine Drive and return across Jericho Park, this time taking the track south of the lagoon, perhaps pausing a little to watch the wildlife in its vicinity, before heading back towards Pioneer Park and the end of your excursion.

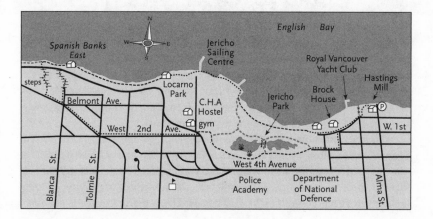

6 ENGLISH BAY

Round trip 13 km (8 mi) or less	Allow 4 hours
Paths and ferry	Good all year

Heritage Harbour.

Here, in one of Vancouver's most attractive areas, you have a walk that may be as long as a 13-km (8-mi) lung-expander or, if you elect to do only the West End part and do not cross the ferry to Granville Island, a gentle stroll of less than half that distance. You may even make it a leisurely one-way walk by using the public bus service for your return.

Walking from north to south, you begin in Stanley Park at the end of Beach Avenue, along which there are several parking lots (or bus stops) that you could use to shorten the walk. Once on foot, your route is along the seawall towards Burrard Bridge, passing the tall inukshuk occupying its own little green space on your right. Then, near the Aquatic Centre is the ferry terminal with boats to Granville Island and, in summer and on weekends the rest of the year, to the Maritime Museum close to Kitsilano Point.

Embark for Granville Island, and once there, head past Bridges Restaurant, following the south shore round to the causeway, which you cross under the shadow of Granville Bridge. Now proceed west, townhouses and gardens on one side, a marina on the other, to Burrard Bridge and Vanier Park, a spot favoured by kite enthusiasts. Here you continue along the shoreline, the mountains of the North Shore before you and, closer to hand on your right, the Heritage Harbour, with the Vancouver Museum and the Maritime Museum successively on your left.

As you move round the point and through Hadden Park, Kitsilano Pool appears, and you may note the parking area (or beyond it Cornwall Avenue and its bus route) if you wish to do this walk in reverse from another of its intermediate points. If you want to go farther, you continue round the bay, now on a narrow path below houses and above the beach, until a flight of steps takes you up to the level of Point Grey Road, here a quiet residential street.

Now head back, first through Kitsilano Park, then Hadden and Vanier back to Granville Island, with its market to distract you as you make for the return ferry. This you may reach either directly or by a counterclockwise detour over Lookout Hill to East Point and round by Sea Village, with its colourful assortment of house boats. Of course, you will miss all these and more if you choose to use the alternative ferry service from the Maritime Museum or take the bus back across Burrard Bridge.

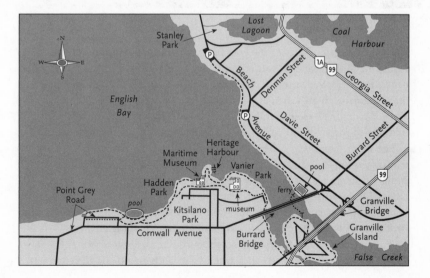

7 FALSE CREEK

Round trip 10 km (6.2 mi)   Allow 2.5 hours
Paths and ferry   Good all year

View under Burrard Bridge.

Urban redevelopment over the past few years has rescued this core-city area from the blight that had settled on it during its industrial age. Thus it has become of renewed interest to walkers, indeed to all people pursuing outdoor activities in an urban environment, providing as it does something for almost everyone—from a children's adventure playground to theatres, from markets to marinas and parks, with a fine stretch of seawall thrown in.

There are many ways to reach Granville Island from downtown Vancouver, one being by Aquabus from the False Creek Ferries terminal near the Aquatic Centre on Beach Avenue. You may even vie for a parking spot on the island itself with all the other visitors, but for the walks described here, approach the area at its east end from West 6th Avenue by the Charleson Park entry, where there is a bus loop and visitors' parking.

For an overview of the whole neighbourhood, turn west from here along Sawyers Lane, then go left on a track that leads up to the development's highest point, the top of an attractive Japanese-style garden, with a waterfall at your feet flowing to a placid lake below. And the views beyond are even more arresting, with the stark landscape of the inner city looming across False Creek set against a backdrop of the North Shore mountains.

Now make your way to water's edge and follow the shore east past Stamp's Landing and a residential area until, at Cambie Bridge, you may note a possible shortcut: a stairway joining the footpath that takes you to the north side. If, however, you wish to make a circuit of the whole creek, stay with the seawall walk as it takes you past the last vestiges of False Creek's industrial era towards the Science World globe at the easternmost extremity of your walk.

Now you turn west, making for the towering Concord Pacific developments via B.C. Place and the Plaza of Nations to where the route over Cambie Bridge joins. From here you remain at the water's edge until, at the head of a little bay, you may wish to make a detour along Davie Street to visit the Roundhouse, a historic building renovated to serve as a community centre. Here, too, you may pay your respects to old CPR Engine No. 374 before continuing westwards past David Lam Park to resume your walk along the shoreline, only briefly leaving it to skirt the False Creek Yacht Club property.

Next, cross False Creek by ferry from the foot of Hornby Street or farther west from near the Aquatic Centre. On Granville Island, make your way east past the sights and sounds of the busy market, past the cluster of floating homes called Sea Village, round or over Lookout Hill to the little footbridge and the final stretch along the south shore to your transport.

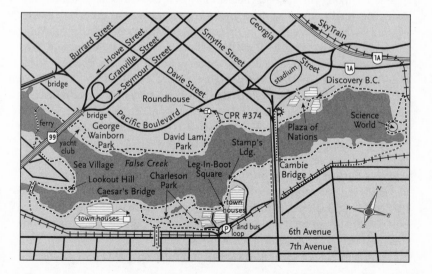

8 STANLEY PARK

Round trip 7 km (4.3 mi) Allow 2 hours
Trails and paths Good all year

West End beyond Lost Lagoon.

For a circuit taking in many features of Stanley Park while leaving some trails for further exploration on your own, try this walk beginning from the Ceperley Park parking lot near the west entrance off Beach Avenue, easily accessible by car or bus.

Make for the seawall to sample one of its most picturesque sections, running north along the shore of English Bay past Second Beach. At the same time, you surely do not wish to plod mechanically round the whole length of the seawall, crowded as it is. Instead, ascend the steps at Ferguson Point to emerge on top of the low cliff opposite the Teahouse Restaurant. Stay close to the cliff's edge, keeping the sea on your left as far as possible, a rule to follow on this stretch to Prospect Point.

The first point of interest is the roughly hewn stone monument to Pauline Johnson, a poet who loved the park, gave Lost Lagoon its name and was thus commemorated following her death in 1913. Having paid your respects, continue along the sidewalk to the Third Beach parking lot, remaining on the landward side of the pavilion in order to pick up Merilees Trail, which runs along the top of the cliffs. From this trail, you catch fleeting views through the trees over the bay to Point Atkinson and Bowen Island. Particularly spectacular is Siwash Rock, seen from the old coastal defence platform that now serves as a lookout point; you may even see a cormorant or some other seabird perched on the rock.

Past the rock, stay with the trail as it works its way round to the northeast in a forest of Douglas-fir, cedar and hemlock, finally rising via a flight of steps to a higher level and eventually coming out on Stanley Park Drive a little south of Prospect Point. Even now, you have no need to pound the sidewalk; cross the road and follow a trail north through the bush to emerge opposite the café. Here you may pause for refreshments, look down at First Narrows, examine the walking beam of the old ss *Beaver* or contemplate the basalt dyke that helped to create the headland by resisting erosion.

To resume, take Eldon Trail downhill from the west side of the café, going under the Lions Gate Bridge and, after dropping to the seawall, meeting the park road near its junction with Pipeline Road. Leave the seawall again, cross the main road and start on the path to the right of Pipeline Road, then go left at the first opportunity onto a track paralleling that road. Next take Hanson, the second trail on the right, which plunges you into some satisfactorily dark forest, with yet one more left taking you to Beaver Lake, with its profusion of marsh plants and bird life.

It is immaterial whether you go round the lake to left or right, though right is shorter; the trails rejoin on the lake's south side. There, turn south onto Lake Trail, which leads through a fine stretch of forest. Now, approaching the settled part of the park, go first left, then right, with one more dog-leg left to take you past the rose garden and on towards the underpass of Stanley Park Causeway. Now you may go along either shore of Lost Lagoon, home of myriad waterfowl, crossing the meadow on its west side to reach the park road and your starting point.

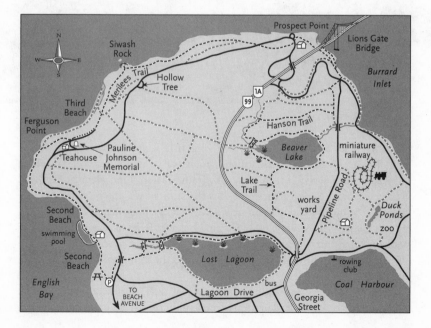

9 RENFREW TRIANGLE

Round trip 5 km (3.1 mi)   Allow 2 hours
Trails and sidewalks   Good all year

Tai chi in Ravine Park.

No, this is not a tale of illicit passion! The title simply indicates that this is a walk with three clearly identifiable points of reference, any one of which may serve as a start: 29th Avenue SkyTrain Station, John Hendry Park and Renfrew Ravine Park. Farthest south is the station, which you may reach by SkyTrain or by bus, though you may drive to its vicinity just as easily, a small park lying just to the west of it. Should you start from here, you first follow Molson Way north, gradually descending and in the process enjoying the wide sweep from Bowen Island in the west to the twin peaks of Golden Ears in the east.

Molson Way is a walking trail, part of B.C. Parkway, that follows SkyTrain for much of its length, its route punctuated by parkway features, many of which represent the local community's ethnic mixture and give an excuse to pause along the way. On your way to John Hendry Park, with its centrepiece, Trout Lake, you must cross Nanaimo Street, after which comes one such feature, the Filipino Garden, a charming little piazza with a traditional arched entrance. Thereafter, your route changes to the east side of the elevated tracks, then parts company with the transit line at Lakewood Drive as you head for John Hendry Park. There you may choose the slightly longer track round the west side of Trout Lake, perhaps dropping in at the community centre en route.

From the northeast corner of the lake, walk eastwards out of the park onto 15th Avenue, on which you recross Nanaimo to the second park of your outing, Beaconsfield. Head diagonally across the park to its southeast corner and another short stretch of residential street, with 18th Avenue bringing you to a crossing of Renfrew Street and the north end of Ravine Park. Your direction now is upstream (south), until, after passing yet another community centre, you must rise to a busy intersection, which you cross to the diagonal southwest corner of 22nd Avenue and Renfrew Diversion.

From here you continue upstream, but at road level, the ravine below on your right, first on a lane, then with a short stretch of trail taking you to a crossing of upper Still Creek, a name that is hardly appropriate for it on this part of its journey to Burnaby Lake. Once on its west side, you may turn left at Atlin, on which, after a block, you find yourself back at 29th a little to the east of your start. Beside you is another parkway feature, the plaza created by Vancouver's German community, with its touch of nostalgia for veterans of World War II: a lamp standard reminiscent of the one Lili Marlene stood under by the barrack gate waiting in vain for her lover. Maybe this walk has its touch of passion after all.

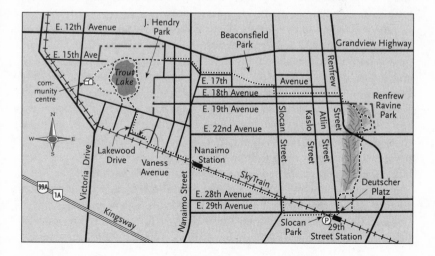

10 CHAMPLAIN HEIGHTS

Round trip 8 km (5 mi)   Allow 2 hours
Paths and trails   Good all year

Morning Glory blossoms.

The east side of Vancouver is not very well endowed with parks. For this reason, it is pleasant to discover in the city's southeast sector a little urban wilderness, Everett Crowley Park, the name commemorating a pioneer Vancouver dairyman and supporter of the area. Nor need you confine your walk to the park alone. The neighbourhood has been laid out for walking, with paths winding through wide grass pleasances and groves of trees.

One suggestion is to turn south off East 49th Avenue a short distance west of Boundary Road onto Arlington Street and to park alongside Sparwood Park, where a track heads off east between the Champlain Villas and a line of trees. Next cut across the grass past Champlain Heights Elementary School, turn right briefly on Frontenac, then go right again on Hurst, a cul-de-sac to the south of the school. From here a path veers left, crossing Matheson Crescent to the beginning of Red Alder Walk, your route through this little urban maze, the trail names telling you something of the present tree cover. At the first fork where left goes to White Birch Trail, stay right, then go left at the next three forks, then right, left, and right again, continuing ever downhill until you pass a small playground and emerge on Champlain Crescent beside a convenience store just below Riel Place.

Cross Champlain to Grey Gum Trail and follow it to a fork where you turn down left to cross two footbridges. After the second footbridge, ascend a

bark-mulch trail on the right into Everett Crowley Park and a choice of circuits. If you go right at the first T-junction, then right again, you may follow
the ravine, with a side trip to investigate Avalon Pond before continuing your
tour west along the northern perimeter, the backs of houses on 62nd Avenue
on your right. Then just after you turn south, you pass a road entrance coming from a parking lot on Kerr Street just south of 63rd Avenue, the access
point if you intend to confine your outing to the park itself.

Next, unless you want to make the short detour left to ascend Mount
Everett, a manmade hill affording a view of the park, continue south to the
escarpment above the Fraser lowlands and, turning east, enjoy three viewpoints from which you see the southern islands of the Strait of Georgia, and
Mount Baker majestic in the southeast. Next, soon after the third viewpoint,
go left, then left again to join the Champlain Loop, which circles Mount
Everett. Go right here, never deviating until you reach the northern perimeter
of the park once more. A final right turn brings you to a small open area with
a platform before which you go left on the path leading out of the park onto
Butler, the continuation of 62nd Avenue. This takes you past a sports field and
a recreation centre to the edge of Captain Cook Park, into which your path
leads just opposite Rosemont Drive. Finally, cross Champlain Crescent and
follow the path along Arlington back to Sparwood Park and your vehicle.

Incidentally, the earlier mention of Kerr Street may evoke from older
Vancouverites recollection of the city dump. Well, Everett Crowley Park was
that very site, now risen phoenix-like from the waste. If you like black-
berries, this park sports a prolific crop of them, interspersed with a healthy
growth of morning glory.

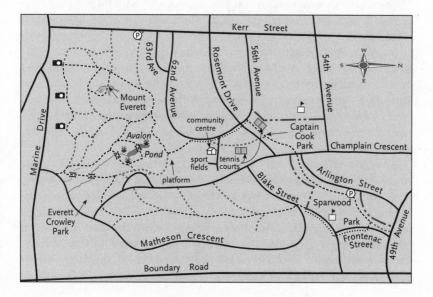

11 BURNABY HEIGHTS/ TRANS CANADA TRAIL

Round trip 5 mi (3.1 mi)	Allow 2 hours
Trails and roads	Good all year

View across Burrard Inlet.

North Burnaby is blessed in its rolling topography, with numerous little eminences to provide vantage points over city, sea and mountain; it is doubly blessed in its many little parks and green spaces with their vistas of the distant North Shore mountains, from The Lions to Golden Ears and its neighbours.

To reach the beginning of this walk, you drive over one such hill going from Hastings Street north on Boundary Road, the whole of Burrard Inlet and its surroundings in front of you as you descend to road's end at little Bates Park. On foot, start your walk at the west end of the park to savour views of the road and railway bridges across the Second Narrows and, beyond their approaches, of the sprawling elevators of the Cascadia Terminal on the waterfront below.

Soon joined by the Trans Canada Trail as it heads eastwards, your route runs north of the houses of Burnaby Heights, while on the left a narrow strip of deciduous forest grows down to water's edge and, in summer, permits only glimpses of the ridges and valleys across the inlet through the leafy screen. Still, as compensation, there are notice boards and photos to inform you about life on the waterfront in its early days. Then your distant views improve but, replacing the forest on your seaward side, the foreground is now a Chevron "tank farm" as you make your way across two little parks to

North Willingdon Avenue, busy with gasoline trucks. Ignoring the TCT signs and starting opposite Eton Street, head east on a rough track north of the miniature-railway compound to join the Penzance Nature Trail in the relatively untouched section of Confederation Park, not far from its western end beside the Rainbow Creek Station. Thus going right offers you a quick escape from nature to the trim bowling lawns, picnic grounds and play areas of the urban precincts south of Penzance Drive.

The more rewarding choice, to the left, is about a kilometre longer and winds through rich second-growth forest. It drops to just above the water's edge, unfortunately separated from the park by the CP Railway line, with only one or two viewpoints to reveal the beauties beyond. But there is plenty of interest by the path itself in the varied undergrowth and enormous cedar stumps, nurses to a new generation. Rising again, your trail emerges on Penzance Drive opposite a dead-end street on the margin of Confederation Park's more developed section, and at this point you may depart from the Burnaby Scenic Trail, leaving the eastern leg for another day (see Walk 12).

Accordingly, cross the road and make your way over the grass in the direction of the picnic area to enjoy the fine views to the northwest, The Lions as centrepiece, before returning to Penzance Drive, there to decide whether to descend the Nature Trail briefly and retrace the unimproved track to Eton Street or to make straight for Willingdon and thus to Eton and a return by your outward route.

A point to note, however: if you travel by bus, your reward is freedom to make a one-way trip along the whole 5.5-km (3.5-mi) Burnaby Scenic Trail, with transport convenient to both ends (see Walk 12).

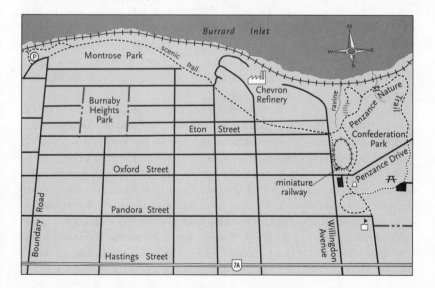

12 CAPITOL HILL

Round trip 6.5 km (4 mi)   Allow 2.5 hours
Elevation gain 150 m (490 ft)
Trails and streets   Good most of the year

Monument in Confederation Park.

Hastings Street, the face that North Burnaby presents to the casual passerby, does not rate high for attractiveness. No, the beauties of the area have to be sought out away from that bustling thoroughfare. And what better destination than Capitol Hill via the Burnaby Scenic/Trans Canada Trail?

To reach this mecca, you may start from Kensington Park, from its north side at the corner of Fell Avenue and Frances Street, one block south of Hastings Street. Better still, drive along the more attractive Curtis (called Parker farther west), the next through street south of Hastings, and turn into the park's southern parking lot between the golf course and the ice rink. Buses are convenient for both approaches as well.

Starting from the south side, make your way along a path west of the playing fields to the north parking area, then cut diagonally through a little woodland to emerge just opposite the sign for the Burnaby Scenic Trail/TCT on Hastings Street. Cross as best you can to where the trail begins on the west side of an oil refinery, the latter fortunately hidden from view by a line of trees. Next comes a stretch of dead-end road, then, from the end of another street, you find yourself entering an area of second-growth forest. As you proceed, ignore successive trails coming from the left, before finally you step out on the quiet Penzance Drive. You are, however, not finished with forest yet. On your right, a short distance to the west, lies Confederation Park's Nature Trail, which takes you downhill, crosses a pipeline right-of-way and bottoms out a little above the CP Railway tracks. From here, you start rising again, meeting and crossing Penzance just east of the Rainbow Creek Station and entering the "civilized" section of Confederation Park.

For your return, you have at least two options: for the easier, make your way to the upper boundary of the park at Gamma Avenue, then north to a five-way intersection. Still bearing left, follow Bessborough briefly, then angle uphill on Brisbane Avenue to Scenic Highway, a road that, despite its grandiose title, is a peaceful dead end, soon becoming a trail. Go straight ahead here until you slant gently downhill to join your outward route.

For a more strenuous but more scenic choice, from the five-way intersection on Gamma, head straight uphill on Cambridge Street. The beauty of this route, besides splendid views of Vancouver's inner harbour when you pause to take breath and look behind, is that a small substation in a grass plot splits it, inhibiting through traffic. Continue upwards to Ranelagh Avenue and turn left on it to reach Harbourview Park, your view of the harbour now obscured by houses.

After consoling yourself with the sight of mountains across the treetops to the north, resume your walk on Grosvenor, thence to Cambridge which does have spectacular views, this time of the head of the inlet and east as far as Golden Ears. Descend to Ellesmere, go left on it to its end, then down a forested track to Bessborough, where you go right as far as Dundas Street. A left turn takes you to Fell and thus back to bus or car, your expedition to the hidden face of North Burnaby over.

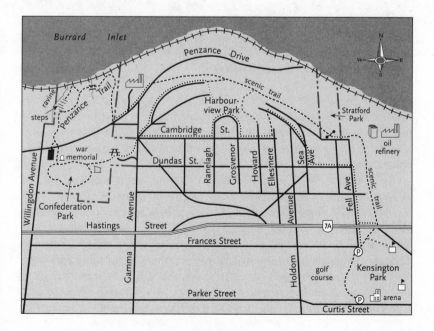

13 BURNABY MOUNTAIN

Round trip 8 km (5 mi)
Roads and trails

Allow 3 hours
Good most of the year

View of Mount Seymour and the mouth of Indian Arm.

Everyone knows that Simon Fraser University is situated on top of Burnaby Mountain; not so many are aware, perhaps, that the mountain is also the site of Burnaby's Centennial Park, which lies about 800 m to the west of its illustrious neighbour. It is in the park that this walk has beginning and end, the two separated by a circuit of about 8 km (5 mi).

One way to reach Centennial Park is to drive east on Hastings Street. After it curves into Burnaby Mountain Parkway and houses are left behind, go left up the steep Centennial Way to a parking lot by the pavilion. Alternatively, you may approach via Gaglardi Way from Highway 1 or Highway 7 (Lougheed Highway), turning left on Burnaby Mountain Parkway and right up Centennial Way. Here on a commanding spur overlooking Burrard Inlet, you may enjoy views of city, sea and mountain.

After paying homage to your surroundings, set off past the Ainu totems, Kamui Mintara, around the perimeter of the park, keeping the wire fence on your left. Pass the rose garden and the children's playground and arrive at a meeting of the ways to the left of the one-way road leading from Simon Fraser University. Here a well-defined trail (Joe's, now also the Trans Canada) strikes off to the left in the second-growth forest on the north side of the mountain, below the crest and out of sight of the university, though linked with it by two trails on the uphill side. Your trail travels eastwards, dropping a little as it progresses until, after about 3.2 km (2 mi), by a small spring, a foot trail—Mel's—strikes off uphill to the right. Turn right on this trail.

The trail rises and descends as it rounds the east flank of the mountain, intersects a power line, then crosses several small streams on wooden footbridges, followed by an old access road where you drop a little to get over a larger creek. Next you rise to cross a major approach to the university, your route continuing up a bank a little to your left. Stay with the more travelled route, now somewhat degraded by bikes, until you come to a trail crossing under a power line. Go straight ahead here to the next crossing, then turn left to a fork with bridges on both branches, the two arms encircling what used to be Naheeno Park. The right fork is slightly shorter, so why not go left? Then, after yet another bridge, turn right through a derelict adventure playground after which either the first or second left brings you out onto South Campus Road opposite Science Road. Proceed along the latter briefly before turning west in front of the university buildings.

Now cross University Drive, then walk diagonally left across the running track in front of the gym to the next sports field, at the end of which a track takes you right to join Residence Lane. There you go left to West Campus Road, where you veer left, passing Chilcotin, Kitimat and Penticton Houses on their south sides. Next head for the northwest corner of Quesnel House to find your trail running gently downhill on the bank above University Drive West. Finally, cross this road and turn back into the park from which you set out, passing a Trans Canada Trail pavilion on your way to the parking lot.

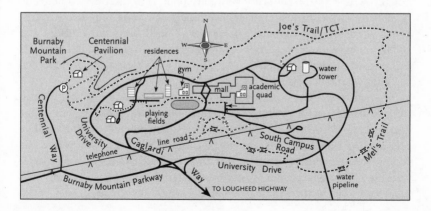

14 BURNABY MOUNTAINSIDE TRAILS

short loop:	Round trip 5.5 km (3.4 mi)	Allow 2 hours
long loop:	Round trip 12 km (7.5 mi)	Allow 3.5 hours
	Elevation gain 210 m (690 ft)	High point 302 m (990 ft)
	Paths and trails	Good all year

Heading up from Production Way.

This loop incorporates the Trans Mountain Trail, not, as you might suppose, an ambitious trail traversing a mountain range, but a delicious little path of less than 1 km (0.6 mi) in length, created as a gesture of good neighbourliness along the margin of its property by the Trans Mountain Pipe Line Co. It may, however, be treated as the prelude to a ramble through the residential clusters on Burnaby Mountain's south face, following a series of linking paths and stairways.

To reach the start, drive (or take the bus) south on Arden Avenue, reached from Curtis or Hastings Streets by turning south on Duthie, then going left on Greystone Drive, which curves into Arden Avenue. Alternatively, you may come north from the Lougheed Highway on Lake City Way and Arden. Turn east on Shellmont and park by the roadside just clear of the corner. The beautifully laid out trail starts at the intersection on the north side of Shellmont and winds its way uphill amongst quite large trees, with here and there a picturesque little bridge. But it is short, only 750 m (0.5 mi), and in no time you come to its end at Trans Mountain's main entry.

Straight ahead, however, beyond a gate, an old road, now a trail, continues eastwards to a fork beyond three tracks on the right into various school and recreational areas. The route on the left, which you may want to explore another day, runs along a power line to Gaglardi Way; the right, which you follow today, trends southeastwards into a residential enclave at Mountainside Village. Maintaining your direction, cross Ash Grove Crescent onto an unimproved track running downhill between townhouses and Forest

Grove Drive to end on that road at its junction with Maple Grove Crescent. Across Forest Grove, descend the series of stairways to a path just above another road, Production Way.

Now turn back west on this trail, which gradually pulls away from the busy thoroughfare as it ascends gently along the face of the slope, joined by successive paths and stairs from the adjoining houses. Soon you come to a trail forking back left from your route which crosses a pedestrian bridge high above a deep ravine and continues to a T-junction in front of another gorge. Ignoring the left branch, turn right alongside the ravine, the air in spring redolent with the sweet smell of cottonwood trees. A second high bridge takes you to the west side of the abyss, and there you remain until you emerge on Forest Grove Drive again. Opposite is a playground, east of which a path heads up beside a creek to join your outward route, where a left turn takes you back to the Trans Mountain Trail.

For a trip more than twice as long with a significant altitude gain, you should take that left fork along the power line west of Mountainside Village and cross Gaglardi Way onto an access road to some water towers, where you will find trails rising from both sides and meeting just above. Continue upwards until you meet Mel's Trail (Walk 13). Go right on it, ignoring bike routes dropping steeply downhill on the right until you come to a power line, on whose north side you descend steeply to the main hydro line, where you connect with the Stoney Creek Trail (Walk 15). Cut in to your right south of Broadway, passing north of Stoney Creek School to Beaverbrook Crescent, then go right to Avonlea, where a path leads you to an overpass of Gaglardi Way and thus to Production Way. Just over 100 m to your left you will rejoin the walk described in the shorter circuit for a gentle end to your outing.

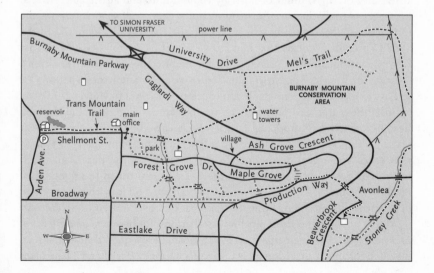

15 SFU/STONEY CREEK

One-way trip 8 km (5 mi)   Allow 3 hours

Trails, sidewalks and roads   Good most of the year

Steps up to Academic Quadrangle.

This walk takes you downhill nearly all the way from Simon Fraser University on the summit of Burnaby Mountain to end at the bus terminal in Lougheed Mall, the busy Burnaby shopping centre. Of some interest is the mountaintop location from which you set out, the start, incidentally, of the 1967 Centennial Trail, so that you retrace a part of the route as you go east from the campus centre. Savour, too, the architecture of Arthur Erickson's creation until, at its Administration Centre, you veer left across a parking lot to East Campus Road, on which you continue downhill to University Drive.

Just below the road junction and its "No Entry" sign, you find the trail heading off left and dropping sufficiently steeply for the macabre student sense of humour to have called it Cardiac Hill. This joins the trail system that takes you right, descending to the junction of the mountain trails, where you go straight ahead when Mel's Trail turns off to the right. Then reaching the power line right-of-way, you head right on it, with the option in dry weather of descending by an informal track in the line of forest to the east.

Watch now for the small pipeline installations, for here you go off left, on another right-of-way emerging on North Road, here a quiet dead-end street. Descend this until, at its low point, you reach Stoney Creek and a lane takes you off to the right along its south bank. (If you cut through the forest, you would reach the lane at a small ford.) Eventually a cross street (Broadway) appears, but a pedestrian underpass takes you beneath it. Your route now gradually diverges from the stream until, at the second track right, you return to the waterway, choosing either bank as you head south for the next cross street, Beaverbrook. This time you must rise to road level at the pedestrian crossing that gives access to Simon Fraser Village. Here, instead of dropping at once to creekside again, cut clear across the subdivision to a little park on its south side, where, from the dead end of Eastlake Drive, your trail resumes. Bounded by a fine split-rail fence, it descends to cross a tributary stream near its confluence with the main creek and pass beneath SkyTrain and the Lougheed Highway in quick succession.

Your walk along Stoney Creek is now almost over, for on Government Street you must turn left, then go left again on the dead-end Halston Road before following the wide parkway that takes you over the hill, the townhouses along your route becoming high-rises as you descend, Keswick Park on your right. Here you turn ninety degrees left and walk via Discovery Place Garden Apartments to an underpass of the Lougheed Highway, beyond which the mall appears.

For a bus back to the top of the mountain (30-minute service on the hour and the half-hour), work right of the Bay to the terminal for a relaxed, mechanically assisted return to your mountaintop starting point.

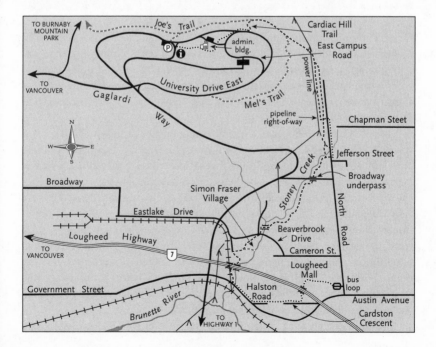

16 BURNABY LAKE

| Round trip 11 km (6.8 mi) | Allow 3 hours |
| Trails | Good all year |

Cariboo Dam.

Completion of the South Shore Trail makes possible a circumambulation of Burnaby Lake, with only the distant roar of traffic to remind you that you are walking in a peaceful oasis surrounded by highways and industrial and commercial endeavours. Numerous access points accommodate many variations to your hike around the lake and also allow you to tailor the length of the outing to time and ability.

One of the most convenient starts to a complete round of the lake is at the Burnaby Sports Complex, reached from the west by going off Highway 1 at Exit 32, turning left on Sprott Street and crossing the highway before proceeding to the traffic lights on Kensington Avenue, just beyond which lies the sports complex and its parking. Approaching from the east, leave Highway 1 at Exit 33, go north on Kensington Avenue to the Sprott Street intersection, then right to the sports complex. A second start may be made from the rowing pavilion, which you reach by turning right on Sperling Avenue after crossing Kensington, then left on Roberts Street to the pavilion parking lot. You may reach yet a third starting point by staying with Sperling as it curves round into Glencarin Drive and following it to the end, where a trailhead kiosk provides maps and information.

If you choose to start at the Glencarin trailhead and go clockwise, you first pass close to the water behind the Wildlife Rescue Association and several other buildings through interesting marsh scenery, crossing a bridge from which you may gaze into the depths of Deer Lake Brook before arriving at the parking lot for the rowing pavilion. Across this and slightly to the left, Pavilion Trail continues through head-high vegetation to reach the sports field behind the complex and the crossing of Still Creek, some 3.2 km (2 mi) from your start. Now you change direction as you embark on the long straight Cottonwood Trail, paralleling a railway and with only a few fleeting glimpses of the lake, eventually coming to the main Piper Avenue entrance with its Nature House, viewing tower and picnic area. (To confine your outing to the short, self-contained walks near Nature House, you may reach this spot from Highway 7 (Lougheed Highway) by turning south onto Brighton Avenue, which lies between Gaglardi Way and Kensington Avenue, then driving west on Winston Street to Piper Avenue, where you go south again, passing the attractive little Warner Loat Park as you near the parking lot.)

Continuing your walk round the lake, follow the trail east of Nature House, emerging into the open just where the Brunette River debouches from the lake, the crossing at the dam a short distance ahead. From here, turn upstream on the south bank to the Avalon Avenue parking lot (for access, see Walk 17). Leave the water here and set off west on the riding/hiking trail before branching off to the right on the pedestrian South Shore Trail. This winds through groves of quite large conifers and deciduous trees and over boardwalks across marshy areas, with here and there a viewpoint and here and there a connecting route to the bridle trail beside the freeway, until a final connector brings you back to the Glencarin trailhead.

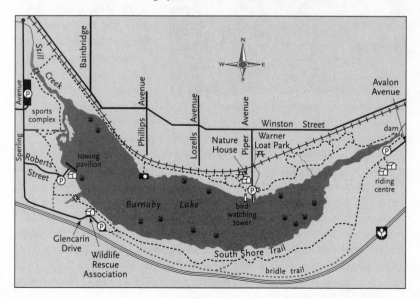

17 BRUNETTE RIVER

| Round trip 8 km (5 mi) | Allow 3 hours |
| Roads and trails | Good all year |

Looking up the Brunette River towards the lower weir.

This walk along the Brunette River, so named for the brown colour derived from the peaty soil through which its headwaters flow, may be tackled from several access points: from the west at the Piper Avenue entrance to Burnaby Lake (see Walk 16) or from the Avalon Avenue trailhead, reached from Highway 1 by turning onto Gaglardi Way at Exit 37. Cross the overpass, stay right at the traffic lights, then go left on Cariboo Road North to descend into the valley of the Brunette beneath Gaglardi Way. Immediately after the underpass, cut back left on Avalon Avenue, passing an equestrian centre on your way to the parking area. From there walk north to cross at the Cariboo Dam and join the trail downstream to Hume Park for a return walk of some 6 km (3.7 mi).

The walk also lends itself to an upstream approach from Hume Park, with an incursion into Burnaby Lake Regional Park as far as its Nature House as a bonus. For this, leave Highway 1 for Brunette Avenue South (Exit 40A), go right at the first traffic light onto Braid Street, then right again on Fader Street, which leads you to parking above the sports fields at Hume Park. Now on foot, make your way westwards to find the nature path that winds along the side of an old riverbank, gradually dropping to the valley floor near a park entrance off the busy North Road. Cross the river on the road bridge, then, to avoid a road crossing, drop to the water's edge and pass under the bridge to its west side. Head right to join the service road, which is your route upstream.

Across the river, on your left, are tall trees, and between you and them the water flows, still and dark, until you reach the little waterfall created by the first of two weirs controlling the free movement of the current. On your right, hidden by a screen of trees, runs the CN Burlington Northern Railway track, bearing the occasional train to disturb the peace. Eventually, though, another kind of traffic becomes audible as you pass under the high arches of the freeway bridge. Next, after crossing Stoney Creek at its confluence with the Brunette, you meet the road into a trailer park and pass under yet another main road, Gaglardi Way. Then you arrive at Cariboo Road and, a few minutes beyond it, the Cariboo Dam, where you may look down on the dark water with its scattering of lilies or westwards, up the lake, to the tall buildings rising, somewhat incongruously, above the rural scene.

Staying on the north side you may now head off on the Brunette Headwaters Trail. Three right turns at successive forks will allow you to sample the outer limits of the Spruce Loop and Conifer Loop Trails on your way to the Nature House at Piper Avenue, with its viewing tower and spit. Farther to the west, another short loop, the Piper Mill Trail, leads you round the sawdust heaps and other signs of the area's industrial past. But, inevitably, the time to return must come, and, back east of Piper Avenue, you may again choose right forks on the Brunette Headwaters Trail for the direct route back to the dam and your downstream walk.

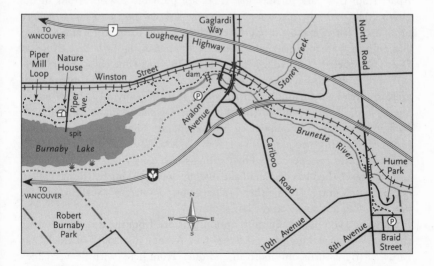

18 DEER LAKE

Round trip 5.5 km (3.4 mi)   Allow 2 hours
Trails and roads   Good all year

Ducks on the frozen lake at Century Park.

Apart from this park in Burnaby, there are probably few locations in the Lower Mainland where you may, from one parking spot, visit an art gallery or an arts centre, explore a re-created village, stroll through formal gardens and enjoy a walk along a trail system by an enchanting little lake. Here, at Deer Lake, the city's art collection is housed in a one-time mansion, its carefully preserved gardens providing a fitting setting also for the magnificent architecture of the Shadbolt Centre for the Arts, Burnaby's 1992 Centennial Legacy Project. Downhill to the east is the Burnaby Village Museum. As well, you may swim or go boating from a separate small recreation area and beach off Sperling Avenue, reached from Canada Way via Burris Street. The other pleasures are approached by turning south off Canada Way onto Deer Lake Parkway, then left on Deer Lake Avenue, with parking by the art gallery or Shadbolt Centre. From either building you may begin a walk round the lake by going due south to the lakeshore.

However, you have yet a third option, this one from the west side, where there is a small parking area off Royal Oak Avenue just south of Deer Lake Parkway (right turns only both in and out). From here, with Beaver Creek through the trees on your right, you may walk east to pick up the lake trail, on which you turn right for a walk anticlockwise round the marshy west end on a boardwalk trail. However, some interesting developments besides the residential in the old Oakalla Prison lands have taken place, and to take advantage of these, you should take the first right after leaving your car. This takes you across some low-lying meadows and up to an observation area overlooking meadows and marsh. Next continue upwards and eastwards along the front of the new townhouses, enjoying wide views of the North Shore mountains east to Golden Ears with Deer Lake as foreground. Resisting the temptation to drop too soon to the lake on the first descending tracks, stay high until you reach a fork just short of another entry, from Oakland Street. Now turn left and make your way down beside a shallow, leafy ravine to the lake trail, then turn east again, heading towards a fence with a missing panel. By going through here into the trees, crossing a small creek and taking the rough trail uphill, you emerge on Strawson Street and veer left on Haszard Street a short distance from a flight of steps down to Sperling and the beach.

From the beach, make a short jog to the north, and after passing The Hart House go left on Dale Avenue, with the Burnaby Village Museum to your right. Cross the creek and turn left again on the park trail to get back to the lake at the foot of Century Park, with its attractions.

Beyond here, you are once more forced away from the lake, past a large white house to another quiet road. Two more left turns take you back to the lakeshore, and soon after is a fork where right takes you straight back to Royal Oak. But if previously you missed the walk along the westerly boardwalks and the bog plants they protect, you may wish to continue to your left, going right only at the next junction to rejoin and retrace your outward route.

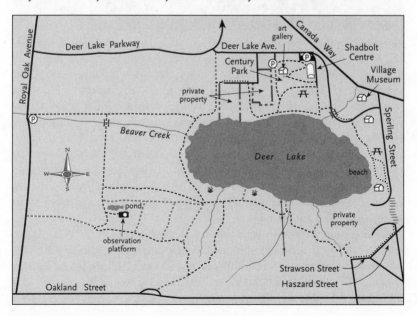

19 MOLSON WAY
(Central)

One-way trip 10 km (6.2 mi)   Allow 3 hours
Paths and trails   Good all year

Peaceful scene in Central Park.

Molson Way, the pedestrian portion of B.C. Parkway, follows the SkyTrain route for 19 km (11.8 mi) from False Creek in Vancouver to New Westminster. In its entirety and using transit for the return, it makes a comfortable one-way outing, its many parkway features, created by communities along its route, a source of recurrent interest for the walker.

But for those who would prefer to sample a little at a time, here is a section of the parkway that links three of Burnaby's parks, one the well-known Central Park, the other two little-known contiguous green spaces with distinctive names and functions—Ron McLean Park, a sports and picnic area, and Byrne Creek Ravine Park, a tiny wilderness.

Your approach is by SkyTrain to Patterson Station in Central Park. (If you drive, you may park and join the walk at the entrance by the tennis courts on Patterson Avenue.) Leaving the station, follow the John Molson markers towards the tall trees of Central Park. On entering the park, however, turn left, away from Molson Way, to embark on a clockwise circuit along quiet forest trails amidst giant Douglas-firs. Ignoring tracks to the right, shortcuts across the heart of the park, pass the tennis courts entry and veer right, following the split-rail fence that borders the pitch-and-putt course occupying the southeast corner. Next comes the model-yacht pond, home to various ducks and geese, its outlet at the east end crossed by a picturesque wooden bridge and, farther west, its inlet straddled by an equally attractive bridge. Now turn right (north), following the stream through a Japanese-style garden to another body of water south of the horseshoe-pitch, then continue through the forest to the picnic areas near Variety Park, an adventure/play area for children.

Here you rejoin Molson Way for your walk southeast, passing first the Rhododendron Garden, the bushes donated by the society of the same name. The next stretch of the B.C. Parkway is further enhanced by other community-inspired floral displays: the Dutch Mile, the Sears Garden and the Garden of the Province, to name a few. Peace, however, is notably lacking as you traverse this busy commercial and industrial section of Burnaby, and it may be with some relief that, shortly after the little garden at Gilley Avenue, you espy on your right the green fields of Ron McLean Park and head for the wooded area across the sward.

From the parking lot there, turn south on Hedley Avenue and proceed to its end, then, passing north of the tennis courts, you'll find the trail starting among trees along the western perimeter and descending into the attractive Byrne Creek Ravine. Soon you reach the low end at Marine Drive, with no apparent return trail on the other side of the creek; however, a search east reveals a steep track heading up the embankment and into the trees to join a braided trail system following the east side of the ravine and finally emerging on a paved path entering from the right. Go left on this until it meets B.C. Parkway once more, follow its markers left as the pathway curves round and under SkyTrain, then go right for Edmonds Station and your speedy return on the elevated railway.

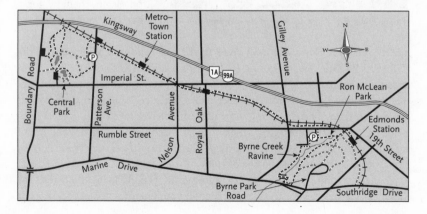

MOLSON WAY
(South)

One-way trip 5.5 km (3.4 mi)   Allow 2 hours
Paths and roads   Good all year

Patullo Bridge over the Fraser River at New Westminster.

You may already have used a stretch of the John Molson feature of B.C. Parkway on one or both of Walks 9 and 19. This time your outing begins at Edmonds SkyTrain Station and ends with a walk along New Westminster's riverfront, culminating in a visit, perhaps, to the Westminster Quay Market, a short distance from the transit station, from which you may return whether you used Sky-Train to reach Edmonds or parked nearby.

Your first task is to find the route, hidden as the walkway is, in low ground west of the station. Begin, then, by going under the right-of-way to where the trail markers greet your eyes. Then the path veers to the east, and you begin to rise, the "City in the Park" on your right, B.C. Hydro headquarters on your left. Now, travelling more south than east, you enjoy the familiar sights of Mount Baker and the flatlands of the Fraser Delta, with the southern Gulf Islands on the horizon. Then, starting your descent to river level, you note over to your right a sign of mortality, Schara Tzedeck Cemetery, with, beyond it, the soaring spires of the Alex Fraser Bridge, the twentieth-century equivalent of the Gothic cathedrals of the age of faith.

Still descending, you come to another of the parkway features, the Japanese Garden, a spot to stop and recoup your energies before tackling the busiest portion of this walk beyond 22nd Street Station. This you pass on its north side, watching the trail signs with extra care as you come to the crossing of 20th Street. Thereafter, Grimston Park provides a respite before your next street crossing, one that has to be undertaken in two stages. Once over, however, though heavy traffic is on your left for a time, you are past the worst, despite the presence of Scott Paper Limited's plant between you and the river.

Now, at the crossing of 14th Street, comes the B.C. Bearing Plaza, at its centre the brick foundation once housing a giant bearing. A few minutes later you turn right to cross an overpass spanning the railway yards, the riverside housing developments ahead replacing the industry of yesteryear. Once over, leave the official Molson Way temporarily at Rialto Court and head for the waterfront to enjoy the full length of the esplanade, the river and its traffic on one hand, the multitude of architectural styles on the other; on the river an old railway bridge, its spans open to permit passage for shipping, and nearby on land the Quayside Children's Place, an ultramodern playground with a nautical theme. Finally, SkyTrain's fine new bridge appears, itself an interesting contrast to the old Patullo Bridge, and, at the market, your walk ends, an overpass of Columbia Street taking you to the station for your return trip.

You might, of course, walk back, but if you want to lengthen without repeating your outing, you might begin or end with a visit to Byrne Creek Ravine Park, a delightful little remnant of wild British Columbia. To reach it from Edmonds Station, head for Molson Way but go right almost immediately thereafter between the verge of a ravine and a row of townhouses. This leads you to Ron McLean Park, from which you follow the directions in the previous walk (Walk 19).

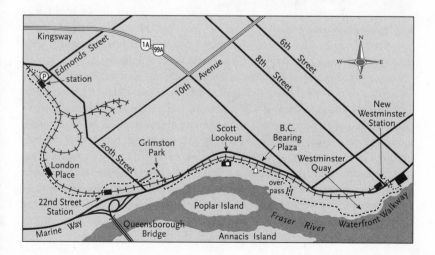

21 BURNABY FRASER FORESHORE PARK

from Boundary Road:	Round trip 8 km (5 mi) or less	Allow 2.5 hours
	Trails and roads	Good all year

At the pier near the eastern entrance.

With development still going on, with new buildings and their linking parkways springing up where once was green space in Burnaby's Big Bend, the recreational picture is by no means complete. Even so, you have numerous possibilities at present.

To reach the central picnic area of Burnaby Fraser Foreshore Park, drive south from Marine Way on Byrne Road. Once parked, you must decide whether to go downstream towards Boundary Road for a return walk of 4.4 km (2.7 mi) or take the slightly shorter distance upstream to the eastern limits of the park, a possible destination being a pier with seats around a wooden structure reminiscent of a ship's masts.

A trailhead on Marine Drive is most easily reached by bus and starts opposite the foot of Patterson Street just west of New Haven Correctional Institution. Your trail takes you south from here towards Marine Drive's upstart successor, Marine Way, but a pedestrian overpass clears this hurdle. Continuing towards the river, you next cross a creek, followed by a B.C. Hydro railway and a roadway, North Fraser Way. Though most of the ground to the right has been industrialized, the trees on your left have been spared, as have the wet brushlands in the immediate vicinity of the trail, which meets the riverside pathway 1.5 km (1 mi) from Marine Drive. Once more you have the choice of going east or west, though you may simply pause to contemplate the river with its traffic.

From the western entrance at the foot of Boundary Road, you have the most satisfying of all, the complete walk to the east. Although industry is not far off, the riverbank is tree-clad, and from the end of the Patterson access onwards, stately cottonwoods grace either side, their perfume in springtime and their golden beauty in fall delighting the senses as you go east, once more a possible target being the pier just within the bounds of the park.

However, to add distance and interest to your outing, you should continue upstream alongside Fraser Park Drive to a gated road on the right of the Correctional Centre for Women and thence to the CNR's bridge, disused and somewhat forlorn-looking at present, with its centre span left open for the free passage of river traffic. Immediately beyond the old railway you come to the Fraser Foreshore Restoration Project with, as well as the wetland habitat surrounding it, Terminus Park, a wide meadow providing a hunting ground for raptors.

Another possibility for extending your outing is to take the Byrne Creek Trail, which runs northwards from just west of the picnic area for some 2.5 km (1.5 mi) alongside the still waters of that stream.

Farther west, your return to Boundary may be varied by swinging right around a pretty little pond and continuing along Glenlyon Parkway to a path going left opposite the Ballard Building back to the riverside trail. Or you may continue on the sidewalk as far as North Fraser Way, turning left there to the Patterson trail, then left again towards the river, where you head west once more for Boundary Road.

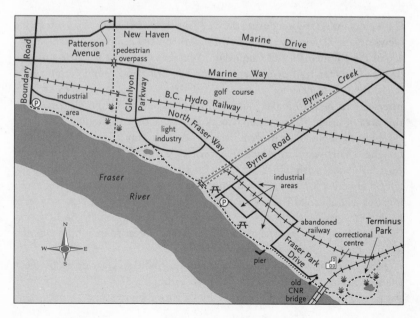

MUNDY PARK

Round trip 7 km (4.3 mi)
Trails

Allow 2.5 hours
Good all year

Reflections in Mundy Lake.

For a pleasant afternoon outing on well-laid-out forest trails with intriguing views of small lakes, try this delightful park located near the eastern boundary of the Municipality of Coquitlam. Whether you wish to circle the park on its perimeter trail or concentrate on the heartland round Mundy Lake itself, there is something to suit most desires. As well, trail plans at main intersections help to make route-finding easy, adding to the pleasure from this area of urban afforestation, Coquitlam's response to Stanley Park.

From Highway 1 turn off north on Gaglardi Way (Exit 37) to join the Lougheed Highway, on which you turn right. Next go left and uphill on Austin Avenue, with which you stay for some 4.5 km (2.8 mi) before going left on Hillcrest Street—and suddenly you are at your destination, the parking area just ahead of the park's main entrance. Here you are close to sports fields with washrooms just to the north. Beyond them is yet another parking lot and, on its right, the Mundy Park Urban Forest Map, which provides an introduction to the park's history and trails.

For a first visit's sampling of the many possibilities, walk north between the small lakes and continue on the path through a disc golf installation to yet another parking area. Cross this, making for its northwest corner, where

Nitinat Trail (blue markers) takes you north, forest on your right and a sports field on your left at first, but giving way to trees on either hand. Stay with Nitinat as it meets and leaves School Trail, then turn right at a point where going straight on would take you to Como Lake Avenue, the first of four such exits on this eastward leg of your trip. Soon, at the next trail crossing, you join Perimeter Trail (which, perversely enough, has avoided the perimeter so far), then, not long after, you cross Waterline Trail, which cuts across the whole width of the park from north to south and may suggest ideas for another walk.

Eventually your trail turns south, and soon you are treated to tantalizing glimpses of water in the forest. Where Interlaken Trail (orange) intersects Perimeter (blue), go left for a closer sight of Lost Lake. Keep going south to a T-junction, at which go right to rejoin Perimeter, now heading west through fine second-growth forest, its floor adorned with trilliums in spring.

Finally, with a sports field ahead, you meet the trail from the main entrance and you are ready for the climax to this trip: Mundy Lake itself. For it, stay with Perimeter going right, then, when Owl Trail (red) goes straight on, turn left briefly before swinging right for the Lakeside Loop Trail (yellow) with its viewing platforms at strategic spots. Towards the northwest end of the lake, you may be interested in making a short detour left to walk Logging Trail, built on one of the originals used early in the century. At the top of the little hill, go right on Interlaken, with another right bringing you back to Mundy Lake to resume the loop, after which a left on Perimeter returns you to your starting point.

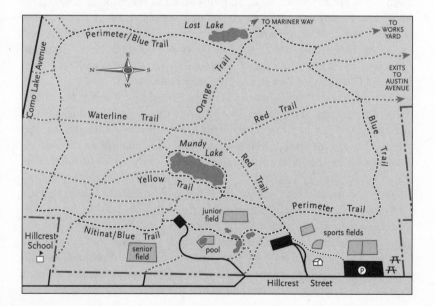

23 SHORELINE TRAIL
(Port Moody)

Round trip 5 km (3.1 mi)	Allow 2 hours
Trails	Good all year

Deteriorating wreck.

Even if you are a regular user of St. Johns Street in Port Moody, here serving as Highway 7A (Barnet Highway), you may well be unaware that between you and the head of Burrard Inlet lies a trail, hidden from the road by a screen of trees. Giving a succession of views and points of historic interest, it follows the line of the original Ioco Road partway between Rocky Point Park and Old Orchard Park in the district of Pleasantside.

To reach Rocky Point Park from St. Johns Street, turn north at the Moody Street intersection. This road takes you over the CP Railway tracks before decanting you on Murray Street beside, appropriately enough, the Port Moody Station Museum, given that this city was intended as the western terminus of the transcontinental railway. On Murray Street turn left, then left again for the parking lot, near the recreation area with its open-air pool, its jetty and its children's playground, built atop an ancient Native midden.

Starting on the trail at the east end of the park, you soon reach your first stream, picturesquely named Slaughterhouse Creek, beside which stands a large board with a map and information about the plants and animals you may see. On the shore you may also note an old wreck, abandoned and forlorn, as you head north among groves of trees, fir and cedar being prominent. Along the way, steps, sturdy footbridges and boardwalks take care of obstacles, one stretch of walkway at the head of the inlet over the thick coarse sedge grass being particularly impressive. Here a notice board tells something of the trail's creation, giving credit to those who helped bring it into existence as well as providing an overview of the area's history, natural and human. Just beyond, a short detour left takes you to a bird-watching platform, complete with seat, which offers fine views down Burrard Inlet even if you are not specially interested in the great blue herons and lesser birds of the tidal marshes. Then cross the mouth of Noons Creek, on which a fish hatchery has been created upstream beyond the old railway bridge, and head west.

The next part of your trip is interesting historically as well. By your path you may spot scraps left from an early steel mill, and fire bricks underfoot bear testimony to a one-time brickworks, Stanley's. On this stretch, too, you may want to diverge from the trail to visit the remains of one of the cedar mills that once dotted this part of the coast. At low tide you may stand on the concrete foundations of the old McNair cedar mill and look around at the rotting stanchions, relics of old wharves, busy with shipping in the mill's heyday. Then, towards the end of your journey you walk through a grove of poplars before the appearance of fruit trees indicates your approach to Old Orchard Park.

Incidentally, if you drive round the head of the inlet on Ioco Road to start this walk from its north end, you must turn left on Alderside Road and pass the little community hall. There is no sign at the road, either, the good folk of Pleasantside perhaps wanting to keep the news of such an attractive park to themselves. And who can blame them?

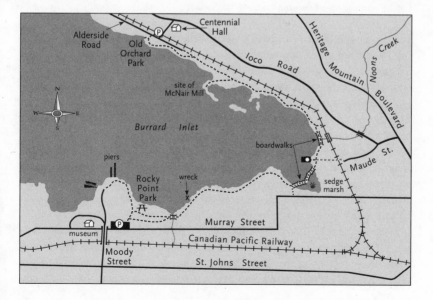

24 SASAMAT LAKE/ WOODHAVEN SWAMP

Round trip 8 km (5 mi)   **Allow 3 hours**
Trails   **Good all year**

Looking across to Main Beach and Buntzen Ridge behind.

For those who like to combine a short walk with some swimming, picnicking or fishing, all within comfortable distance of Vancouver by bus or car, Sasamat Lake is an ideal spot, for the lake is reputed to be the region's warmest and the trails are well treed, providing shade on hot summer days.

From Highway 7A (Barnet Highway), turn onto Ioco Road just east of Port Moody and drive west, following signs for Belcarra. Turn right on 1st Avenue at Ioco School, left at the next fork onto Bedwell Bay Road, then go right for White Pine Beach shortly thereafter. On foot, make your way down to the main beach and turn right past the building at its north end, where the trail starts off into the trees along the lake's edge. Quite soon you rise to an access road on which you turn left to meet the approach to the Sasamat Outdoor Centre, a private camp run by the Association of Neighbourhood Houses.

Across this road the trail resumes, dropping to and crossing the lake's outlet, before coming to a T-junction. For a short walk of 3 km (1.9 mi) around the lake, go left along the shore, the noise of traffic from Bedwell Bay Road above on your right. (Indeed, you might very well start from that thoroughfare, descending one of the two rough tracks conveniently placed for small parking spaces on the verge. These start 200 m and 700 m beyond the junction of the Bedwell Bay and Burrard Thermal Plant Roads and may provide attractive alternatives on a busy summer weekend.) Next you come to the floating bridge, with its fishing and swimming decks, which saves you a long trip on pavement round the marshy area at the south end of the lake. Take this direct route to the east side and continue on the final lap of your circumambulation, assisted here and there by little bridges over feeder streams. Soon you come to South Beach, with its picnic tables backing onto Pine Point, the natural separation from Main Beach and the end of your walk.

But what of Woodhaven Swamp? To make the connection, you must turn right after crossing the outlet by the Sasamat Outdoor Centre, follow the creek, Windermere Creek, downstream for about 200 m, then rise to road level at the Belcarra Village welcome sign, where a crosswalk takes you to a flight of steps. These start you on a trail ascending between private properties, beyond which the route veers briefly east of south, the lake visible below through the trees, then you swing away again, gaining height and crossing a long bridge en route over a damp hollow. Thereafter, still rising gently, the trail works its way round the side of a bluff before it levels and comes to a power line access road, which in turn is joined by a bike path and emerges on the park road to Belcarra Picnic Area directly across from the swamp. Cross the road and follow the bike path briefly until, just below a small parking lot, you drop to the walker's route round the margin of this little wetland, a long boardwalk at its north end a strategic spot from which to survey the scene. Then, the circuit complete, retrace your steps to Sasamat Lake to resume your course round its shore.

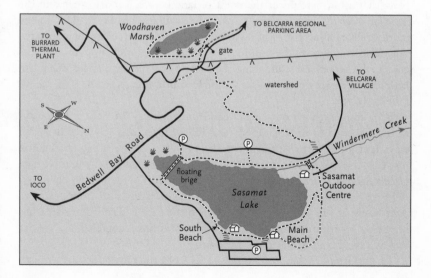

25 BELCARRA REGIONAL PARK

to Jug Island Beach:	Round trip 5.5 km (3.4 mi)	Allow 2.5 hours
to Burns Point:	Round trip 5.2 km (3.2 mi)	Allow 2 hours
	Trails	Good all year

Jug Island with Raccoon Island beyond on right.

Now that a fair amount of the point of land between Indian Arm and the head of Burrard Inlet is regional parkland, walking has been added to the more traditional activities of swimming, fishing and picnicking associated with Belcarra. Besides the trail round Sasamat Lake (Walk 24), you have the choice of a woodland walk along the spine of the peninsula to a delightful little beach at its north end or a ramble south along the shoreline above Burrard Inlet.

For a start, turn left onto Ioco Road from Highway 7A (Barnet Highway) at the eastern end of Port Moody and follow it to Ioco School, where you turn right for Belcarra. At the next fork, stay left on Bedwell Bay Road, until, just past the approach to White Pine Beach on Sasamat Lake, you leave it to go left again for Belcarra Picnic Area and Burrard Thermal Plant, then fork right for the former after a kilometre of rising, twisting road. Your next concern comes at the gate, which closes when the park is filled to capacity, but once over that hurdle you are free to enjoy this novel approach to Belcarra as it winds up and down to the parking area.

For Jug Island Beach, head northwards from the picnic shelters through the trees and cross Bedwell Bay Road to an opening opposite, there ignoring the trail on your right to West Road. A few steps on, two trails have their beginnings: the Bedwell Bluffs trail on the right is a 35 to 40-minute round trip to a tidal flat; your route, an old logging road, continues on the left working its way north along the ridge. After some 30 minutes you come to a fork with the original trail, now closed, going left beyond a barrier. Going right on its successor you rise quite steeply on a rocky path alongside a mossy slab to a viewpoint just below and east of the ridge crest. Then the track drops to rejoin the former route, levelling briefly before the final descent to the little secluded beach.

Contrasting with the inland northward walk is the gentler excursion that takes you south along the shore past Cod Rock, Periwinkle Notch, Maple Beach, Admiralty Point and Whiteshell Bank on the way to Burns Point. This time you start from below the concession stand on the south side just above the shore.

Heading south, you first cross a footbridge, then a road leading to a piece of private property before beginning to rise in pleasant forest to continue a little above the waters of Indian Arm's southern reach. As you proceed, you will note small cleared areas with their garden flowers gone wild, the few relics of squatters' homes from the 1930s. Next comes Cod Rock, your first extended viewpoint, followed by the other features, with the trail descending to sea level at Maple Beach.

Five minutes more brings you to a major fork. Left takes you on towards your destination, right a few steps to Admiralty Point. There, where the waters of the Arm meet those of Burrard Inlet, you may enjoy the view down the inlet to the Ironworkers Memorial Bridge or lift up your eyes to Mount Seymour; in fact, this makes a satisfying destination for a short walk. If, on the other hand, you continue eastwards on the main trail, you first find yourself down at Whiteshell Bank before rising fairly steeply prior to your final descent to the present end of the trail at a bluff above Burns Point, with its sheer drop-off and its views up, down and across the inlet.

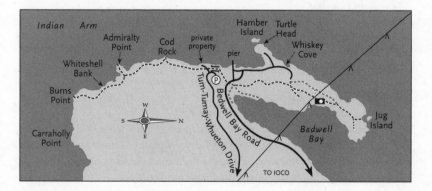

26 BUNTZEN LAKE

Round trip 10.5 km (6.5 mi) or less   Allow 5 hours
Roads and trails   Good all year

Looking west towards North Beach, Mounts Seymour and Elsay above.

Where do you have the choice of several delightful walks, ranging from a gentle stroll to a lung-opening circumambulation lasting several hours? The answer: Buntzen Lake, that attractive body of water, manmade though it is. Here, B.C. Hydro has done a superb job of creating recreational facilities: developed beach areas, launching sites for pleasure craft (no power boats) and trails for horse riders and hikers, the whole set in an impressive basin with tree-clad mountain slopes on either side.

To partake of what Buntzen Lake has to offer, turn left off Highway 7A (Barnet Highway) at the Ioco exit and drive uphill on Heritage Mountain Boulevard, thereafter following signs for Buntzen Lake as you work through developments springing up apace on the mountain slope. Finally, from East

Road go right on Sunnyside Road to the entrance gate at Anmore (where you may also arrive by bus), the parking lots lying 2 km (1.2 mi) beyond.

From here, to sample outings along the lake's east side, walk right along the beach, cross a footbridge and embark on an exceedingly fine forest trail that undulates gently as you proceed north. Various lakeside viewpoints give you short there-and-back outings, but if you are more ambitious, you may reach North Beach, beyond the tunnel that carries water from Coquitlam Lake on the other side of Eagle Ridge.

Here, at 4 km (2.5 km) from your starting point, you may feel that honour is satisfied, but if you wish to complete the circuit, you have two options: for the shorter, cross the footbridge west of the picnic area and bear left to join the power-line trail, here designated for both hikers and riders; on the longer, the original Buntzen Lake Trail, you go north on the road by Trout Lake to the dam. Here you fork left, then left again just after a bridge onto a forest track that winds south to emerge near a water intake building. Continuing south on the power-line trail, you soon meet the shorter route from the suspension bridge and part from the horse route (Lakeview Trail), which goes uphill to the right. Then you descend into a hollow and climb up again over the next bluff, with views of Swan Falls across the lake to raise the spirits.

In forest again, the track undulates along, crossing and recrossing the right-of-way, before eventually approaching the shore once more and bringing you back down to lake level beside a pumphouse. Now you walk south on the service road, then cross a long wooden floating bridge spanning the lake's southern extension and the surrounding wetlands to the final lap, through another attractive stretch of forest back to your starting point.

And the short outing at South Beach? For it, go left past the boat launch and follow Energy Trail to a knoll with a view along the whole length of the lake, once so appropriately called Lake Beautiful before it was renamed for a power company official.

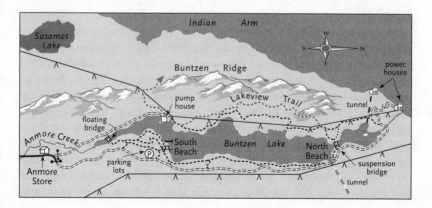

27 COLONY FARM REGIONAL PARK

river loop:	Round trip 5 km (3.1 mi)	Allow 1.5 hours
	Dykes and trails	Good all year

In Riverview Arboretum.

Colony Farm was long known as one of the most fertile and productive farms in B.C. Straddling the lower Coquitlam River, it was farmed intensively for more than 70 years and, until recently, provided food in abundance for Essondale, Woodlands and the Forensic Psychiatric Institute as well as rehabilitative employment for the patients of these institutions. Despite its agricultural potential, however, in the 1980s much of the land ceased to be farmed actively and began to revert to its wild condition, and now the GVRD Regional Parks Department manages it for wildlife, recreation and a little horticulture. Containing marshes, grass and trees as well as streams, ditches and sloughs—and the wildlife attracted by these diverse habitats—the dykes are wonderful places for walking and nature study.

To sample some of the pleasures of the area, leave Highway 1 at Exit 44 following signs for Highway 7 (Lougheed Highway). Turn south (right) from Highway 7 onto Colony Farm Road, just east of the United Boulevard overpass, and drive to the parking area at the end, near the Forensic Psychiatric Institute. On foot, start along the west side of a ditch, which you soon cross to proceed northwards, with the canal on one side and the river on the other. Almost immediately you come to a bridge, a millenium project to replace one built early last century to give access to the lands on the eastern side. Continuing, your course dictated by the meandering stream, you next come to a fork where a track runs left to join the farm road at a small parking spot by the Lougheed Highway. Staying with the right branch, however, brings you into woodland and across Mundy Creek and several ditches, noting, as you proceed, the signs of beaver gnawings on a few trees. At the next junction a track goes right to a small sandy beach by the river, a pleasant spot for a pause, while the route left heads out to Pitt River Road, whose bridge enables you to cross dry-shod to the eastern bank to begin your return.

After travelling pleasantly through bush and trees and past an extensive wetland, your dyke breaks out into the open and you keep right at a fork with the sight of residential developments to confront you until, with another bend in the stream, you turn away, passing a second track on the left leading out to Shaughnessy Street. Then you are back at the new bridge, by which you may return after a walk of some 6.5 km (4 mi). But you may also continue downstream, turning right to ford a muddy ditch and make your way under the Mary Hill Bypass, up onto the bridge and thus back to the west side. There, you drop to river level once more and, perhaps after making a brief side trip to the marshes at the confluence of the Coquitlam with the Fraser River, head north towards the parking lot and the end of an interesting walk.

Across the Lougheed Highway from Colony Farm lie the Riverview Lands, home to the hospital and Western Canada's first arboretum, with its fine collection of native and exotic species. The future of the area is still to be determined, but in the meantime it is possible to include a visit by going left when you reach Pitt River Road and crossing Lougheed Highway at the traffic lights, near which an approach road takes you into the grounds. After a tour of the area, you may return to continue your walk down the east side of the Coquitlam River or depart by the main approach road, which takes you out opposite Colony Farm Road.

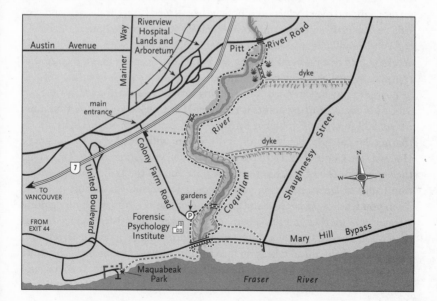

28 RIDGE PARK LOOP

Round trip 5 km (3.1 mi)
Elevation gain 245 m (800 ft)
Trails

Allow 2 hours
High point 400 m (1310 ft)
Good most of the year

Bunchberry with maidenhair fern.

For a Vancouverite returning to the lower Fraser Valley after an exile of a decade or two, the population explosion is painfully evident, and nowhere, perhaps, is it more visible than on the once-forested south slopes of Eagle Ridge, where residential development creeps relentlessly upwards from the town centres of Port Moody and Coquitlam. Fortunately a few areas along streambeds and over rocky outcrops have been saved from the debacle and provide an escape from pavement to some pleasant green oases. Such a haven in the Westwood Plateau area of Coquitlam is Ridge Park, with a loop trail and access points from several existing streets. Plans exist for other recreational routes to be available as developments are completed, so that eventually it will be possible to make extended walks linking various green strips across the area.

One of many starting points is the West Hoy Creek trailhead on Panorama Drive, 300 m west of Johnson Street, which runs north from Highway 7A (Barnet Highway), just west of its junction with Highway 7 (Lougheed Highway) in Coquitlam. Here the street is wide, with room for parking along the verge convenient for the steps that start you on the trail. You rise with a thin fringe of trees separating you from nearby houses for a short distance. Then you reach a power line and a crossing of trails, with left climbing quite steeply to another access point on Parkway Boulevard opposite the Westwood Plateau Golf Academy, and right dropping to Johnson Street.

Going straight ahead takes you into the forest that is Ridge Park, and quite soon you must ford another branch of Hoy Creek, the North Fork, beyond which comes the beginning of the loop encircling the park. It is immaterial which way you go: left starts rather more steeply then eases, while right begins by losing height and saves its stiff section for later, but unless you bail out onto one of the adjacent streets, you will arrive back at this point.

Choosing to go counterclockwise takes you down to level just inside a thin margin of trees, then you swing left and up, ignoring tracks from the right, which would take you out to residential streets east of the ridge. After some 20 minutes of climbing blissfully free of sights and sounds of human endeavours, you begin to get glimpses of a golf course with mountains beyond, and the less pleasant sight of another power line as your trail begins to curve left and south. Now approaching the high point on the main loop, you may be tempted to go still higher on a short loop to the top of the ridge, where a bench invites you to pause, though there is no view of distant scenes to beguile you.

Continuing, you soon come to a three-way fork, with a map giving you the choice of a quick plunge to meet the main trail at another exit point or a more leisurely zigzagging descent to join it a little farther south. Then you walk roughly parallel to and above the golf fairways for a short time before turning away and dropping quickly to the end of the loop, thereafter retracing your steps to Panorama Drive.

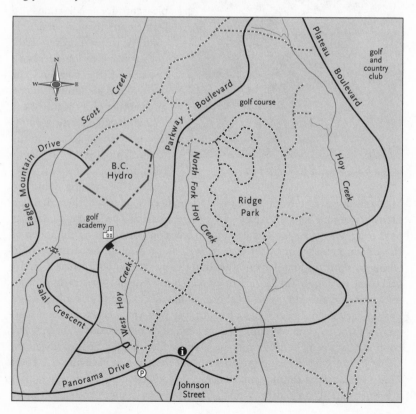

29 POCO TRAIL

| Lions Park to | One-way trip 10.2 km (6.3 mi) | Allow 3 hours |
| Dublin Docks Inn: | Dykes, streets and trails | Good all year |

Restored stream in Coquitlam River Park.

More than three decades ago, the idea was conceived of a walk round the municipality of Port Coquitlam with transverse trails running east and west to link the two south-flowing rivers, the Pitt and the Coquitlam, that enclose it. Sad to say, development, both residential and commercial, has played havoc with the original design, reducing the part still pleasant for pedestrians to little more than a semicircle confined to the northern half, with transportation necessary to connect the two ends or with your walk limited to one or the other of its segments.

One possible starting point, if you wish to focus on the Coquitlam River, is Lions Park on the river's east side, reached by turning south on Shaughnessy Street from Highway 7 (Lougheed Highway), then right on Lions Way. From here, you may walk upstream using a pedestrian underpass at the highway, a screen of cottonwood trees on your right hiding much of the urban growth from your eyes as well as perfuming the air sweetly in spring. A short distance beyond the footbridge at the end of Patricia Avenue, you come to Coquitlam River Park, in which the federal Department of Fisheries and Oceans along with local groups has, according to the information board, "reclaimed 2 kilometres of historic stream channels, ponds and wetlands vital to fish and wildlife." The area is a maze of old roads and trails, but confined between the river and the Oxbow Sidechannel, it is easily negotiable if you wish to experiment with different routes. Leaving the PoCo Trail and travelling through mixed deciduous and coniferous forest, you pass a former equestrian centre, a small pond beside a trailer parking lot and a dead-end trail into an oxbow lake in the midst of a private development before reaching the northern end of the project at the intake channel flowing into a dyked pond. If you turn around here, you give yourself a return trip of some 7.5 km (4.7 mi).

Alternatively, you might have stayed with the PoCo Trail, now also designated part of the Trans Canada Trail (TCT), crossing Shaughnessy Street onto a track into the trees and walking clear across the municipality from west to east, following park and woodland trails to Lincoln and Patricia Avenues, then along Hyde Creek to Cedar Drive and the head of De Boville Slough, a one-way distance of 2.8 km (1.7 mi). A slightly shorter, but less interesting, route takes you right from the pedestrian bridge and straight along Patricia to its crossing of Coast Meridian Road and the beginning of the Hyde Creek Trail.

The slough itself is a respectable 1.5 km (0.9 mi) in length, and it could be the destination of a walk along the Pitt River, its start the Dublin Docks (formerly Wild Duck) Inn, just south and west of the Pitt River Bridge. This stretch of dyke gives unimpeded views to the east and north, and its marshlands provide a total contrast to the treed banks of its neighbour stream.

On its own this route makes a return trip of 7.2 km (4.5 mi) between the Highway 7 bridge over the Pitt River and the mouth of the slough, a walk conveniently approached from a parking spot located on the river dyke near the inn and using the pedestrian underpass to launch you on the open dyke, popular with bird and nature watchers.

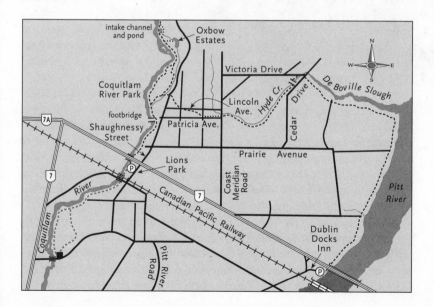

30 WOODLAND WALKS
(Lower Burke Ridge)

Woodland Walk:	Round trip 8 km (5 mi)	Allow 3 hours
	Elevation gain 180 m (590 ft)	High point 500 m (1640 ft)
	Trails and roads	Best May to November
Coquitlam Lake	Round trip 9.5 km (5.9 mi)	Allow 5 hours
Viewpoint:	Elevation gain 610 m (2000 ft)	High point 930 m (3050 ft)
	Old roads	Best June to October

Dwarfed by a large cedar stump.

Here is a perfect walk for a hot summer's day, with shade to protect you and filtered sunshine to relieve any gloom cast by the massive stumps, memorials to the magnificent trees clothing the slopes of Burke Ridge for hundreds of years until the logger arrived less than a century ago. The Woodland Walk is the gentlest route of several created by the Burke Mountain Naturalists from the maze of abandoned logging and skid roads on the ridge to introduce walkers to its treasures, biological and historical.

To start, go north off Highway 7 (Lougheed Highway) on Coast Meridian Road and continue for some 5 km (3.1 mi) to Harper Road; turn right and drive another 2 km (1.2 mi) to a parking spot near the entrance to the gun club. Walk up the road on the right for about 10 minutes beyond the gate, then go left for a short distance to another fork. The left branch bears a wooden sign inscribed "Woodland Walk" and right, "Coquitlam Lake View and Burke Ridge."

Go left, following the blue markers, at first still on the old logging road through second-growth forest, traversing a power-line cut and keeping left, but soon coming into the open at the power line again. Shortly after crossing a stream with a fine waterfall you reenter the trees to embark on a circuit on which going right at successive forks gives you the longest loop. The trail rises quite high amongst myriad huge stumps and lengthy deadfalls before descending to another old road. Going right brings you to a halt at a ravine, where, near a great Douglas-fir on the verge, a moss-covered, ruined bridge crosses above a spectacular waterfall.

With no means to go ahead, you must turn back. This time stay with the road when you pass the turnoff to several loop trails until finally, after bypassing a collapsed bridge, you find yourself back at the beginning of your circuit, not far from the power line, where a left turn sets you off on the home stretch.

Another possibility in this area is the Coquitlam Lake View Trail, which goes right at the second fork. Travelling in concert with the Burke Ridge route, it soon goes right again and crosses a power line, entering trees on the far side. The trail, an old logging road becoming washed out and overgrown, continues gently uphill to another fork with wooden signs, where the routes part company and you go left through a stretch of tall second-growth timber before arriving at an attractive little waterfall. Some 90 minutes from the start, this makes a satisfying destination for a short walk.

The hike all the way to the Coquitlam Lake Viewpoint is a more ambitious outing. To continue, ford the stream below the waterfall, go right at a fork, then right again shortly thereafter, ascending more steeply now on an old road eroded oftentimes down to bedrock. Eventually the grade eases and a variety of mosses and other plants carpet the trail as you approach your destination on a wooded knob. From it, you may enjoy excellent views of the lake with its surrounding ridges, enjoyment perhaps tempered by the sight of a gravel operation in the valley downstream.

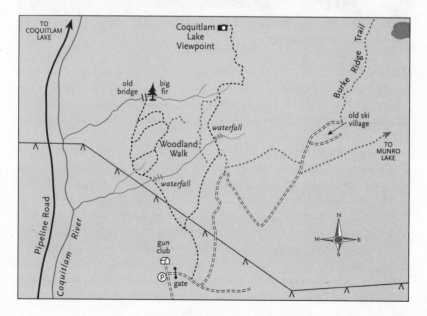

31 MINNEKHADA REGIONAL PARK

long circuit:	Round trip 6.5 km (4 mi)	Allow 2.5 hours
	Trails	Good most of the year

View over the marsh from Low Knoll.

This former estate northwest of Port Coquitlam is now a regional park with a lodge sometimes open to the public and a trail system that supplies the walker with as much variety as anyone may desire, including a miniature mountain, steep enough to test many, and a viewing pavilion giving a wide outlook over the Pitt River Valley.

To reach the parking area, travel north for 2.5 km (1.5 mi) from Highway 7 (Lougheed Highway) on Coast Meridian Road in Port Coquitlam, then follow directional signs via Apel Drive and Victoria Drive, taking the left fork of Victoria, which later becomes Quarry Road. From the fork continue for 3.5 km (2.2 mi) to parking on the right at the park entrance. The trail system starts here, with the choice of colour-coded routes to either right or left.

Going right, you come to a marsh that you keep on your left, but after a picnic area and the approach road to the lodge on your right, the forest reasserts itself. Then comes the parting of the ways, at a four-way crossing, the right-hand fork taking you to a striking viewpoint across Addington

Marsh to the UBC Malcolm Knapp Research Forest with the great peaks of Golden Ears beyond. After gazing your fill, instead of retracing your steps, follow the track north parallel to the marsh to a fork just before a bridge, and turn left and uphill to return to the four-way crossing, where you go right to rejoin the circle trail. Next, after a detour to the Low Knoll viewpoint over the central marsh, you reach a major junction: left (green) here leads you across the marsh on a dyke before returning you via Log Walk (green) or Meadow Trail (orange) to your starting point; right (red) commits you to the long circle trail.

On this you soon come to yet another fork, the right-hand branch of which sends you panting to the top of the sharp rise to High Knoll lookout, from which once more the valley lies before you. On your return to the T-junction, go first right, then left, gaining height and losing it again as you turn west, eventually reaching a small parking lot beside Quarry Road. From here, Quarry Trail parallels the road south, two successive left forks giving you access to the marsh dykes again before you meet your outward route, Lodge Trail, and keep right for the parking lot. Of all the trails, the one along Quarry Road is the least attractive, so you may well decide on your descent from High Knoll to turn back left, retrace your steps for a short distance, then keep right to cross the marsh and join Log Walk or Meadow Trail for the final stretch back.

Note that the house, Minnekhada Lodge, previously owned by two lieutenant governors of British Columbia, is now open to the public on the first Sunday afternoon of the month from February to December. It may also be booked for private functions. (For details, call 604-432-6352.)

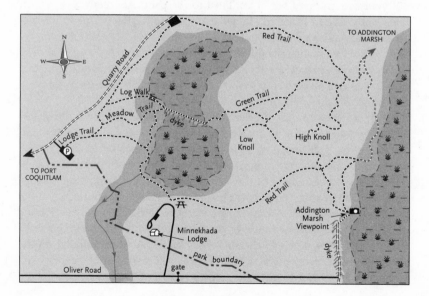

32 WHYTECLIFF

Round trip 5 km (3.1 mi) or less	Allow 2 hours
Trails and roads	Good all year

Whyte Island.

From the viewpoint in Whytecliff Park, on the most westerly point of West Vancouver, you may be content with a view across Howe Sound to Bowen Island or, if the tide is favourable, a walk over the causeway to Whyte Island. But your activity need not be confined to the park's southerly area; a high ridge, aptly named Panorama Ridge, may be a satisfying outing in itself or the start to more ambitious walks.

Travelling west along Highway 1/99 (Upper Levels Highway), take the Squamish fork at the Horseshoe Bay junction, turn left almost at once and cross the overpass, then stay with Marine Drive as it winds its picturesque way round Batchelor Bay and ends in Whytecliff Park.

On foot, head towards the overflow parking lot on the fringe of the forest. There find the start of the steepish trail to Panorama Ridge, with first, on your right, a diversion to a viewpoint over Batchelor Bay. Back on the route, you may enjoy the mixture of trees, arbutus being prominent, before emerging on top for views of Howe Sound and its surrounding mountains. Choosing left forks as you progress brings you to the northern margin of the park. If you wish only a short outing, turn back right, then left, rejoining your outward route for a return to the busier regions of the park, this time, perhaps, dropping down to the shore at Whyte Bay, then working up the steps and round the point to savour every aspect of Whytecliff.

For longer circuits, when you reach the park's northern extremity, descend Hycroft Road, going left at its bend on a track connecting with Isleview Road, down which you continue to its junction with Copper Cove Road, sharing as you go the fine views of the local homeowners. Next travel right on Copper Cove to its meeting with Marine Drive, and here again you have a choice. A jog right, then a left turn down Dufferin Avenue brings you to Batchelor Bay, a secluded little beach enclosed by rocky cliffs, a pleasant spot for a swim or a picnic. But if you prefer to explore even farther, back at Marine Drive go briefly left to find and ascend an inconspicuous track up to Madrona Place, thence to Madrona Crescent on which you go left to Wellington Place.

Now it's plain sailing as you stride down Wellington with the occasional backwards glance over your left shoulder at Mount Harvey and Brunswick Mountain. Next you cross Rosebery Avenue and Marine Drive in quick succession, then, just when you think you are approaching a dead end, you go right on Imperial Avenue, another cul-de-sac! But don't despair. The stone stairs between #6265 and #6268 are public and will take you back to Marine Drive. Nor are you yet condemned to walk that busy road, for a few metres to your left, you may escape down another set of steps—down, down to Batchelor Bay.

But by whichever route you arrive here, there's no escaping a final walk along Marine Drive if you want to complete the circuit, so climb the steps at the west end onto the road, here bereft of sidewalk, turn left and cautiously make your way back to Whytecliff Park.

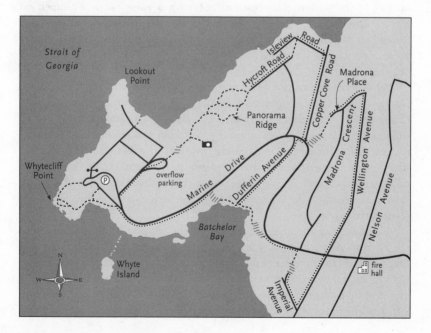

33 SEAVIEW/BADEN-POWELL

Round trip 8 km (5 mi)   Allow 3 hours
Trails and roads   Good all year

View over the golf course to Brunswick Mountain and Mount Harvey.

The main drawback to the Seaview Walk, on this abandoned railway right-of-way, is its western termination, not with a bang but a whimper, on Marine Drive at Gleneagles. By including in your itinerary a little of the Baden-Powell Trail and a few connecting residential streets, however, you may avoid most of this ignominy and add some distance to the 2.5-km (1.5-mi) one-way walk.

The eastern end of this excursion is in Eagle Harbour, approached from Marine Drive with a right turn in the 5700 block onto Cranley Drive. Cranley takes you uphill to a crossing of Nelson Creek, and it is here, east of the stream, that a path takes off on the road's north side, crossing the waterway on a footbridge and continuing upwards to a flat stretch below the viaduct that carries the highway. A glance to the right shows the rerouted railway track disappearing into the tunnel that replaced the right-of-way following a derailment in 1972, caused by the sharp change in direction from southwest to north.

Although your main preoccupation on the Seaview Walk is surely with the marine views, you may be fascinated, too, by the modern-day cliff dwellings and the plants, notably the arbutus, that cling to the rocks on your right. Soon, however, even before the 1-km marker, you leave the level walk and turn up a short track that takes you onto Falcon Road, where you turn left, heading more or less parallel to the trail below and ignoring cul-de-sacs on your left until you reach Eagleridge Drive, where you go right and uphill, passing Raven Place on your way to the highway overpass, beyond which lies the western terminus of the Baden-Powell Trail.

Now you head for the high point, literally and scenically, of your outing, for soon you come to a little track on the left leading to the top of a rock with a commanding view of Horseshoe Bay and the headlands and islands at the mouth of Howe Sound. Back on the Baden-Powell proper, you next join an old road and go right—up, over and down to meet the Black Mountain Trail beside a little pond. Turn left here, taking your leave of Baden-Powell, descend to the trailhead and go right along Highway 99, which you must cross as best you can to the overpass connecting with Marine Drive, on which a left turn would provide a direct route via Marine Drive to the Seaview Walk.

For more interest, however, cut along Rosebery Street and past the school onto a track that leads out to Fox Street and thence to Nelson and St. Georges Avenues, heading back with the Gleneagles Golf Course on your left. Then, with the clubhouse in sight, you may take a few more minutes to explore the charming little trails down Larson Creek to the secluded bay of the same name.

After this pleasant interlude, return to St. Georges Avenue, which curves into Orchill Road and meets Marine Drive opposite the western end of the Seaview Walk, whose whole length with its sea and mountain vistas you may now enjoy as you return to your transportation.

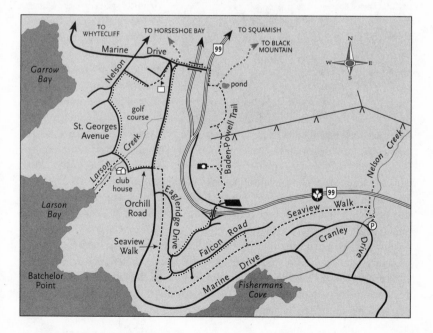

34 TRANS CANADA TRAIL/ NELSON CREEK LOOP

Round trip 9 km (5.5 mi)   Allow 3.5 hours
Elevation gain 418 m (1370 ft)   High point 460 m (1510 ft)
Trails and roads   Good most of the year

Forest's edge above Nelson Creek canyon.

If you have traversed the Seaview Walk east from Horseshoe Bay (Walk 33), you have already sampled the most westerly mainland section of the Trans Canada Trail. Now comes the next, more demanding part, which starts you off on the trail's upsy-downsy march across the face of the North Shore mountains.

Start as you did for the Seaview Walk (Walk 33) by driving north off Marine Drive on Cranley Drive to the trailhead at Nelson Creek. On foot you cross the creek and rise to the Seaview Walk, where you turn right and immediately mount to a vantage point above the entrance to the tunnel that replaced the original right-of-way. Then you continue to ascend, passing under the present Upper Levels Highway to reach the roadbed of its predecessor. Here you may enjoy a brief respite as you cross the 1956-vintage bridge with a view down Nelson Creek under the viaduct.

Beyond the bridge the route goes left towards a water tower, to the right of which you embark on a delightful trail through ancient forest above the canyon of Nelson Creek, climbing steadily through the fine old trees to arrive at the end of an abandoned road. This you follow for a few minutes before the trail heads off left, zigzagging a little at first to gain altitude and oftentimes making use of old forest roads, for you are now amongst quite large second-growth trees. Descending into a damp bottom, you approach, then swing left away from a small creek (Eagle Creek), arriving at a fork where turning right offers you a shorter circuit. (If you so choose, ford the little creek, turn right again and follow a rough road down.) Electing to go left, you stay with the Trans Canada Trail as it rises, finally crossing the creek on a makeshift bridge and emerging shortly thereafter on the grassy right-of-way of a water pipe, just below a tower.

From here, the high point of your outing, you go right, descending on Eagle Lake Road to a split where, if you go right, you find a track to a bluff top with a splendid view. After this break, continue downhill to a wide turnout. From here the Trans Canada Trail goes left, ascending steeply for another 500 m (1640 ft) on the route of the original access into Cypress Bowl. Your goal is lower, however, and you turn downhill again—on the road, if you wish, though you may cut the first corner using a faint trail that drops off on the east side, following a washed-out forest road. Whichever route you choose, you will eventually arrive at a junction close to the McCrady Bridge over Cypress Creek. Now you go right on the wide right-of-way to another T-junction. Turn left here and down before going right above a residential area, your path adorned with a disclaimer of liability by British Properties, its owner.

Next, after passing a second gate with another warning, you note a track angling in from your right—the route you would have taken had you bailed out earlier—and then you continue westwards across Eagle Creek and gently upwards to rejoin the Trans Canada Trail and retrace your steps to Cranley Drive.

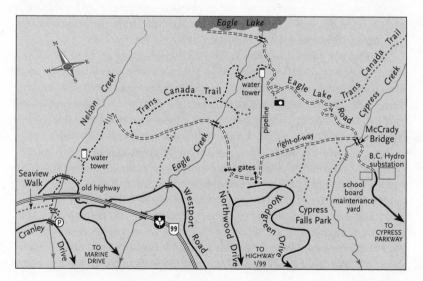

35 POINT ATKINSON

west circuit:	**Round trip 5 km (3.1 mi)**	**Allow 2 hours**
east circuit:	**Round trip 4 km (2.5 mi)**	**Allow 1.5 hours**
	Trails	**Good all year**

Point Atkinson lighthouse from the historic cairn.

Even urban troglodytes who emerge only infrequently from the built-up sections of Vancouver must be aware of this landmark on the north shore of Burrard Inlet, if for no other reason than that its lighthouse sends friendly beams of light over the waters during the hours of darkness and its foghorn bellows its warning during periods of gloomy overcast. But Point Atkinson is well worth a visit for its own sake, located as it is at the southern tip of Lighthouse Park, which features old-growth coastal forest, rocky headlands and narrow bays, and is the haunt of varied wildlife, from the humble organisms of the intertidal zone to majestic birds.

To reach the park, drive or take Bus #250 west along Marine Drive from the north end of Lions Gate Bridge for a distance of just over 9.6 km (6 mi). A little past a firehall, after a small rise in the road, Beacon Lane lies on the left. Turn and follow it to the designated parking area, at the end of which a gate bars further progress, though a service road does continue beyond it. Below the gate, a main trail goes off through tall conifers towards the southwest.

For a trouble-free walk, you may simply follow the trails with the yellow/white markers until they split, when you opt for white, adding little excursions seawards as fancy takes you. You may, for instance, follow a track going off right beside an interesting cedar and working its way out to Juniper Point and a fine view; then, at the next divergence, you may go right and descend gradually to an attractive cove with dykes of igneous rock penetrating the granite and contrasting with it. A little farther south, another short diversion right leads to Jackpine Point, giving views across to Bowen Island

and exhibiting all the beauty of a combined marine and forest landscape. Here, too, note the grooves in the rock, mute evidence of past glaciation.

As you turn towards the point, you get your first sight of the lighthouse, and soon you find yourself on the rock just behind it, where a plaque gives its history, dating back over a century, though the present tower was erected only in 1912. Before leaving, you may be able to walk into the grounds. Once you start back, your direct route is to the right (east) and virtually parallel with the service road.

Side trips are possible, the first being the short detour right to Arbutus Knoll, a rounded bluff overlooking Starboat Cove. Once you have rejoined the trail, the trip back to the gate at the south end of the parking area does not take long; that is, if you have not followed another track heading up from the valley and linking up with the less-developed trail system on the park's east side.

By so doing, you almost double the length of your walk, so you may wish to save this for a separate trip, given that you may go east over the spine of the peninsula from a track that starts close to the gate. On this, if you keep right, you come to the summit trail. Another right turn takes you to the park's highest point, after which, still staying right, you come to a four-way crossing. Here you may go right or straight ahead, both trails eventually rejoining close to a small point on the park's southeast coast with a nice view over English Bay.

After this diversion return to the white-marked trail heading up left then meandering along for a little before descending steeply to meet the main valley trail beside some impressive cedars. Here, going right soon brings you to the service road a short distance south of the gate.

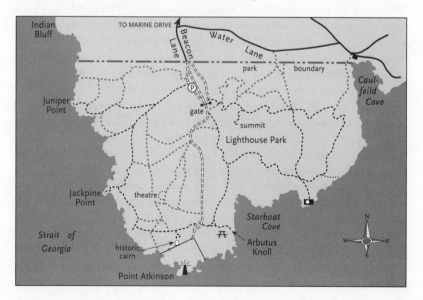

36 CYPRESS FALLS PARK

Round trip 3 km (1.9 mi) or more   Allow 1 hour
Trails and roads   Good all year

Sword fern.

Given that the semi-wilderness Cypress Falls Park, with its groves of fine Douglas-fir, is little more than a stone's throw above Highway 1/99 (Upper Levels Highway), it is not as well known as it might be. For access to it, take the Woodgreen Drive turnoff (Exit 4) from the highway, turn right, then right again at Woodgreen Place to park in the open area on the left beyond the tennis courts. Cross the clearing towards the forest, then turn left and uphill, but for the best view of the lower falls, abandon this trail almost immediately and drop to an old pipeline route on a bench just below on the right.

On this you soon reach a fine viewpoint overlooking the tumbling waters in their little canyon. Then you must scramble up to your left to regain the main trail, which descends to a lookout above the waterfall. Next a footbridge takes you across the creek to its east side and you start rising, eventually emerging on a service road with various power lines leading to a power station. Turn left and uphill towards that installation and a School Board Facilities Workshop opposite it. Ignoring a B.C. Hydro service road on your right, in a few more minutes recross the creek on the stout McCrady Bridge. Then go left on the pipeline right-of-way where Eagle Lake Road goes right, rising quite steeply. A little more than 100 m along, a trail to the left takes you to a view of the upper falls, particularly impressive during spring runoff. From here many routes descend through the park, providing opportunities for viewing its grand old trees. Staying left at forks, however, brings you down close to the creek, with glimpses of its rapids an added bonus. At a fork within sight of your first bridge you may go right, rising slightly to pass a final few large Douglas-firs and a grove of young hemlocks before descending to rejoin the main trail within steps of the clearing from which you set out.

This, however, by no means exhausts the area's possibilities. Given that the park route abuts on the previously described Trans Canada Trail/Nelson Creek Loop (Walk 34), you may wish to incorporate part of that walk into your outing. For instance, you may defer your return to the park, continuing on the pipeline right-of-way westwards and going left at the T-junction, then right past the British Properties gate with its disclaimer of liability. Next, after passing a second gate, watch for a track angling in from the right at a widening of the road. Slightly overgrown and eroded, this leads up to a fork where you turn left, soon arriving at a ford over a little creek (Eagle Creek) and a junction with the Trans Canada Trail shortly after.

Now you may choose whether to go left towards Nelson Creek, returning on the British Properties road, or to go right, rising to the high point at the water tower and descending by Eagle Lake Road. Either way you arrive back at the right-of-way with the previously described alternatives through the park at your disposal. And either way you will have more than doubled the basic park outing, so allow lots of time.

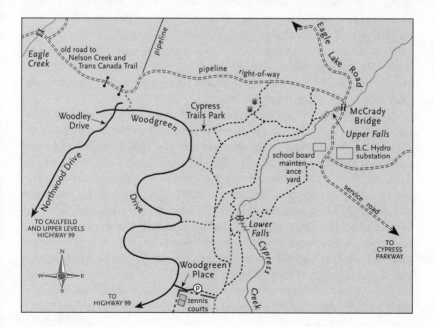

37 BLACK MOUNTAIN LOOP

Round trip 7.5 km (4.7 mi)
Elevation gain 300 m (985 ft)
Trails and roads

Allow 3 hours
High point 1217 m (3992 ft)
Best June to October

Looking towards the north summit, Brunswick Mountain (left) and The Lions behind.

Until the late 1970s this summit and its picturesque subalpine plateau were attainable only by those prepared to hike from just above sea level at Horseshoe Bay. Now, thanks to Cypress Parkway, they may be reached with a fraction of the energy required before.

From Highway 1/99 (Upper Levels Highway) turn off at Exit 8 for Cypress Bowl and drive to the downhill ski parking area at the end of the road. From there start at the west end, turning uphill immediately, your route's beginning identified by a Baden-Powell Trail sign. First you rise southwards, with a variety of views over Point Grey and the Strait of Georgia until you reach a sharp curve, at which point you double back right and proceed, still uphill, the floor of Cypress Bowl now well below you. When the grade eases, take a track going left and up to join the main Black Mountain ski run, on which you double back left to the next bend, where you may leave the Baden-Powell. Watch on the left side for a small cairn that marks a trail going off south into the forest.

Though this trail may be a little difficult to find at first, following it in preference to staying with the ski run is well worth the initial effort, as it winds its way westwards to intersect the Black Mountain Loop about 20 m south of its junction with the Baden-Powell Trail. From here, you turn left (south), descending and crossing the outlet from Theagill Lake on your way to Sam Lake and an area dotted with little lakes. This area you reach by bearing southwest and up a gully to another meeting with the Baden-Powell Trail, on which you go right; that is, unless you want to visit the Black Mountain plateau to the west and Eagle Bluff 1.7 km (1 mi) away.

Now you work your way up a series of switchbacks to the south summit, from which your outlook extends all the way from the lowlands in the southeast to the peaks of the Vancouver Island mountains in the west. From here, follow the Baden-Powell Trail down to Cabin Lake, with a short side trip to the north summit, the so-called Yew Lake Viewpoint, though Lions View would be a more apt name. In fact, the vista to the north is outstanding, with the snow-capped peaks of the Tantalus Range clearly visible.

For your descent, rejoin the Baden-Powell Trail and follow it to the next fork, where it parts company with the Black Mountain Loop, which stays right. There, for variety, you may go left, rising a little uphill to the upper terminal of the chairlift. Descend its ski run to the right, eventually meeting the trail by which you ascended. Actually, any of the runs would provide a route down; they all meet at the foot near the parking area. The only difference between one and the other is in their steepness.

Should the Black Mountain chairlift be operating on summer days, you may, if you feel lazy, confine your outing to the mountaintop loop and the North Summit for a round trip of 2.5 km (1.5 mi), with an elevation gain of only 65 m (212 ft).

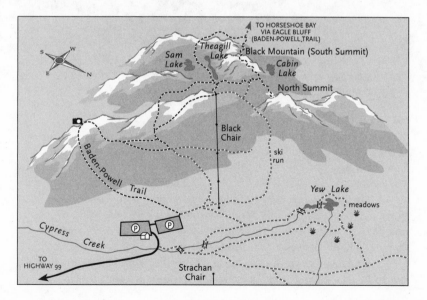

38 CYPRESS BOWL

Round trip 4 km (2.5 mi)
Elevation gain 145 m (475 ft)
Trails and roads

Allow 2 hours
High point 1060 m (3475 ft)
Best late June to October

Yew Lake.

If the preceding hike on Black Mountain (Walk 37) appears somewhat strenuous, you may find this loop, using in part the Interpretive Trail round Yew Lake, more to your taste. The circuit of the lake alone from the ticket office at the downhill ski area is rather short, involving as it does only a walk west along the valley floor beside Yew Lake's outlet creek, called Cypress (hence the name Cypress Bowl), the whole amounting to no more than 1.4 km (0.9 mi), all of it wheelchair accessible.

For a slightly longer outing, head off northeast on the trail across the marsh to visit a stand of old-growth trees enclosed within a short loop in an unlogged band of forest. Continue, connecting with an old road near a shed on the far side. Going left to the end of this road brings you to a viewpoint overlooking Bowen Island's Deep Bay and Snug Cove across Howe Sound. After this diversion, retrace your steps to rejoin the main lake trail and complete the loop.

For a still longer, more energetic trip, go right on the old road to the sign for the Howe Sound Crest Trail (HSCT), the high-level route that links Cypress Bowl with Highway 99 (Sea to Sky Highway) just south of Porteau Cove. On this route, turn left and zigzag through a belt of trees to another, higher road, on which you turn left again. Here you may enjoy views across to Bowen Island over the fireweed and shrubs now cloaking the logged-off slopes before once more entering the tall timber. Next, on your left, comes a sign for Bowen Lookout, at which you go left for views to the west over Howe Sound.

Before you do so, however, you may go a few paces farther on the HSCT for a view of The Lions, framed in trees. You could even follow the trail to the meadow north of Mount Strachan, though this is likely to be wet most of the year. The Bowen Lookout itself, despite its promising title, has a somewhat restricted view of the east side of the island for which it is named; in fact, its best outlook is across Cypress Bowl to Black Mountain.

From here you may have to retrace your steps; however, if you have a taste for shortcuts, you may descend on a rough, flagged route to the road below and turn right to enjoy the view at its end. Return via the grove of old-growth trees and the marsh to join the Yew Lake trail and go right to complete the loop, which makes its way along the margin of the marsh and then the shore of the lake before crossing and eventually recrossing the stream to join the other branch for the last lap back to the parking lot.

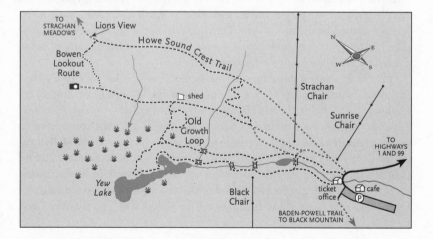

87

39 BADEN-POWELL TRAIL
(Hollyburn Ridge)

Round trip 11.3 km (7 mi) or less	Allow 4.5 hours
Elevation gain 260 m (850 ft)	High point 1068 m (3500 ft)
Trails and roads	Best late June to October

Heritage Hollyburn Lodge beyond First Lake.

Use of the Baden-Powell Trail as part of its circumference permits you to undertake an interesting circular outing in the Hollyburn-Cypress area, which includes unspoiled forest and various small lakes but, alas, some human-spoiled landscape as well. Or, if you do not wish to make the complete circuit, you may hike only the more appealing ridge section, of some 5.6 km (3.5 mi), using a two-car operation.

Your best point of departure is Parking Lot 5 on the left side of Cypress Parkway, located about 11 km (7 mi) from its beginning at Exit 8 off Highway 1/99 (Upper Levels Highway). By starting here, you get the least aesthetic part of your excursion over at the beginning, when you have to walk a short distance uphill on the road, noting as you pass it the Hollyburn fire access road opposite that will be your return route. After some 200 m, turn left on the road to the resort maintenance yard, walk to its northwest corner, and from there proceed via the one-time logging road up the valley of Cypress Creek, your route being joined at the power line by the Trans Canada Trail.

After about 30 minutes you come to the Cypress Creek crossing. Then, having climbed out of the valley, continue right and uphill, keeping right when the Trans Canada Trail heads off southwards and finally reaching the downhill ski area parking lot. Traverse this and cross the access road. Opposite the administration and ticket office, look for an orange Baden-Powell sign at the start of the trail's Hollyburn Ridge section. On this part of your journey you are in original forest with some fine old trees close by the trail, which winds upwards crossing some interesting creeks en route to its junction with the old Mount Strachan Trail. Stay right, cross the bridge over the final creek and continue for 10 minutes more until you meet the main trail to Hollyburn Mountain as you reach the ridge proper.

Stay right at this junction also, descending gently to pass the first of the little lakes that you meet on this stage of your outing. Soon you see power lines running at right angles to your route and you reach the right-of-way near several other small bodies of water, Fourth Lake being closest to the trail. (Second and Third are a little farther west.) At the warming hut, you see the main hiking trail heading southwards, on its way to First Lake and Hollyburn Lodge; follow this after you have savoured the views over to Crown Mountain.

At the lodge, you say good-bye to Baden-Powell, your route turning right behind the building and following the main service road back to the park highway. On the way, ignore a trail going off to the right; it leads to the cross-country ski parking lot some distance above the point at which you wish to reach the road.

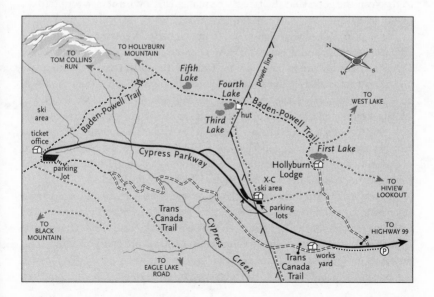

40 LOWER HOLLYBURN

Round trip 12 km (7.5 mi) or less
Elevation gain 500 m (1640 ft)
Trails and roads

Allow 4.5 hours
High point 930 m (3050 ft)
Best May to November

West Lake.

With snow lying late on Hollyburn's higher reaches, it is fortunate that a well-established trail system on its south-facing lower slopes permits an earlier start to the hiking season. The bad news is that the trails are wet early in the year, the good that the tree shade makes this a wise choice for hot days in summer.

For a start, leave Highway 1/99 (Upper Levels Highway) at Exit 8 for Cypress Parkway and drive to HiView Lookout at the second hairpin bend. Cut across the corner to pick up your trail on the north side of the highway and almost immediately note the trail coming downhill from the left; it will be your return route. Next your track, the Millstream Trail, drops sharply to cross a stream and rise again, repeating the process for a second creek before it settles to a gradual descent on its way eastwards. Then, some 30 minutes along, a narrow track signed "Brewis Trail" leads up to the Skyline Trail if you want a shortcut. The main route continues east to a T-junction not far from the junction of Eyremount Drive and Millstream Road.

Go left on the trail, rising steadily on the eroded surface and, ignoring a right fork to the Shields Incline Railway (Walk 42), eventually reaching the fork where your route parts from the Brothers Creek Trail. Keep left, making a second left just beyond a power line. From here you are on the Skyline Trail, now also designated the Trans Canada Trail, sometimes in the open close to the power line, sometimes in the forest as you cross one creek after another, with, before long, signs for the Brewis Trail again, the uphill leg this time leading to the former Westlake Lodge road via the Hollyburn Douglas-fir.

At last comes a four-way fork adorned with a pile of stones supporting the old Forks sign as well as some newer ones. Here you turn left and follow the steepish trail downhill, emerging just above the original lookout for a round trip of 6.8 km (4.2 mi), having risen in all the best part of a thousand feet.

For a longer walk, stay right at the fork above the power line and follow the Baden-Powell Trail uphill, ignoring the Crossover Trail, which you intersect en route to the next decisive fork. Going straight ahead and still on the Boy Scout trail, you would pass the site of the one-time Westlake Lodge, then continue on the Grand National ski trail. But right is more attractive, leading you quite soon to Blue Gentian Lake, where the damp environment encourages a healthy growth of that plant plus other moisture-lovers. From here turn left and uphill to West Lake, beyond which you may travel via the Jack Spratt ski trail until it too joins the Grand National, on which you reach the literal high point of your walk: the outlet from First Lake and the old Hollyburn Lodge. Just across the creek and close to the ranger station, turn left on the one-time main trail, descending through the cabin area and staying right at the first two forks, then going left at the third.

At the next, however, take the steep, dark and narrow track going down right to the Westlake road just west of and below a TV relay tower. Now jog right some thirty paces, then continue downhill on the foot trail, cross a very old road and finally turn left on an eroded stretch of logging road to the Forks. From here your downhill route duplicates that of the shorter circuit.

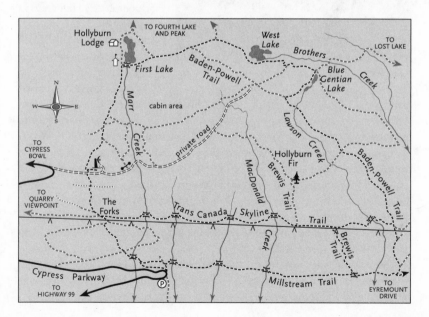

41 BROTHERS CREEK TRAILS

Round trip 11 km (6.8 mi) or less
Elevation gain 435 m (1425 ft)
Trails

Allow 4 hours
High point 800 m (2600 ft)
Best May to November

Lost Lake.

One nice point about the trip described here is that the route's elongated shape allows you to sample slices of suitable length if you do not wish to indulge in the whole delicacy. It provides rich variety, too: maturing second-growth forest with, here and there, survivors of the original giant trees, a creek with three sets of falls and canyons, and two forest lakes as well, if you make the longest trip.

To reach its starting point, from Highway 1/99 (Upper Levels Highway) at Taylor Way (Exit 13) continue north into the British Properties, turn left at the T-junction and pick up Highland Drive at the first four-way stop. Stay on Highland until, finally, you turn left on Eyremount Drive and continue to its junction with Millstream Road. Park here close to a gated forest road with West Vancouver Parks trail signs and map. Take this trail, and in about 5 minutes turn right and uphill for another 5 minutes to a fork where you have a choice: to go right on the recently cleared old railway bed that meets the Skyline Trail close by Brothers Creek and then takes a jog left; or left on the traditional route, going right at the next fork signposted for Brothers Creek and Lost Lake and, a few minutes thereafter, crossing a power line right-of-way and the variously named Skyline/Baden-Powell/Trans Canada Trail.

Now you plunge into forest, the creek well below you on your right, and thus you remain until, after track and waterway have both levelled slightly, you come to the second point of decision: a footbridge takes you right, over the creek on the Crossover Trail, to an eventual meeting with the return route, giving a round trip of 6 km (3.7 mi) for which you should allow about 2 hours.

If you stay left and continue up the main trail, you have first of all a level stretch where the creek is just another pleasant forest stream, but then you rise again and soon you are viewing your first set of falls, above which you are faced with yet another choice: to cross the creek or not. Here again you may start your return by staying right after you have crossed to the east bank, then descending on a fire road to link up with the lower circuit trail for a round trip of 8.7 km (5.4 mi) and a time of nearly 3 hours.

For the longest walk, stay west of the creek. Another 20 minutes or so of walking brings you to pretty little Blue Gentian Lake, where there are picnic tables and, in summer, an abundance of water-lily flowers as well. From the lake stay right, drop a little to cross a small creek, then, following signs for Lost Lake, cross Brothers Creek, just beyond which are interesting views into the gorge of the upper falls. After a half-hour walk, traverse the outlet of the lake you are seeking, another possible stopping point.

For your return trip, use the trail downhill on the east side of Brothers Creek to join and descend the fire road. On this stretch the road coincides briefly with an old cable-railway bed (Walk 42) before parting again at the next bend. Lower still, the Crossover Trail enters from the right and departs a few bends later for Ballantree by the site of a one-time sawmill. Keep right and continue down to the power line, turn right on Skyline Trail, rise some 100 m (350 ft), then drop sharply to Brothers Creek's lower falls. Here you recross the creek, rise equally fast out of its ravine and return to your starting point by whichever route you choose, your walk on Brothers (once Sisters) Creek over.

If, however, when you reach the power line on the fire road, you want no more climbing, you could go straight ahead, crossing Skyline (Baden-Powell) Trail out to Millstream Road and thence back to your car.

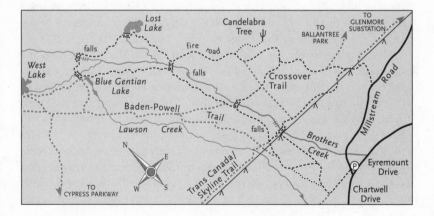

42 HOLLYBURN HERITAGE TRAILS

Round trip 6.7 km (4.2 mi)
Elevation gain 314 m (1030 ft)
Trails

Allow 3.5 hours
High point 665 m (2180 ft)
Best May to November

View downstream under Pinecrest Drive.

Hollyburn has not one but two heritage trails commemorating its logging history, with self-guiding brochures available from West Vancouver Parks and Community Services (604-925-7200). The walk suggested here combines the two to produce one satisfying ramble that avoids as far as possible those sections of routes described elsewhere (Walks 40 and 41).

To start, leave Highway 1/99 (Upper Levels Highway) at Exit 11 and go right on Cross Creek Road, then left onto Chartwell Drive. Stay on Chartwell, winding uphill until, just after the fifth elbow bend, you go left (west) on Pinecrest Drive. A small cairn and the distinctive blue-and-green heritage trail sign marks the beginning on the west side of the bridge spanning Lawson Creek.

Almost immediately you reach a viewpoint for the Shields Log Dam and pass on up the pleasant woodland trail to meet Millstream Trail, an old logging road. Turn right and across Lawson Creek to a T-junction, where you go left. Stay on this, an old truck road, for about 5 minutes to the next fork, leaving it for what was the route of an inclined cable railway, running straight ahead until it reaches the banks of Brothers Creek, the remains of an old bridge still visible across the stream. Following the deepening canyon you next come to the Skyline (Baden-Powell) Trail and turn right, dropping steeply to cross Brothers Creek and rising again to continue past a small lookout with views over the city to a fork at the foot of another section of cable railway, again straight and smooth except at creeks where old trestles have collapsed and disappeared. Next you cross a transverse trail (Crossover Trail) and shortly thereafter join a fire road occupying the place of the railway for a short distance to the next bend, where you go straight ahead on the railbed to its upper terminal, only a few scattered artifacts to mark the one-time loading site. After visualizing the scene in the 1920s, return downhill almost to the fire road and descend by a rough trail on the left (east) for about 5 minutes to a large Douglas-fir, now dead and called the "Candelabra" tree for its distinctive fork-like shape. Continuing downhill, the track passes several other huge snags before ending at an old-growth Douglas-fir, a living giant among the dead.

Next retrace your steps to the fire road, and thereafter to the former railbed as far as the Crossover Trail, where you turn right, heading gently uphill towards Brothers Creek and its trail beyond the bridge. A few metres right on this brings you to the continuation of the Crossover Trail, now making for the Baden-Powell Trail and Lawson Creek and across both on the way to the high point of your outing—the Hollyburn Douglas-fir, a giant quietly growing here for nearly eleven hundred years.

Close by, Brewis Trail runs roughly north-south, north eventually arriving at the old Westlake Road via the MacDonald Canyon, but today turn left and south, descending quite steeply to the Skyline Trail. Go left on it for a short distance before resuming your downhill plunge on Brewis, which returns you in short order to the Millstream Trail. Going left again soon brings you back to your outward route from Pinecrest Drive.

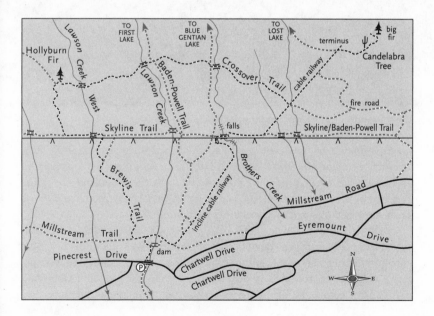

43 BALLANTREE

Round trip 3 km (1.9 mi)
Elevation gain 145 m (475 ft)
Roads and trails

Allow 1.5 hours
High point 465 m (1525 ft)
Best April to November

Crown Mountain over the rooftops on Ballantree Road.

Looking for a short walk within easy reach of the British Properties? Try this circular outing on the lower slopes of Hollyburn Mountain for a forest trail ending in Ballantree Park with a return through the woodland above the homes of the area and views across to Crown Mountain, to Grouse Mountain, and over the city and inner harbour.

As with Brothers Creek (Walk 41), your approach through the British Properties is via Highland Drive and Eyremount Drive. This time, however, turn right off Eyremount onto Crestline Road. Follow Crestline to its junction with Millstream Road, where you go left to the next junction. Park there a little before the Glenmore power station, then ascend the power line westwards, noting that it carries the Baden-Powell Trail sign and the markers for the Trans Canada Trail. Ignore a faint trail on the right alongside a creek that you reach after about 10 minutes and keep left again shortly thereafter, but do go right on the fire access road.

At the next fork you pass several pieces of B.C. logging history—a stone foundation, all that is left of a long-gone sawmill, and the remains of a donkey engine hidden in the bush opposite. Turn right at this point on Ballantree Trail, which takes you north and east through the forest towards the watershed boundary. Finally you come down off the trail, very eroded in the last section, into an open space, part of Ballantree Park. With the trail sign behind you, turn right again over a bridge and cross a clearing prior to picking up a trail that runs southwards above the houses on the west side of Ballantree Road itself.

The route you are following brings you out at the end of Kildonan Road, and a short walk along it and Craigmohr returns you to your parking spot. Incidentally, given that most of the street names have a Scottish flavour, it looks as though "Ballantree" may be a slightly distorted version of "Ballantrae," the setting of Robert Louis Stevenson's historical romance.

Another and more practical point: since this walk abuts on the Brothers Creek one (Walk 41), you may combine parts of that outing with the trail just described. For example, stay with the Baden-Powell (Skyline) Trail beyond the fire-road crossing, go up to the Brothers Creek Trail just west of the lower falls and go right on it. Recross the creek at the first junction and follow the Crossover Trail downhill through the forest to the fire road. Descend on that road for about 5 minutes until you reach the Ballantree Trail going off left. Since this extension would more than double the length of the walk, adding roughly 5 km (3 mi), and would also double the elevation gain you should allow an extra 1.5 hours.

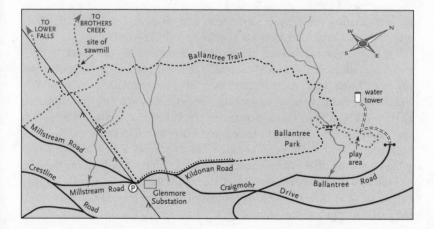

44 CAPILANO CANYON

to dam from park road:	Round trip 4.5 km (2.8 mi)	Allow 2 hours
to dam from Keith Road:	Round trip 8 km (5 mi)	Allow 3 hours
to dam from Ambleside Park:	Round trip 12 km (7.5 mi)	Allow 4 hours
	Trails	Good all year

Pipeline Bridge.

The walker in this scenic valley lying between the twin communities of North and West Vancouver has a number of outings from which to choose, ranging from various circuits in Capilano River Regional Park itself to an upriver approach, following in part a one-time logging-railway right-of-way that links Keith Road in West Vancouver with the Cleveland Dam.

For walks within the park, drive or take a bus north on Capilano Road in North Vancouver. Your first access is reached by forking left onto Capilano Park Road from a little north of the traffic light at Edgemont Boulevard and parking near a salmon hatchery on the valley floor below the dam. For another approach, at dam-top level, with views across the reservoir northwest to The Lions, turn left at the top of Capilano Road where it curves into Nancy Greene Way.

From the former, you may complete a circuit below the dam taking Coho Loop, a short level loop using the park's two footbridges. Of course, once on the river's west bank, you may take one or other of the trails leading to the dam top. A detour to the Second Canyon Viewpoint provides a fine spot for appreciating the canyon's grandeur, and an extension, Giant Fir Trail, gives you a sight of that monster conifer as well. Thereafter, having crossed the spillway, you may return by one of the routes on the east bank.

For a walk from the south, you may use the Capilano Pacific Trail, starting from Keith Road, itself reached by going east from Taylor Way in West Vancouver. From here, after parking a little beyond the underpass of Highway 1, you head first upstream on the old railway grade, then leave it for forest, meeting the Rabbit Lane trail farther on. High above the river, the park trail hugs the side hill, majestic trees all around until Houlgate Creek causes a detour, after which you must make a choice: stay high for the dam or drop into the valley. For the dam, the second trail to the left, still Capilano Pacific, provides a relatively level route, with the trails from the valley joining from the right as you embark on the final rise to the dam.

A more ambitious walk, adding a good 4 km (2.5 mi) to the round trip, follows the Capilano Pacific Trail all the way from its beginning in Ambleside Park, which you reach by turning south from Marine Drive on 13th Street. From your start eastward along the seawall, you swing north, following closely the river's west bank until, after crossing Brothers Creek at its mouth near Capilano Care Centre, you approach the Woodcroft residential complex. Now you go left and uphill to meet and go right on Keith Road, continuing as in the previous paragraph.

Yet another possibility exists if you want to explore the downstream trails on the east side. For this option, start on Capilano Park Road at a small parking area about 200 m beyond the turnoff from Capilano Road and walk north on the sidewalk a short distance to where the trails, Chinook and Pipeline, go off left. Both take you to the Pipeline Bridge crossing of the river, with Chinook winding up and down closer to the river—longer, more adventurous and altogether more interesting. North of the Pipeline Bridge you may join Capilano Pacific Trail on its way upstream to the dam crossing, with a return via the hatchery and Camp Capilano on the river's east side. Then, back on Pipeline Trail, your outing ends with a gentle little rise back to the road and your transportation.

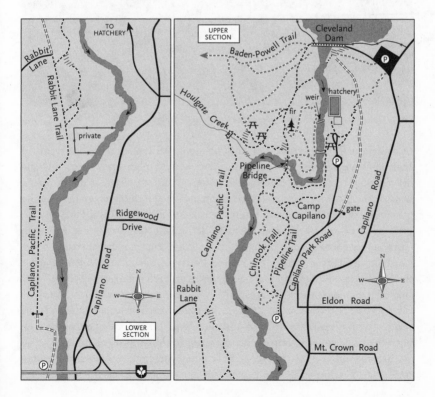

45 BOWSER TRAIL

Round trip 6 km (3.7 mi) or more **Allow 2 hours**
Trails and streets **Good all year**

View upstream to Crown Mountain beyond the Upper Levels bridge.

In its official entirety, this trail running along the foot of the slope north of Marine Drive and linking Capilano Road with Pemberton Avenue has one drawback: it is too short, less than 30 minutes being required for the complete walk. Fortunately it does lend itself to expansion at either end, giving you the possibility of a walk that may stretch as far as 7.5 km (4.7 mi) if you wish.

You may, for instance, start from Klahanie Park (reached by a left turn on Curling Road from Capilano Road just north of Marine Drive, with a short jog right on Glenaire Drive). From the parking lot, turn left on Glenaire, pass the barrier at the road end and go left again on Fullerton Avenue to the near side of the bridge leading across the Capilano River to Woodcroft. Drop to the riverbank on the north side here and follow the track that runs along it, some townhouses on your right and the Upper Levels bridge ahead of you, with the ridge running north from Grouse Mountain as a background.

Just beyond the last house, a track takes you right among some young conifers to Sundown Place and hence to Capilano Road. This you must negotiate with care, given the speedy traffic, to reach the start of the trail proper. Along it you walk in a screen of tall trees, noting on your way the high flight of steps from Pemberton Heights by which you may return. Finally, behind a shopping centre at Pemberton Avenue, the official trail ends; however, you may continue by ascending the many flights of wooden steps upwards to the attractive little Zig Zag Park, with its view of Vancouver's inner harbour.

Now you go right on Keith Road, starting to lose the height you just gained, as you pass 19th Street and reach Mackay, with a track into Heywood Park just opposite. Once in the park, you descend to cross Mackay Creek and its grassy valley before you turn north to experience its ravine. Ignore the first steps heading upwards to the right, taking instead the second set to emerge on the plateau by Lucas Education Centre.

Your business is not with education, though, and you continue north along some playing fields, with the choice of recrossing Mackay Creek directly or of looking for a track starting just behind the right-hand goalpost of the soccer field. This detour gives another experience of mini-wilderness, the illusion spoiled only by the sounds of traffic on the Upper Levels Highway. Descend gently to the creek on this forest trail and rejoin the direct route at a bridge. Here you are faced with the inevitable climb out of the ravine, after which, by turning right at the edge of the trees, you emerge on 23rd Street at a little sports field. Now on quiet treed residential streets, work your way west on 23rd, then south on Pemberton, its pedestrian steps taking you a little uphill before again you turn west then south, cross Keith Road and descend by the 200-odd steps from the end of Bridgman Avenue to the Bowser Trail again.

You may retrace your steps to get back to Klahanie Park directly from here, but an alternative does exist. On Fullerton, cross the river, turn back left on the Woodcroft side and follow the west bank downstream, staying with it until you come to the bridge that carries Marine Drive traffic. Recross the river here, drop to the riverbank and follow the trail north to your starting point.

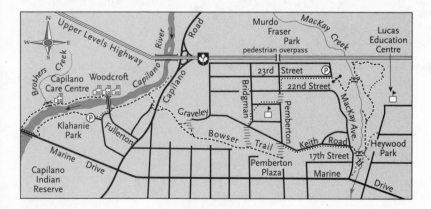

46 BADEN-POWELL TRAIL
(Grouse Mountain)

current route:	Round trip 5 km (3.1 mi)	Allow 2 hours
	Elevation gain 215 m (705 ft)	High point 533 m (1750 ft)
original route:	Round trip 6 km (3.7 mi)	Allow 3 hours
	Elevation gain 380 m (1250 ft)	High point 686 m (2250 ft)
	Trails and roads	Best April to November

The Lions seen from Powerline Trail.

The basic walk on this circuit linking the Grouse Mountain Skyride with Skyline Drive uses the current Baden-Powell Trail one-way with a return trip on B.C. Hydro's power line right-of-way for a round trip of 5 km (3.1 mi) and an altitude gain of 215 m (705 ft). If, however, you do not mind having to gain some extra height on a rough trail with a bit of a drop-off here and there, you may add to your options by hiking part of Baden-Powell's original route.

Whatever your choice, a start from the west end is preferable, despite its greater altitude gain, for on the return along the power line you face views southwest to the Strait of Georgia and northwest to The Lions. To begin, therefore, drive or take the bus to the Skyride area at the top of Nancy Greene Way. Just above the overflow parking lot, you will find the trailhead blazoned with statistical data for the much-touted Grouse Grind with the blue fleur-de-lis on orange background, the distinctive Boy Scout sign, taking second place.

Rising quite steeply at first, in a few minutes you reach a fork. The Grouse Grind heads up even more steeply to the left, while the Baden-Powell

Trail works its way along the front of the slope in deep forest. Finally levelling, you come to a junction with signs, the steep trail on your left to the old British Columbia Mountaineering Club (BCMC) cabin site being assigned a deceptive 0.3 km only. Continuing, you undulate along until you arrive on the verge of a washed-out ravine, its bridge swept away in a savage flood. At low water, however, the creek, Mackay Creek, is negotiable with care. Carry on, gradually descending to the next significant fork, where the Baden-Powell Trail heads left towards Mosquito Creek. But you go down right, emerging in a few minutes on a bend at the top of Skyline Drive and going right again to the second bend down the road, where a gated track starts along the power line right-of-way. With nothing now to worry about but the views, you are soon back at the Skyride and the end of your circuit.

And what of the older route of the Baden-Powell? For this, start as before and at the first junction go left on the Grouse Grind, a newcomer that has usurped the route of the old trail for its initial stage. After some 20 minutes (less if you are running like a Grouse Grinder), you come to a fork where you leave the improved trail for one going right, signed to the BCMC Trail and angling precipitously up the side of the mountain's south slope. Having made your height, you come to another fork, where an alternative to the Grind goes left for the ridge top, while your old Baden-Powell Trail drops gently to an open bluff with views over Burrard Inlet and the cities along its shores.

Close by is the site of the former BCMC cabin and the meeting of several trails: left and uphill, the Larsen Trail to Grouse Mountain; straight ahead, the joint BCMC and former Baden-Powell Trail, now impassable because of a massive landslide at Mackay Creek. To complete your circuit, therefore, you must keep right and descend the steep 0.3-km (0.2-mi) trail to join the current Baden-Powell, going east with it as before described or, if you wish a shorter outing, turning back west for a direct return to the Skyride.

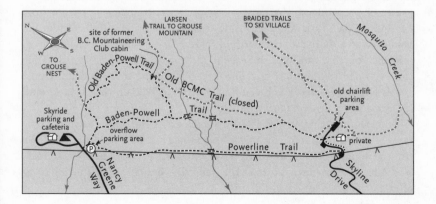

47 MOSQUITO CREEK

to Montroyal:	Round trip 6.8 km (4.2 mi)	Allow 2.5 hours
to Mahon Park:	Round trip 3.5 km (2.2 mi)	Allow 1 hour
	Elevation gain 206 m (675 ft)	High point 220 m (725 ft)
	Trails and streets	Good all year

Heading up Mosquito Creek to Montroyal.

Like its neighbour to the west, Mackay Creek, some of this valley has been preserved as parkland, the most scenic sections stretching upstream from Mosquito Creek Park on its west side at the intersection of Fell Avenue and Larson Road a short distance north of Marine Drive. A kiosk at the trailhead informs you that you will share your route with the Trans Canada Trail, then you plunge almost at once into trees. Next you travel beneath Upper Levels Highway, after which you find yourself in William Griffin Park, with its recreation centre on Queens Road.

For a short outing, you may walk uphill east of the centre towards some trees before turning south on a little upland ridge separating Mosquito Creek from a tributary stream, dropping down into the park again near the lacrosse box. A bridge provides a return to the trail and eventually your starting point after a walk of about 3.2 km (2 mi).

If, however, you wish to continue, you must cross Queens Road for the dead-ended Del Rio Drive where the trail resumes, the creek invisible in a culvert extending uphill as far as Evergreen Place. Beyond here the stream, now carefully tailored, is in a surprisingly wide valley, the route beside it taking you as far as Montroyal Boulevard, a little beyond which it peters out at present, though it could easily be linked to the Baden-Powell Trail higher up. You may, however, vary your downstream route by crossing to the east bank on Montroyal, then going right on Glencanyon Drive until that street turns away left at a sign saying "Mosquito Creek Walking Trail." Descend on this trail, emerging on the creek again a short distance above the bridge at Evergreen. Thereafter, retrace your steps to William Griffin Park and your return as for the shorter option.

Back at your starting point, if you still have some energy left, you may add a circuit of the smaller Mahon Park by crossing on the footbridge to the east side of Mosquito Creek and going up to 17th Street. At the end of the street a short descent takes you into the ravine of Mahon Creek, along whose east bank you may go left or right: left takes you upstream to some playing fields, where you walk east along the crest of the ravine to Jones Avenue; by going right you can explore the inner park, walking downstream to the bridge above the confluence of the two creeks, Mahon and Wagg, then going left up onto the little ridge separating them. At a crossing before a little meadow you may continue straight ahead to emerge alongside the fields and thus to Jones Avenue.

You then descend to Wagg Creek and follow it down to just above the meeting of the waters before you cross both streams and go right to mount the steps to 15th Street. Across Bewicke Avenue this street ends at Mosquito Creek, where a waterside track takes you right to Larson Road, on which crossing at the traffic lights brings you back to your original park a good hour after leaving it.

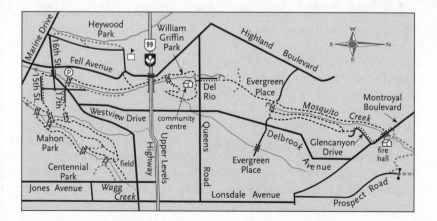

48 UPPER LONSDALE TRAILS

Round trip 3.3 km (2 mi)   Allow 1.5 hours
Elevation gain 137 m (450 ft)   High point 490 m (1600 ft)
Trails and roads   Good most of the year

Worn boardwalk on Baden-Powell Trail.

This walk has plenty of variety, with its forested stretch along the Baden-Powell Trail in one direction in contrast to a return along an open power line between St. George's Trail and Mosquito Creek. That trail itself links the Upper Lonsdale area with the old Grouse Mountain Highway, the road that gives access to the upper Mosquito Creek for hikers on the way to Mount Fromme and the wilderness north of Grouse Mountain. You, however, may use it to reach the Boy Scout trail, which intersects it partway up the slope.

To reach the starting point by car, head up Lonsdale Avenue above Highway 1/99 (Upper Levels Highway), turn right at Braemar Road E., left on St. Georges Avenue, right on Balmoral, with a final left taking you uphill on St. Marys. At the very top of this road, even after it has narrowed, you may find limited parking close to the gate on the power line right-of-way. Your walk starts with a short spell to the west on the power line before you turn uphill to the right on the main St. George's Trail, though if you feel like a little exploring, you may take the narrow trail angling off to the right immediately after the Baden-Powell Trail sign. This track leads to an old logging road that takes you to a fork where you go left, straight uphill, to join the Baden-Powell Trail and start back west along it, heading for the highest point of your walk, a little before the intersection with St. George's Trail.

On the west side of this junction is a viewpoint furnished with a seat from which you may look over Vancouver harbour before resuming your walk, now descending steadily until, with a pair of green-topped water towers below you and Mosquito Creek a little beyond, you cut back left to leave the screen of trees for the open power line. Of course, if you wish, you may descend the last steep section of the Baden-Powell to the footbridge over the creek or walk upstream a little to the site of its predecessor before returning, though having done so you must regain the height you will have lost.

This was the sylvan part of your walk, and even though you were in second-growth forest, the original logging took place sufficiently long ago for the trees to look impressive. In spring, too, the open banks are clothed with yellow violets, giving a touch of colour. Now, however, you are returning on an open right-of-way, the homes of North Vancouver just a short distance below, though often barely visible through the shrubbery, which, despite being regularly shorn, persistently grows back as healthy as before.

Near the end of your walk, a trail goes off downhill through the bushes on your right, the true end of the St. George's Trail connecting with the avenue of the same name. Should you desire to prolong your outing and have no objections to walking on the street, you may follow it down, then go left on Wooddale Road and left again on St. Marys back to the start.

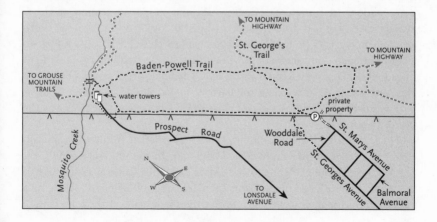

49 LYNN HEADWATERS LOOP

Lynn Loop Trail:	Round trip 5.1 km (3.2 mi)	Allow 1.5 hours
to debris chute:	Round trip 9.5 km (5.9 mi)	Allow 3 hours
	Elevation gain 168 m (550 ft)	High point 380 m (1250 ft)
	Trails and roads	Good most of the year

Bridge and cascades near the beginning.

Although this regional park is intended to provide wilderness experience, some of its trails are short enough to make satisfying walks, notably certain combinations of Lynn Loop, Cedars Mill and the lower section of Headwaters itself. Nor is it difficult of access: just follow Lynn Valley Road north from Highway 1/99 (Exit 19), passing the approach to Lynn Canyon Park on your right and continuing along the one-time Intake Road by going straight ahead where Dempsey Road goes off left. The final part of your approach to the park is somewhat winding and narrow, so you should exercise caution as you approach the main parking lot close to the bridge over the creek and the start of your walk.

Having crossed the creek, you must choose whether to turn left and follow it upstream or, for a more demanding walk, to go right and uphill, turning left just before the gate to the Lower Seymour Conservation Reserve (LSCR) at the south end of the Lynn Loop Trail and following it back along a raised bench, the moss-covered trees giving an indication of the high rainfall in the area. Some way along a hiking trail to Lynn Peak goes off to the right, then a little later a short, steep track rises some 70 m (230 ft) to a viewpoint overlooking the Seymour Valley and Burrard Inlet. Still later another path to the right takes you on a side trip to a pair of huge boulders, erratics left by a retreating glacier. Next comes another point of decision: to continue north on what will be Headwaters Trail or to complete Lynn Loop by dropping to the creek via a steep connector, a left turn at its foot giving you a round trip of 5.1 km (3.2 mi).

If you decide to go forward, you reach first of all, beside an ancient cedar, a viewpoint over the valley to the wooded slopes of Mount Fromme (named for the founder of the company that logged the area). Then you gradually start descending, the trail crossing one or two debris torrents, perhaps dangerous when in spate during spring runoff. At the third such feature, a major one, you drop to the open ground by the creek, where the lower trail joins the upper that you had been on. From here Headwaters Trail continues north, but the round trip to Norvan Falls, the next objective, involves an extra 5.5 km (3.4 mi), so this may be a satisfactory destination, with its superb view across the valley towards Kennedy Creek and the wild country north of Grouse Mountain.

A return downstream from here on the creekside trail has you passing the site of the long-vanished Cedars Mill, the only signs of its existence a few pieces of rusty machinery. Somewhat farther downstream you reach the T-junction at the lower end of the Lynn Loop connector, and from here back to the dam your walk is enlivened by the sight of wire coils, remnants of wire stave pipes that carried water to North Vancouver. You might also be on the lookout for the giant cedar on the west side of the creek, one of the largest remaining examples of the species, as recorded in the late Randy Stoltmann's *Hiking Guide to the Big Trees of Southwestern British Columbia.*

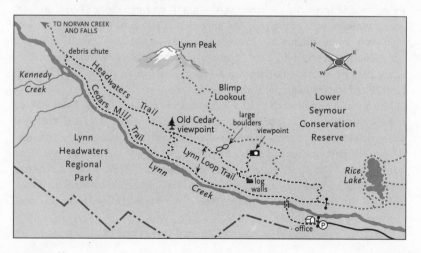

50 RICE LAKE

from LSCR:	Round trip 3 km (1.9 mi)	Allow 1.5 hours
from Lynn Headwaters:	Round trip 8 km (5 mi)	Allow 2.5 hours
	Trails and roads	Good most of the year

Mount Seymour reflected in Rice Lake.

This feature of the Greater Vancouver Regional District's Lower Seymour Conservation Reserve (LSCR) is a major recreation area within the outdoor educational complex, and as such is worth a visit in its own right. It is readily accessible from the entrance at the north end of Lillooet Road; in fact, many walkers may argue that the approach is too easy to ensure a reasonable walk even when that distance is added to the lake circuit, which is wheelchair accessible to boot. Fortunately that objection may be met in some part by starting not from the forest gate but from the neighbouring Lynn Headwaters Regional Park instead.

For the direct approach to Rice Lake, drive north on Lillooet Road, having left Highway 1/99 at the Capilano College exit (Exit 22) and travelled through a cemetery onto a gravel road with a concealed pipe on its east side. The public part of the road ends at a parking lot beside the guarded gate that bars access to the upper valley, though bikes are permitted on the main road on weekends. From the parking lot, you go straight ahead towards a yellow-painted gate beyond the Learning Lodge at the north end, with the lake trail next on the right.

Starting from Lynn Headwaters Regional Park, cross the bridge and turn right as though you were making for the south end of the Lynn Loop Trail (Walk 49), but where it branches off to the left, pass through the boundary gate between the two parks, after which you have a possible access going left to the lake. You may, however, wait for the next approach, which brings you to the shoreline farther south, as does the trail from Lillooet Road, having passed a flume and shinglebolt demonstration en route.

Making your circuit clockwise, your next point of interest a little farther north is the Forest Ecology Loop Trail, which makes a short detour on your left. Then, working your way round to the east, you see a broad multi-purpose trail heading north and come to a path going left to connect with it. Staying with the lake, you next come to a fork where you may go right along the shore or straight ahead to arrive at the Douglas Mowat Memorial Special Fisheries Wharf, a pleasant spot to pause. Shortly thereafter comes the dam at the south end of the lake and reunion with your outward route. Now you may start your return to Lynn Headwaters, first making your way out to the connector, then going right on it.

However, you may add distance and variety by electing to return by the Varley Trail, dedicated in 1998 to the memory of Frederick H. Varley, a founding member of the Group of Seven. To do this, start by going left on the Lynn Headwaters connector and back to the LSCR entrance. Now go west on the track that descends to cross Lynn Creek on a footbridge high above its turbulent waters. Turn right immediately on crossing and follow the road briefly to where the signed trail begins and heads northwards along the low-lying lands west of the creek, rising finally to the main parking lot and the end of your outing.

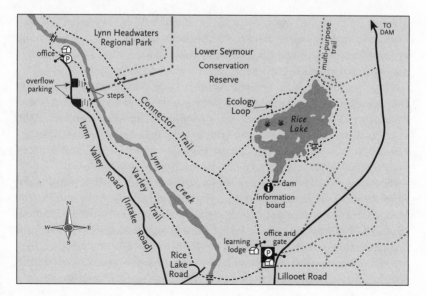

51 TWO-CANYON LOOP

Round trip 8 km (5 mi)   Allow 3 hours
Trails and roads   Good most of the year

Looking up the Seymour River from the viewpoint.

The proximity of the Lynn Creek and the Seymour River canyons near North Vancouver makes a scenic circuit possible with the use of connecting trails in Lynn Canyon Park and the Lower Seymour Conservation Reserve (LSCR), plus a stretch of the Baden-Powell Trail for good measure.

For this loop the best departure point is Lynn Canyon Park. To get to it from the west, leave Highway 1/99 (Upper Levels Highway) at Lynn Valley Road (Exit 19), go northeast and cross Mountain Highway, then turn right at the park sign on Peters Road and drive to the parking lot near the Ecology Centre. Arriving from the east, depart Highway 1/99 at Exit 21, drive north on Mountain Highway and go half right on Lynn Valley Road.

First you cross Lynn Creek on its suspension bridge, walk forward away from the canyon, then turn left on a trail that takes you to the entrance of the LSCR at the north end of Lillooet Road. From there, cross the main access road and head into the trees again on a dirt road bound for Twin Bridges, a demonstration plot on your left.

Soon Homestead Trail goes off left, and on this you may descend to the river before turning right to go downstream, passing the mossy gate of a long-abandoned settlement on your left and a Spawning and Rearing Habitat Loop on your right. At the surviving Twin Bridge, if you opt for a shorter walk you may turn uphill on the road back to the gate and thence to Lynn Canyon Park for an outing of some 6.5 km (4 mi). (An even shorter outing of 4.8 km or 3 mi would start at the LSCR entrance itself.) If, however, you are not seduced by the appeal of an early return, cross the river and head downstream on the remnants of a road cut into the canyon walls with viewpoints here and there to the river far below. And on the last stretch, where a small tributary has washed away most of the original trail, angle off left through the forest to intersect the Baden-Powell Trail.

On this you turn right, heading downhill for the river crossing on a pipe bridge at a point where the narrowness of the canyon causes the water to come through with explosive force. But now comes retribution, for you must mount a steep flight of steps then zigzag upwards, gaining some 110 m (350 ft) in the process, until you emerge on a power line right-of-way, Mount Seymour standing up proudly on your right. Continue west, cross Lillooet Road and stay with the Baden-Powell Trail as it takes you through open forest, until, just above Lynn Creek, you turn right for the descent into the depths of a small side valley, then use the boardwalk to return to the creek by a gravel beach.

From here, you must regain your lost height. This you can do on either side of the creek, staying on its east side to the suspension bridge or crossing Twin Falls Bridge for your return on the west side at the end of an energetic but rewarding outing.

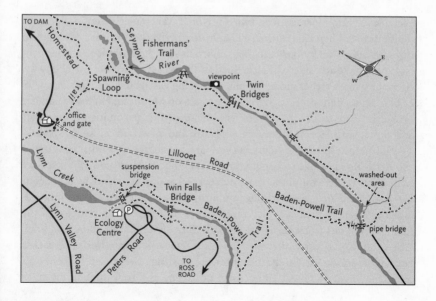

52 HASTINGS/LYNN LOOP

Round trip 9 km (5.6 mi)   Allow 3 hours
Trails, sidewalks and roads   Good all year

Bridge over Hastings Creek.

Feel like a lung-opener over two of North Vancouver's semi-wilderness ravine trails? Then this outing will suit you perfectly. You may even get to the starting point by bus; the 232 service passes the entrance to Bridgman Park on the south side of Keith Road, a little east of Mountain Highway. Arrival by car is rather more complicated: going east you leave Highway 1/99 at Exit 22, go right on Fern Street, right again on Mountain Highway and left on Keith Road; from the Ironworkers Memorial Bridge coming north, go off at Exit 21, turn left on Mountain Highway and left again on Keith Road.

The park's eastern boundary is Lynn Creek, and first you must pass under the Keith Road bridge to begin your journey north. Next you join a service road that takes you under Highway 1/99 and pass the Kiwanis/Scout Canada Camp area, then you enter mixed forest and choose between woodland or waterside routes, which meet again near a pedestrian bridge over the Lynn. Now your track turns off left and rises on a flight of steps to a road, Arborlynn Drive, on which you go right. After a few minutes you reach a right fork, and immediately thereafter the Hastings Creek trail branches off left. Once over the creek, you travel upstream, the trail undulating, until eventually you rise to level ground in a school yard. Here you head for the dead end of Allan Road, which leads you to Ross Road and another right turn. Going east you enter the tall trees of Lynn Canyon Park and stay with the road, its surface now gravel, until you go right again on a gated service road that takes you to a clearing. From here a flight of steps—at its top a pair of larches, vivid in fall—takes you down to cross Lynn Creek on Twin Falls Bridge, with its spectacular view of the canyon's lower end. Still going right, drop to creek level by a gravel beach, where you may draw breath before traversing a boardwalk over a piece of marshy ground and tackling the steep rise to the canyon rim. Once on top, your route stays right, taking you downstream, while the Baden-Powell Trail, which you have been using for the last short while, turns off left. You continue, high above the creek at first but gradually dropping to its level to converge with it.

The forest now ends on your side of the water, and you reach the service road to the former Premier Street Dump, now sporting playing fields on top. Stay beside the creek, and soon you will recognize the footbridge you saw on your outward journey. Finally comes your underpass of Highway 1/99, followed by a climb to street level on Keith Road to cross on its north-side footpath. Once more on the west bank, you drop to the underside and reverse your outward route.

A final note: the two parks, Bridgman, where you started your walk, and Lynnmouth, its neighbour to the south, extend all the way to Main Street if you want a short, easy stroll or want to lengthen the one just described.

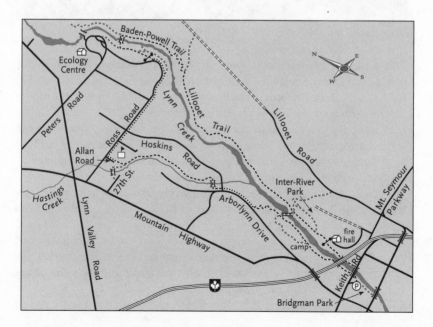

53 HISTORIC MUSHROOM LOOP I

Round trip 8 km (5 mi)
Elevation gain 380 m (1250 ft)
Trails and roads

Allow 4 hours
High point 503 m (1650 ft)
Best April to November

Historic Mushroom.

This walk lets you encounter some social history, sample a less-developed part of the Lower Seymour Conservation Reserve and experience another attractively forested stretch of the Baden-Powell Trail on slopes of the mountain low enough to be free of snow most of the year.

A good place to start is at the Hyannis Drive trailhead, which you can reach comfortably by bus or car by going north off Mount Seymour Parkway onto Berkley Road, then left briefly on Hyannis to where it is intersected by the Baden-Powell Trail, with a map and signs to mark the spot.

On foot you set out eastwards beside a pretty little creek in a wooded valley for some 30 minutes, ignoring trails to left and right and always with signs at the forks to keep you on track. Then your trail, much eroded from many years of use, becomes steeper as it rises past the intriguingly named Good Samaritan Trail and then eases before coming to a major junction.

Here you leave the Baden-Powell, itself now passing thirty years of age and old enough to claim its own place in history, and go left to the power line right-of-way. Crossing this wide swath and reentering the trees, you soon come to a fork at which you may go right or left; both routes lead to the Historic Mushroom, now quite decrepit and protected by a wooden fence with a picture and the story of the one-time parking lot and past generations of hikers who set out here on their long walk up the mountain.

This is the highest point of your walk, so having imagined those bygone days, turn west to find your route down, a one-time logging road descending left of a dilapidated bridge. Stay with this, at first through spindly second-growth trees then into more mature, more attractive forest as you proceed beyond the crossing of Mystery Creek. Eventually you come to a T-junction, where left takes you to the power line once more and here you go right until just before the next pylon, you go left again down the side of the shady Mystery Creek ravine to Fisherman's Trail, on the verge of the Seymour River canyon.

Now you are at your low point. But not for long: a few minutes beyond the bridge over Mystery Creek, go left and ascend on Bridle Trail, traversing a long, curving boardwalk that takes you back towards the south brim of Mystery Creek ravine. Soon the trail, quite eroded on the steep slope, improves and levels in a fine stretch of forest. Going right at the next T-junction, then left over another boardwalk brings you to the Hyannis Point trailhead only a few steps from where you started.

As an alternative to the steeper Bridle Trail, and no more than a kilometre greater in distance, you might continue south on Fisherman's Trail to meet the Baden-Powell and, going left, return along the lower stretch of the self-same creek on which you set out.

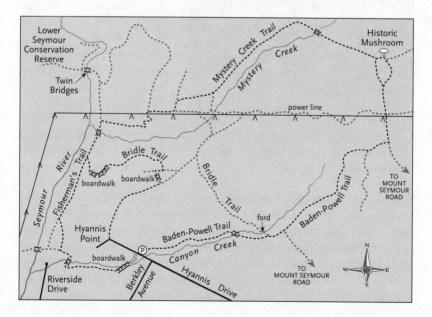

54 HISTORIC MUSHROOM LOOP II

Round trip 6.4 km (4 mi) Allow 2 hours
Elevation gain 275 m (900 ft) High point 580 m (1900 ft)
Trails Best May to early November

Trailhead at Mount Seymour Road.

Here is an accommodating walk in Mount Seymour Provincial Park that allows you to enjoy the lower reaches of the park when higher trails are snowbound earlier and later in the season. In addition to the Historic Mushroom Parking Lot, you may experience some of the park's logging history and yet another stretch of the Baden-Powell Trail at the outset. Turn off Highway 1/99 at Exit 22 and drive east on Mount Seymour Parkway, then go left and uphill on Mount Seymour Road to reach your start at the little parking lot opposite the Boy Scout trailhead about 2.5 km (1.6 mi) from the park entrance.

Once over the road, you rise gently in forest westwards to an intersection with the Old Buck Trail that is your return route, then after about 30 minutes, you forsake the Baden-Powell Trail to go right across a power line right-of-way. Shortly thereafter comes your trip into the past as you inspect the Historic Mushroom, that stump rich in memories for earlier generations of mountain lovers, who, condemned to hike from this point if they wished to go higher, used it to leave messages for others.

Though you may turn back from here, the remaining distance to the so-called Vancouver Lookout is not great. Continuing, you soon reach the park highway, to find that the view is being obscured by the growing forest. To get the best glimpses, you should cross the road to the little picnic site above the corner, where the route back starts on a connector with the Old Buck Trail via a picnic area with a history of its own. It is situated on the one-time road to the upper parking lot that was superseded by today's highway.

You are now on one of the most pleasant parts of your route, descending gently round the spine of the mountain to the junction with your return trail. A right turn here on the Old Buck, once a logging road, takes you down to the highway, where you must walk a short distance uphill for the trail's continuation. As on your outward trip, you must cross the open power line, the right-of-way giving you a view eastwards over Indian Arm to Buntzen Ridge, with Eagle Ridge behind. Reentering the forest, you continue to descend. Watch for the sharp turn left onto your original trail, which will bring you back to your starting point, a change of direction signalled by the distinctive Baden-Powell signs.

For a walk taking another hour or so, you may start lower on the mountain, going left off Mount Seymour Road onto Anne Macdonald Way, then right into a small parking lot at the Old Buck trailhead. From here the rehabilitated Old Buck Trail rises 215 m (705 ft) in 2.3 km (1.4 mi) to meet the Baden-Powell Trail.

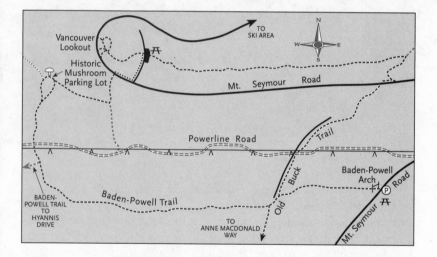

55 GOLDIE LAKE

combined loops:	Round trip 6 km (3.7 mi)	Allow 2.5 hours
	Elevation gain 150 m (500 ft)	High point 1000 m (3300 ft)
	Trails and roads	Best June to October

Looking southwest over Goldie Lake.

"What do you know of Seymour, who only Seymour know?" Such a question may well be asked of the many visitors to Mount Seymour Provincial Park who drive to the top parking area, inspect the downhill ski facilities around it, then depart wondering what all the fuss is about. As an interesting way of finding out more, this hike over park trails may provide an answer, taking you as it does through cool forest to a small picturesque lake situated a little below the level of the parking area and to the east of it.

For the start of your journey of exploration, drive Mount Seymour Road to the parking lot on the west side of the hairpin bend at km 11 (mi 7), the prominent "Cabin Trail" sign just before the bend being another point of identification. Cross to the highway's east side at the corner and pick up the trail as it angles off downhill to bypass the lower end of a ski run. After this, the forest reasserts itself and the only signs of human activity among the trees are some elderly log cabins, survivors of the days before this area acquired park status. When you come to a trail junction, go left on Perimeter Trail, designed, as its name suggests, for straying skiers. To give B.C. Parks credit, it has carried out some improvements without making them too obvious, providing footing in soft spots and bridging creeks where necessary. The first crossing, reached just after the junction, is over Scott-Goldie Creek, where you may admire a miniature canyon before you continue northwards.

After some 50 minutes, you leave Perimeter, going left to Goldie Lake and arriving at a trail junction by two small ponds just south of your objective. For the nature trail round Goldie, you may go in either direction (each is attractive). You finish your circuit at this same junction with two choices: staying right for a direct walk to the upper parking lot via Goldie Tow, or going left and taking in the pretty little Flower Lake as well before heading for the area with its cafeteria and comfort stations.

From here, you may retrace your steps, but for a succession of views stretching from the southern islands in the Strait of Georgia to the peaks and ridges of Mount Seymour's companions on the North Shore, you may cross to the west side of the parking lot and walk back to your vehicle on the park highway's broad shoulder, this return being much shorter also—less than 1 km (0.6 mi).

Should the outing just described seem a little strenuous, you may try a shorter circuit of the lakes themselves from the top parking lot, starting on the sawdust track parallel with the rope tow. To include Flower Lake in your walk, go right at the first and second junctions, the circuit being a modest 3.5 km (2.2 mi) with no great change of elevation involved.

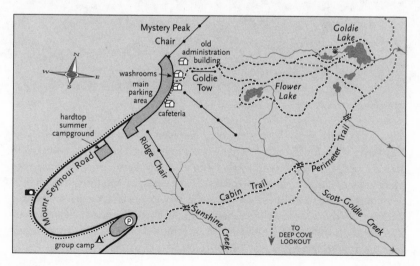

56 DOG MOUNTAIN

direct:	Round trip 6 km (3.7 mi)	Allow 2.5 hours
via Dinkey Peak:	Round trip 8 km (5 mi)	Allow 3 hours
	Trails	Best July to October

Westward view from Dog Mountain.

This walk, with virtually no climbing involved despite its title, takes you from the top parking area in Mount Seymour Provincial Park to a point overlooking the Seymour River, one that gives breathtaking views of Vancouver and its sister municipalities to the south and west, of Mount Garibaldi and Mamquam Mountain to the north, while Mount Baker provides a majestic backdrop to the eastern Fraser Valley. The trail itself is pleasant also, lying in open forest for much of its length and interrupted only by First Lake, set in its subalpine meadow.

To start, park near the chairlift terminal at the north end of the main parking area. Just left of it, the main Alpine Trail heads off northwards to Mount Seymour. Follow this briefly, then turn left en route to your own mountain, and very soon the works of humans are left behind. After some 20 minutes, you reach the little lake, its name sadly uninspired in terms of its surroundings—a picturesque wooded basin with, surprisingly, quite a large cabin perched on a bluff above.

Cross at the lake outlet, noting as you do the trails that join from the right, as they can provide a variation of your return route. Again you enter forest and in it you remain until, practically at your destination, you emerge on a rocky outcrop with an almost sheer drop to the valley below. Here is the panoramic view of the features already mentioned as well as the great mass of Cathedral Mountain to the northwest and—to move from the great to the small—the remains of a cabin just in front of you, a relic of the time when the Vancouver Water District kept a lookout here.

When you start your return journey on the main trail you may, if you are experienced and properly equipped and the season is summer, follow the taped route that stays left, going straight ahead where the path turns right. This, however, winds up and down—sometimes quite steeply—over several minor summits; it is, besides, on occasion somewhat close to Suicide Bluffs for comfort, so if you decide against it but wish a slightly longer walk on your return, there is another possible variant from First Lake, with a miniature mountain, Dinkey Peak, for good measure.

At the lake, therefore, turn left and north, then east following the trail uphill. Gradually you rise towards the main Mount Seymour Trail, coming to a T-junction as the trail levels. Go right here and soon you are enjoying a series of views, culminating in a vantage point directly above the parking lot. Thereafter, continue to the junction with the main trail, on which a right turn brings you back to your original starting point.

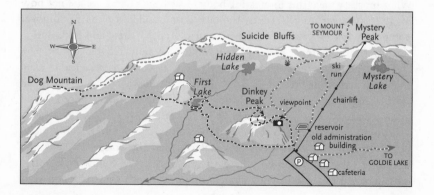

57 MYSTERY LAKE AND PEAK

to lake:	Round trip 3 km (2 mi)	Allow 1.5 hours
to peak:	Round trip 4.5 km (2.8 mi)	Allow 2.5 hours
	Elevation gain 215 m (700 ft)	High point 1220 m (4000 ft)
	Trails	Best July to October

Near the outlet on the lake's east side.

What mystery gave this interesting body of water its name we are not now likely to uncover. At all events, the lake does provide a pleasant stopover point on what may be a circular hike or a straight there-and-back outing starting from the upper parking lot in Mount Seymour Provincial Park.

From the lower terminal of the Mystery Peak chairlift, take the marked trail right across the little basin beneath the right-of-way, beyond which you start rising among trees, soon losing sight of pylons and, indeed, of all human activity. After 20 minutes or so of walking, you pass tiny Nancy Lake, with a rocky outcrop above it to the south. A brief detour to this viewpoint rewards you with views of Vancouver and the Fraser lowlands. On resuming, take the trail round the west side of the lake, following it north, crossing a ski run and heading along a nice ledge with small cliffs on your left and forest elsewhere. As you advance, the trees gradually thin, and the surroundings become subalpine as you near your objective in its rocky basin.

Here is a spot for rest and contemplation, even if the intrusion of the chairlift does spoil the setting to the west. Otherwise, all is natural, and it is pleasant to sit on clean rock and let the peace wash over you. Now, however, comes the moment of decision: to return by the trail you have just traversed, a total distance of 3 km (2 mi) for the trip; or, if you are energetic and adventurous, to continue round the back of Mystery Peak to reach the main Mount Seymour Trail.

To do this, follow the track north on the lake's east side, rising slightly, dropping, then rising again to the foot of the Brockton Point chairlift. From here a sign points to Mount Seymour, and you may follow its route round to the junction with the main trail. If, however, you want to enjoy the all-round views from Mystery Peak, you should leave this almost immediately for another track rising left and circling round to the summit. After you have savoured the panorama, your descent takes you north on the Manning ski run before you swing west and join the main Mount Seymour Trail, on which you go left.

Nor need you tramp down the ski run, barren as it is of shade and vegetation. If you look carefully to its right as it starts to descend, you will see below you the original well-used Mount Seymour Trail, which takes you down a little valley. On your way down the hiking route and not far from the parking lot, you will pass the two ends of the Dinkey Peak Loop Trail (Walk 56), an interesting little outing in its own right or a means to prolong your exploration of the hidden corners of this popular park.

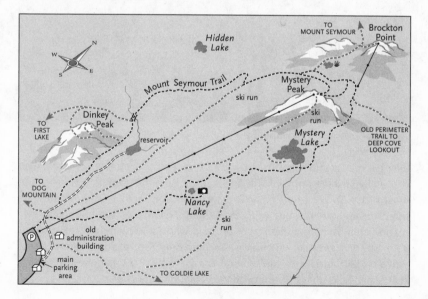

58 BADEN-POWELL TRAIL
(Deep Cove)

Round trip 5.3 km (3.3 mi)   Allow 2.5 hours
High point 200 m (660 ft)
Trails and roads   Good all year

View of Deep Cove from bluff viewpoint.

One possible destination for this walk, a high bluff overlooking Deep Cove, is actually visible from your starting point in Panorama Park, but to make the most of the Baden-Powell's most easterly section you should continue farther, turning part of your walk into a loop. The park itself, a popular recreation area fronting Indian Arm in Deep Cove, is actually a little south of your trail's beginning, but unless you arrive by bus, parking on Panorama Drive's 2500 block is so limited and the view from the park so interesting that leaving from it is recommended.

In any event, you arrive by Deep Cove Road, with a right on Gallant Avenue followed by a left on Panorama. Then, on foot, you may descend to the waterfront and rise again to Panorama Drive on the north side of some private dwellings to where the trail goes off uphill left, with a few houses at the start soon giving way to forest. After swinging right, continue to follow the Baden-Powell fleurs-de-lis that mark the route as you descend into and climb out of little ravines, until, after about 1.6 km (1 mi), you note a heritage Douglas-fir to the right and nearby a track going off uphill left—a possible return route.

After another kilometre, you reach a viewpoint on the right, the great bluff visible from Deep Cove. This is an ideal spot to rest and contemplate the scene before you: across the waters of Indian Arm to Belcarra on the left, Burnaby Mountain ahead and Deep Cove below you on the right. A short distance farther on comes a power line, its final pylon to the west of Indian Arm standing on a rocky eminence just to the right of the trail.

Here is another turning point if you do not wish to follow the Boy Scout route into the forest beyond the right-of-way as it turns uphill, parallel with the power line, to meet Indian River Drive. On this you make your way west for 0.5 km until, at the road's high point, beside a small water tower, the Baden-Powell Trail goes off right, making for Mount Seymour Road, while you go a few metres farther, then turn downhill on the opposite side from a fire hydrant.

This track, marked with red and yellow tapes, was the one that you passed on your outward journey, and it drops straight down through a windfall area to join the main trail. There you turn right, once more on the Baden-Powell Trail, for your return to Deep Cove and its eastern terminus.

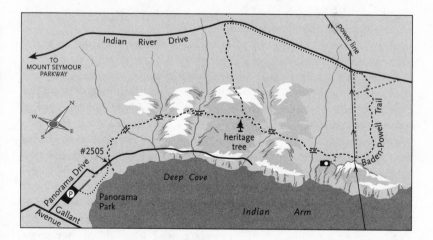

59 INDIAN ARM PARKS

short circuit:	Round trip 4.5 km (2.8 mi)	Allow 1.5 hours
long circuit:	Round trip 9 km (5.6 mi)	Allow 3 hours
	Streets and trails	Good all year

View from Deep Cove Park across Indian Arm to Eagle Ridge.

Along with Cates Park at its south end, lower Indian Arm boasts no fewer than five public recreation areas, the round of which, either in whole or in part, gives you an interesting variety of scenery. Cates Park on its own is reached from Dollarton Highway, but for its incorporation in the total outing, it may also be approached from the northern loop, where four smaller recreation areas vie for your attention.

From the north, the starting point is Panorama Park, accessible by bus or car from Deep Cove Road by going right on Gallant Avenue then left on Panorama Drive to the park. From here, you turn south, heading past a yacht club, following the shoreline on either of two routes through Deep Cove Park to a small creek. Cross this and turn south again on Parkside Lane to Raeburn Street, where you go left to cross Lockehaven Road and enter Wickenden, your third park. In it you continue east amid tall trees, staying first right over a bridge, then left up some steps, and right again to emerge a little above Roxbury Road, which you follow down to the tiny but very attractive Strathcona Park in its little bay.

From it, a track takes you westwards across Noble Bridge to Myrtle Park. Staying left allows you to make a clockwise circuit to emerge on Cove Cliff Road near Banbury Road, on which you go north briefly before turning right on a path behind Cove Cliff School. Ignoring a bridge on your right, traverse a children's playground on the way to a small parking lot and thus to Raeburn Street again. Cross this and walk north on a track flanked by a creek on your right. Once more in Deep Cove Park, a left turn takes you back to your transportation after a round of 4.5 km (2.8 mi) lasting less than 1.5 hours.

To include Cates Park in this outing, go left after Noble Bridge, then left again through a narrow screen of trees to cut through a school down to Strathcona Road. Here walk right to Kinloch Lane, thence to Mount Seymour Parkway. Jog left to Beachview Drive and continue south before going left on Bakerview and right on Lowry Lane to a viewpoint on a corner. Now you must return to Beachview for one block, then drop down again to Seashell Lane and your entry to Cates Park, site of the World War I Dollar Logging Mill and once the home of the novelist Malcolm Lowry.

To sample this park's trails, you might try a "figure of eight" course. Start along the path above the shoreline then, just after a bridge, swing right, ascend a series of steps to join Upper Trail and continue left then right on the track leading towards the parking lot by the main entrance. Across the paved area Upper Trail resumes and circles down through the trees to a viewpoint just above water's edge.

Your return route takes you along the waterside past a boat-launching ramp, the main recreation area and a Native war canoe to the Malcolm Lowry Trail, on which you stay until, immediately beyond the bridge, you arrive at another fork. To vary your return, take the left, inland route to rejoin Upper Trail near the margin of the park, then walk back on Roslyn Boulevard, enjoying vistas of mountain and sea. After Mount Seymour Parkway comes Kinloch Lane again, and thereafter your return to Myrtle Park and continuation to your left of the shorter circle route back to Deep Cove.

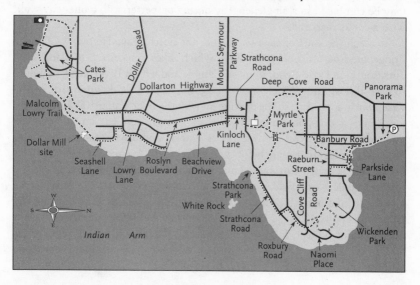

60 LULU ISLAND DYKES

total distance:	Round trip 23 km (14.3 mi)	Allow 5.5 hours
	Dykes	Good all year

Scotch Pond in front, North Shore mountains in far distance.

This excursion represents at least two walks, with a self-contained down-river portion along the Fraser's Middle Arm and an equally self-contained walk along the West Dyke Trail overlooking Sturgeon Bank, though they may be combined in a single lengthy outing or, better still, a one-way walk with a car at each end.

To reach the start of each walk from the north, leave Highway 99 at the Bridgeport Road turnoff (Exit 39A), which takes you onto Sea Island Way. Turn south on No. 3 Road, right on Cambie and left on River Road, stopping to park almost immediately if your intention is to walk downstream; otherwise, continue to drive to the parking lot near the river's mouth at Terra Nova, location of a long-gone cannery. For the approach from the south, however, you are best to stay on the freeway to Exit 32 and drive west on Steveston Highway, almost to its end, before going left on 7th Avenue as far as Chatham Street, where a right turn takes you to parking in Garry Point Park.

On Middle Arm Dyke, water and air traffic contribute to a busy scene, and the riverbank itself promises activity with its marinas. Once beyond the Dinsmore and No. 2 Road Bridges you come to a viewing pier, then a marsh enhancement project, followed by a natural stretch with shore pine, briars and broom an attractive sight in spring. Waterfowl are present in numbers, with herons, geese, even cormorants beside their humbler companions. On your elevated walkway, you travel past Swishwash Island to the mouth of the river, with its little park and the connection with the rest of the walk. You may feel, however, that a round trip of 11 km (6.8 mi) is sufficient and save the West Dyke Trail for another occasion.

For it, begin where River Road ends at Terra Nova, working left as the dyke changes direction to the south, bordering the rich tidal marshes of Sturgeon Bank, with its abundance of birds. Towards the south end of your walk, you come upon a line of radar reflecting towers, marching on stiltlike legs across the marshland and warning passing ships of the proximity of the mud flats. On the landward side, a succession of townhouse developments also becomes evident, threatening to engulf the old farmhouse home of the Steves family, still holding out at the end of Steveston Highway.

Next you reach a lagoon, beyond which is your destination at Garry Point Park, itself a fairly recent creation, its origins a long strip of sand at the mouth of the river. Now, much altered by humans, amongst other things it boasts a Japanese garden honouring the citizens of the old Steveston, for whom also a Fisherman's Memorial is located at the manmade point to the south, overlooking the entrance to Steveston Harbour.

With its sea and mountain views this makes a fine destination for your walk, though you may, if you wish, continue eastwards into Steveston Village to savour some of the atmosphere of the revitalized fishing community: the Gulf of Georgia Cannery National Historic Site and the Public Fish Sales Float along the waterfront and, in the heart of the village, the one-time Interurban Railway and its restored coach, beside the grand community and Japanese-style martial arts centres.

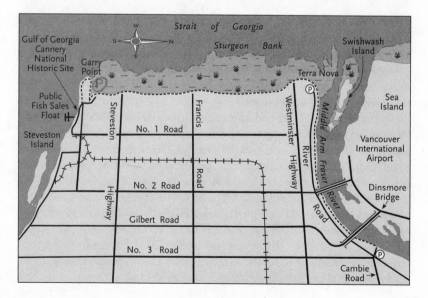

61 RICHMOND SOUTH DYKE TRAIL

Round trip 12 km (7.5 mi)	Allow 3 hours
Dykes, trails and roads	Good all year

Britannia Heritage Shipyard.

On this outing along the South Arm of the Fraser River the walker must share the trail with cyclists and, on the road sections, with motorists as well, but that should be no deterrent to the cooperatively minded. It is an ideal cool-weather walk when shade is of no consequence, for there is none; it is also a walk that may be started at either end, and even partway along, for there are numerous access points.

To reach the upstream end, drive south through Richmond on Highway 99, turn off west on Steveston Highway (Exit 32), then almost immediately go left on No. 5 Road, driving south to its end, where it veers right into River Road. Continue past the Dominion Bridge building to just beyond the bridge over a slough to find parking by the Woodwards Landing picnic area.

Horseshoe Slough, as it is called, boasts a little 15-minute trail up one side and down the other, the commercial buildings nearby obscured by a line of trees, whose reflections in the water enhance its attractiveness, as do the pedestrian bridges from which you may take in the scene, before you finally cross on the third one to return to the river. The next section, though nominally part of the South Dyke Trail, is on paved road, so unless you are a purist and would disdain to compromise, you may drive the next 1.7 km (1 mi) to No. 4 Road and begin your walk proper at Finn Slough, a narrow backwater with a fascinating array of old buildings on stilts, some rescued from decay and still lived in, some with evocative names such as Dinner Plate Island School.

Continuing westwards you arrive at Woodward Slough, slanting down to the Fraser beside a discharge building, and begin a detour around a packaging plant that has usurped the waterside. Cross Garden City Road at the farthest point before returning to the riverbank a short distance from No. 3 Road, with its pier and picnic area. The next stretch is well endowed with picnic tables, attesting to its popularity in summer for its fishing, beachcombing and nature observation as well as for its historic interest at London Farm, a late-nineteenth-century farmhouse, the restored building gracious in its spacious garden. The first land dyked and cultivated on Lulu Island was in this area.

Opposite, on the river side, you may also dally at Gilbert Beach or continue to London's Landing, which, established in 1885 as a government wharf, is part of the fabric of local fishing and canning history. Since its purchase by Richmond in 1994, the pier has been upgraded and its immediate surroundings developed as a little park, commemorating the area's past. Here, at the foot of No. 2 Road, with Mount Baker dominating the upstream landscape, is an attractive destination for your walk down the river.

If, however, you have arranged transport farther west in Steveston or at Garry Point Park, you may make this a one-way trip and continue westwards past Paramount Pond, with its many and varied craft, and past the Pacific Coast Cannery, en route to the Britannia Heritage Shipyard, thence to Steveston Park and the village community centre. From here you may head directly to Garry Point or detour to take in the sights and sounds of the waterfront, a popular area on a fine summer's weekend. (See also Walk 60.)

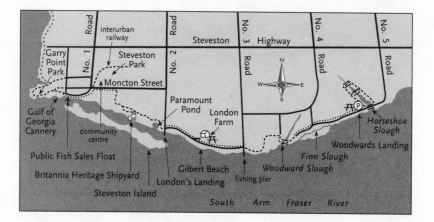

62 RICHMOND NATURE PARK

Round trip 3.2 km (2 mi)
Trails

Allow 1.5 hours
Good all year

On Bog Forest Trail.

Motorists speeding south from Vancouver on Highway 99 are very likely unaware of the outdoor pleasure available to them only a few yards from the freeway in Richmond. Here, fronting Westminster Highway, is Richmond Nature Park, the creation of a devoted group of conservationists.

To find this hidden treasure, leave the highway on the Shell Road turnoff (Exit 38) and drive south to the traffic light at Westminster Highway, where you go left to the park entrance, also on the left. Across the parking lot lies the park office, in which various useful guides are available as are bags of seeds for the inhabitants of the waterfowl pond nearby. There is a picnic area for humans, too, if you wish to make a leisurely round and need sustenance afterwards.

Although the park's total area is small, it is so skillfully laid out that covering its three interwoven circuits in their entirety provides a satisfying walk. For a start, stay left to cross the end of the bird pond, take in the scene from the viewing tower, then set off on Time Trail, the short, 30-minute self-guiding nature loop, armed with its accompanying pamphlet. This course in nature study complete, you may set out, with your newly assimilated knowledge, on Quaking Trail, keeping the other circuit, Bog Forest Trail, for the third and last. By now you should have acquired some familiarity with, at least, the commonest features of the area, from its shore pines to the shrub Labrador tea, a plant particularly colourful in spring.

Gray squirrel near park entrance.

But this is not all, should you be in the mood for exploring, for you may still walk the circuit of the Richmond Nature Study Centre, situated on the east side of Highway 99. To reach this relatively undeveloped tract by car, turn left from the nature park onto Westminster Highway. Go left again on Jacombs Road, its east side adorned by an auto sales mall but its west side mercifully untouched. Immediately after turning, go left again into the small parking lot for the study centre, a more natural area than its neighbour across the way.

Besides a few trail improvements, nothing has been done to modify the environment, and the marshlike surroundings give you some idea of the nature of the peat bog that must have covered much of Richmond in the not-too-distant past, only a few traces of which now remain.

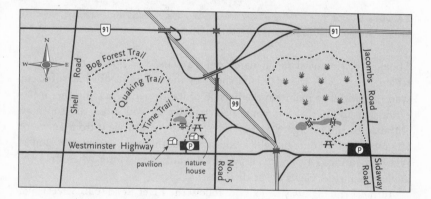

63 DEAS ISLAND

Round trip 4.4 km (2.7 mi)   Allow 1.5 hours
Trails   Good all year

Heritage buildings, Burrvilla and Delta Agricultural Hall.

Though this is an island in name only, a causeway now connecting the regional park with the mainland south of the Fraser, it still has sufficient water around it to maintain the illusion of its former status. Another interesting feature is that on your walk westwards you cross the southern entrance to the George Massey Tunnel, giving you a view from above of Highway 99, the route on which you travel south from Vancouver to undertake this outing. This walk is especially rewarding in winter when the trees are bare and river views are at their best.

Turn off the highway at Exit 28, follow the River Road (62B Street) sign back left across the overpass and continue east for 2.5 km (1.5 mi). Turn left off this road a little before a sand and gravel operation and enter the park, leaving your vehicle at the first designated parking area on the left. Here you are close to the heritage Inverholme Schoolhouse, and beyond it, also on the left, are two more heritage buildings, the imposing Burrvilla and its plain neighbour, the Delta Agricultural Hall. To your right, at the Tinmaker's Walk trailhead, are a commemorative tablet and a lookout tower, the latter providing fine views of the river's main channel below Gravesend Reach.

As you proceed, you pass another parking area on your left, and here you may see the plaque—mounted on an old piston-drive air compressor—that commemorates the park's opening. Continuing, you arrive at a fork, the left arm of which, Dyke Loop Trail, takes you back by Deas Slough to your point of departure. By staying right on Riverside Walk, however, you veer closer to the river, being joined quite soon and in quick succession by Island Tip Trail and Sand Dune Trail, the latter a combined horse/hiking trail. Thereafter horses and hikers travel in tandem as the trail crosses the tunnel access, passing the cairn that commemorates its opening in 1959 by Queen Elizabeth. Your trail west stays close to the river now as you make for the island's tip, passing an attractive little beach en route.

From there, you look south across the mouth of Deas Slough, with its marina lying just to the east of Ladner Marsh. Southwest lies Kirkland Island, a navigation beacon marking its shoal waters. North, of course, is the river, and Lulu Island beyond, the shoreline marked by commercial and industrial operations—freight terminals and the like—though the B.C. Ferries refitting dock does add a touch of maritime romance to the scene.

On your return across the tunnel, you want to go right on Sand Dune Trail and again on Dyke Loop Trail to complete your circular tour of the park. At first you have an interesting sample of dune ecology; next you have views south across the waterway that is Deas Slough. At the second viewpoint, stay right on Slough View Trail as another trail forks left to the central picnic area at Fisher's Field and plod along the sandy route with the recreational activity on the slough to entertain you. Then, just behind Burrvilla, keep right again and cross the bridge on Tidal Pond Trail, the pond replete with vegetation and a blaze of colour in summer. All too soon, you emerge at the picnic area near which you started, your expedition over.

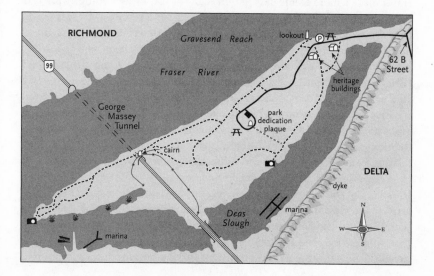

64 BRUNSWICK POINT

Round trip 14 km (8.7 mi) or less   Allow 4 hours
Dykes   Good all year

Walking north, potato field at right front.

Where you start or end your walk is a matter of preference; certainly the site of a one-time cannery fronting on Canoe Passage and the estuarine flats of the Fraser make a more scenic destination than the causeway leading to Roberts Bank Terminal, but even the latter is not without a certain stark attractiveness—seen from a distance. Besides, on this kind of outing, there is really no need for a specific destination; you may turn around any time you choose.

To reach Brunswick Point, turn right off Highway 99 onto Highway 17 (Exit 28) south of the George Massey Tunnel, then go right again on Highway 10 (Ladner Trunk Road) after 1.6 km (1 mi). This becomes 48th Avenue, from which you curve left onto 47A Avenue at a traffic light before veering left again on River Road to resume your course westwards. Eventually you pass the single-lane bridge onto Westham Island and a little later the picturesque floating Canoe Pass Village, a short distance beyond which, opposite the end of Mason Road (34th Street), there is limited parking on the dyke. Here, with the sweep of the river ahead, you may start downstream towards its mouth, arriving after less than 1 km at a gate on the dyke, another possible beginning, with yet a third option available where a barrier across the road prevents farther progress by car, 1.8 km (1.1 mi) from Mason. Now you are close to the site of the old cannery, of which few signs survive—some pilings and assorted bits and pieces by the riverbank, while landwards on your left lush blackberry bushes hide the remains of an old farmstead.

Beyond here your direction gradually changes to the southwest and your gaze is directed across the wide marshes separating you from the sea— wonderfully colourful in summer and home to a large population of resident birdlife at all times of the year, with transients increasing their numbers when they arrive to overwinter or pass through on their remarkable migrations; in addition you may see the occasional raptor, probably because the seaward-side marsh is balanced by arable land, with great fields of potatoes and other crops beyond the drainage ditch. Of the latter you become more aware when you reach the point proper and the dyke swings to the southeast, with the large cottonwoods surrounding a farmstead in the centre of your view. As you proceed, the marshes on the seaward side shrink, the mud flats become more exposed, and after you explore what may have been an orchard at one time on the opposite side of the dyke from the farm, you may wish to turn, retracing the 4 km (2.5 mi) you have come from Mason Road.

If you continue, you finally come to the landward end of the coal-port causeway, Deltaport Way, an anticlimactic end to any walk, but you have the whole stretch of the dyke back to Brunswick Point to restore your spirits as you gaze across the marshes to the distant mountains.

With abundant opportunities for wildlife observation at any time of year, these estuarine marshlands, with their heart in the nearby George C. Reifel Migratory Bird Sanctuary, are especially worth a visit in late fall, when the sight of the snow geese on the move almost defies description, as does the sound of their mass takeoff.

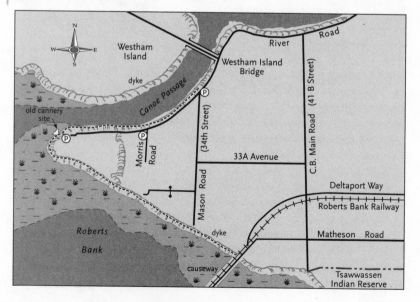

65 BOUNDARY BAY REGIONAL PARK

north section:	Round trip 8 km (5 mi)	Allow 3 hours
south section:	Round trip 4 km (2.5 mi)	Allow 1.5 hours
	Dykes and trails	Good all year

Pond at Centennial Beach.

Since the total distance from Mud Bay in the east to Beach Grove at the bay's western end is 16 km (10 mi), only the superfit, cyclists and two-car groups are likely to attempt this route in its entirety. Fortunately, there are numerous intermediate access points, so you may choose the distance you wish to cover in this interesting regional park, with its marine and mountain views and variety of birds.

The whole area is particularly rich in birdlife and is of international importance to migrating and wintering birds. Waterfowl and shorebirds are common, but you may come across a snowy owl if you are lucky, and hawks and eagles may also be seen on the stretch between the dyke and the sands of the bay. There, too, you may spot small mammals such as the coyote.

From Highway 99 a short distance south of the George Massey Tunnel, go right on Highway 17 (Exit 28) and follow it for 2.3 km (1.4 mi) to its intersection with Highway 10 (Ladner Trunk Road). Turn left here and, as you drive eastwards, the various beach access roads are on your right. The first, 64th Street, provides a short walk to the southwest before the dyke ends at Beach Grove Spit. The next, 72nd Street, gives you a nice round trip west and southwest covering nearly 8 km (5 mi), just the thing to bring colour to your cheeks on a cool winter day.

Eastwards from 72nd lie Boundary Bay Airport and Delta Air Park and, possible noise apart, the uniformity of the landscape towards Mud Bay makes access from 88th, 96th, 104th and 112th Streets less than inviting unless you are a keep-fit buff with distance covered your main object.

At the west end, between 12th Avenue and Delta Centennial Beach, you may use the shore dyke for one leg of your trip and another, a little farther inland, as a start for your return route. For this section, turn left off Highway 17 on 56th Street (Point Roberts Road), go left again on 12th Avenue and drive east to the small parking area at road end. Once through the gate, follow the dyke east then south, noting on your right a track coming in from across the drainage ditch at the pumping station.

As you continue and your dyke becomes indistinguishable from the beach, a trail veers inland heading towards the facilities at Centennial Beach, a loop on the left providing instruction on dune ecology. Then, to vary your return and enjoy an undeveloped part of marshland, strike off from the far northwest corner of the parking lot on a rough trail that first approaches then departs from the main pathways. Thereafter, you should keep left until, close to the main dyke, you veer right to meet it by the pumping station you noted near the beginning of your walk.

Yet another possibility exists, should you wish to connect the two ends without squelching through the rather oozy stretch at the head of the bay: when the dyke ends at Beach Grove on your trip from 72nd or 64th Street, continue beyond the gate along the lane leading to Beach Grove Road and walk the kilometre or so south to 12th Avenue, where the dyke resumes.

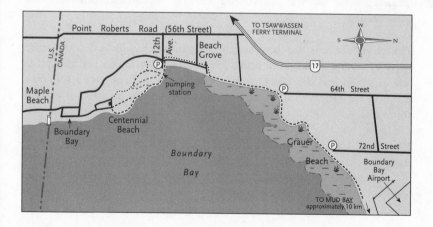

66 CRESCENT BEACH

north loop:	Round trip 5 km (3.1 mi)	Allow 2 hours
south loop:	Round trip 8.4 km (5.2 mi)	Allow 3 hours
	Beach, roads and trails	Good all year

Crescent Beach.

This stretch of coast on the east side of Boundary Bay gives you the possibility of several walks, both north and south, focussing on Blackie Spit in one direction and the beach itself, towards and perhaps round Kwomais Point, in the other, with White Rock as a conceivable objective if you are ambitious.

Having left Highway 99 at the King George Highway interchange (Exit 10), follow Crescent Road westwards. Turn right off it at Sullivan Street, then go right on McBride Avenue to its end at a parking area close to a sailing club, a short distance from Blackie Spit with its numerous tracks. From here you are ready for the northern part of your walk, taking one of the trails round the point bordering on tidal marshes as far as you can to best experience the resident or visiting waterfowl and shorebirds. After the spit, go through the gate on the east side and work your way round the dunes, returning to the main trail that runs south, passing on the east side of tennis courts and washrooms and coming to a fork by a flight of steps.

By descending and going right here, you may return via Gilley Street for a short walk; however, by keeping left on a narrow dyke, well endowed with broom and other plants, you can travel east to the end of a wide lagoon. If you go right here, you come to Maple Street, a gravel road; then, passing Dunsmuir Farm Community Gardens, you meet Crescent Road again just opposite Heron Park and its petroglyph. From the park you pick up the lanelike Maple Street as you head for the seafront, this popular promenade taking you north to Wickson Road, where a right turn leads you back to your car.

For the southern loop, you may start along the seafront, staying left as you reach the end of the esplanade, then continuing along the beach, pebbly and shingly though it is, with the Burlington Northern Railway running between you and the cliff. After about 40 minutes, you may note a flight of steps descending, a possible return route should you decide to mount the so-called 1001 Steps, about 35 minutes farther south, and make part of your return along the roads of Ocean Park.

Having used the pedestrian underpass of the railway, therefore, you begin your walk back from 15A Avenue, turn left and follow 126A Street north as it becomes Ocean Park Road then 124 Street until on 22nd Avenue you go left for one block, then continue right on Harbourgreene Drive to 24th Avenue, a total distance on roads of 2.2 km (1.4 mi). On 24th a left turn takes you to the steps down the cliff and your return north, this time with views to west and north.

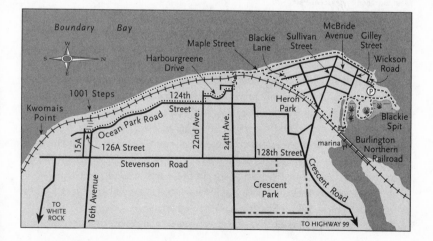

67 SOUTH SURREY URBAN FORESTS

Sunnyside Acres:	Round trip 4 km (2.5 mi)	Allow 1 hour
Crescent Park:	Round trip 4 km (2.5 mi)	Allow 1 hour
	Trails	Good all year

Main entrance to Crescent Park.

Looking for a shady walk on a hot summer's day? Why not try one or both of these delightful little oases located within a stone's throw of each other in South Surrey? To make a day's outing you might start with Sunnyside Acres, a small area of second-growth forest rescued from development by the local heritage society, which provides guided tours and information about the plant and animal life of the forest; and afterwards move on to Crescent Park, which has picnic and sports facilities as well as trails.

Driving south from Vancouver, leave Highway 99 at Exit 10 for the King George Highway (99A) and continue south to 24th Avenue where you go right (west) to a recessed parking area on the north side of the road shortly after 148th Street. You may also reach this spot from Highway 1 at Exit 48 by going south on 152nd Street to 24th Avenue.

A large board with trail maps and pictures of the plants and animals you may see stands at the trailhead. Having absorbed this information, plunge into the forest to test your memory, keeping right twice within the first 5 minutes. Thereafter, keep left twice (right would take you back onto 24th Avenue), at first enjoying the shade of Douglas-firs before entering an area with a more open canopy and an abundance of bushes and shrubs. Soon your path debouches on a busy street (148th), on which you go left, fortunately for only a minute or two, before reentering the forest. Still keeping left at main intersections and ignoring all unofficial tracks, make your way past windfalls—some old, some recent—and great cedar stumps, relics of the forest logged a century ago, until finally you come to a T-junction. Here you go right, retracing your outward route the short distance back to your car.

To follow with a visit to Crescent Park, turn right when you leave the Sunnyside parking area and drive west to 132nd Street, then north to 28th Avenue, which leads you west to the park's main entrance. Here you are near a wide clearing and picnic area. For a short stroll to the heart of the park, take the path to the right behind the washrooms, which leads to an interesting little pond circled by several trails, from which you may view the various waterbirds resident there.

Going left at the entrance, however, takes you onto a bridle trail to begin a ramble round the perimeter of the park in fine second-growth forest, from which you must emerge to pass several sports fields and their associated parking lots along 132nd Street. At the third you may opt to remain in the open and follow the walkway westwards, from there going right at forks and arriving at the central pond and its picturesque little bridge, on the near side of which lies your return path; or you may prefer to remain with the shady perimeter trail, on which you work round back to your start, your exploration of two contrasting urban forests complete.

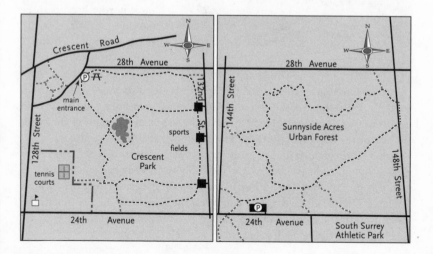

68 TYNEHEAD REGIONAL PARK

Round trip 4.8 km (3 mi)
Trails

Allow 2 hours
Good all year

Bigleaf maple blossom.

Its statistics suggest that this walk may be a little lacking in distance. The relative shortness of the current trail system is, however, more than compensated for by the points of interest along the route, as you wend your way through lush meadows and mixed deciduous-coniferous forest among the headwater feeders of the Serpentine River, with, as culmination, the Tynehead Salmon Hatchery, open at certain times to the public (call 604-589-9127 for details).

To make the most of the little park's winding trail system, a start at the most northerly of its three parking areas is best. To reach it from Highway 1 going east, turn off at Exit 50, go left on 104th Avenue, right on 160th Street, then left again on 103rd Avenue, which curves south onto 161st. Go east again on 102nd Avenue, continuing until this road begins to turn south onto 168th Street and you see, on the right of the bend, the site of the one-time Tynehead House, now a shady parking lot.

From here your trail heads off roughly southwest in rich meadows flanked by interesting old trees, the bigleaf maples being particularly fine; in fact, this part of your route is in parkland uncannily reminiscent of southern England. That all changes when you reach the parting of the ways: left, the direct trail to the picnic area and salmon hatchery at its southeast end, the other reaching the same destination by a much longer route.

On this latter trail, the northern segment of the Serpentine Loop, you cross successive headwater tributaries of the river, normally dry in summer and seen at their best in early spring. On your way, you may notice a short track heading off right to a small clearing, then another that declines to a faint track across a meadow, presumably giving access to 164th Street. Next comes another fork, with the Serpentine Loop leading left to a crossing of the main waterway. Staying right, however, brings you to an attractive picnic area with tracks going off in various directions: right to a parking area on 161st Street and ahead round a butterfly garden and up the Trillium Trail to a viewing platform overlooking a small pond, a safe rearing area for coho and steelhead fry before they migrate to the ocean. Turning your back on the picnic area, you now start downstream on the aptly named Nurse Stump Trail, soon meeting the shorter Serpentine Loop, in trees mostly with one glimpse of a parklike area, home to the Raven's Nest group camp. Then you approach the river again and a fine, arching bridge, on the near side of which you may investigate a short interpretive loop before crossing. Here going right brings you into the open at another picnic area, another parking lot and the hatchery, while left continues the Loop and is your return route to the 168th Street parking lot.

Vehicle approach for those who wish to start at the hatchery is by a turn north from 96th Avenue, itself reached by continuing south on 160th Street from Exit 50 and turning left. Alternatively, you may stay on Highway 1 to its 176th Street turnoff (Exit 53), go south for a short distance, then turn right on 96th Avenue.

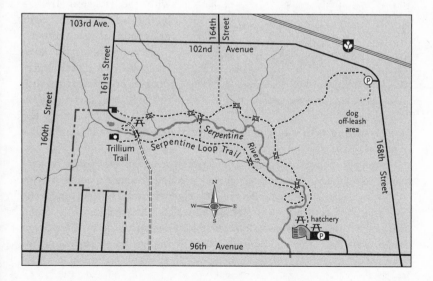

69 DERBY REACH REGIONAL PARK

Round trip 8 km (5 mi)	Allow 2.5 hours
Trails	Good all year

Looking beyond Fort-to-Fort Trail to Golden Ears.

Long a favourite destination for fishermen and picnickers, Derby Reach has become more attractive to those of us who like to stretch our legs now that a trail along the river links the Edgewater fishing bar to the eastern section of this park at the cairn marking the location of the original Fort Langley. Built in 1827, in its heyday the fort was a centre of pioneer agricultural settlement and trade in the lower Fraser Valley. Today, from the heritage area focussing on this early period, a short path connects with the Houston Trail, a hiking and equestrian circuit meandering through forest.

To reach the park leave Highway 1 on 200th Street (Exit 58), go north to 96th Avenue, then east to 208th Street, on which you go left (north), staying with it as it curves east onto Allard Crescent. The entry to Edgewater Bar is on your left. Park here.

Begin your walk by approaching the river, then going east to the right of the campground on the Edge Trail and winding through woodland with imposing cottonwood trees. Beyond the campground, the trail nears the river again and continues upstream as part of the Fraser River Trail. Soon, after a short diversion onto the road and a crossing of Derby Creek, you reach the heritage area and pause to read the inscription on the commemmorative cairn.

The Houston Trail connector starts across the grass from the parking area opposite and meets the trail proper in some 10 minutes. If you go left, your trail borders some low-level meadow and swamp at first, passing through a mixed forest with some fine cedars and bigleaf maples, the leaves of the latter rustling underfoot in fall. Then the path rises on the first of its many ups and downs, and you may glimpse the road below, with the river in the distance across a pond. Next comes an intersection with a sign indicating that left will take you to the Fort-to-Fort Trail. In fact, it takes you down to Allard Crescent and you must walk some 200 m east along the road to connect with that trail. So you stay with the Houston Trail, which pursues its roller-coaster way, eventually arriving at another trailhead and the horse-unloading lot off McKinnon Crescent.

Across the parking area some large maples welcome you to the final lap of the Houston Trail, which winds down towards the Derby Bog, skirting to the right of the swampy ground before coming to your original fork and the path back to the heritage area, from which your return lies downstream once more on Edge Trail.

Alternatively, instead of, or perhaps in addition to, your circuit of Houston Trail, you may wish to sample the Fort-to-Fort Trail, the beginning of which runs upstream for about 1 km (0.6 mi) from the heritage area, affording magnificent views from the Derby Bluff lookout across the Fraser River to the North Shore mountains and east to Mount Baker. Negotiations are under way to acquire rights of access all the way to Fort Langley. If these are successful, the trail may indeed live up to its name, connecting the original with the present-day Fort Langley.

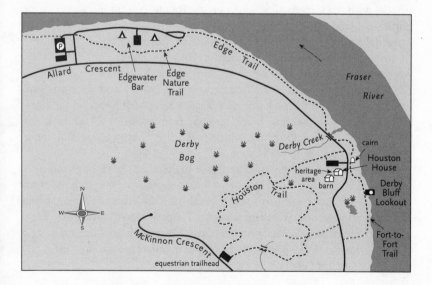

70 CAMPBELL VALLEY

Round trip 12 km (7.5 mi) or less   Allow 4 hours
Trails   Good most of the year

Springtime in the marsh.

The stream that flows through this regional park rises at the south end of Langley Township and pursues a gentle course westwards, running roughly parallel with the Canada-U.S. border except for one hairpin-like swing to the north followed by a return to its original direction. Thereafter it ends uneventfully in Semiahmoo Bay, just south of White Rock.

On its jig northwards, it is crossed by 16th Avenue (North Bluff Road), which you reach from Highway 1 by turning south on Highway 15 at Exit 53 (or on 200th Street at Exit 58). A little east of 200th Street the road drops into its valley, with the park's north entrance and parking area on the right. From here you have several choices, ranging from a short walk on the valley floor to a half-day circuit of the whole park using Shaggy Mane Trail, open to both hikers and horseback riders.

For a short walk, simply head east past the picnic area, through tall trees to a raised boardwalk over the extensive wet meadows bordering the river. On the far side your trail turns south, paralleling the verge of the marshland to another bridge, which returns you to a T-junction on the west side. Here you turn north, heading back on the Little River Loop Trail and crossing a wide meadow, with the possibility of several detours through the woodlands on its east side for variety.

If you decide on the hiking/riding trail, you may head back north for a little before you turn east, crossing the stream just south of the road, then rising to level ground above. More attractive, however, is use of the pedestrian route across the boardwalk and south to a fork where a minor trail rises to the left out of the valley and joins Shaggy Mane Trail, passing south of an equestrian centre; or you may stay with the loop trail to the next junction, then go straight ahead across a meadow to enter the trees beyond. This route, aptly named Deer Trail, takes you southeast by the Little River Bowl, finally joining Shaggy Mane as it descends to the valley floor.

Next comes a turn to the right at a major fork and your crossing of the watercourse. A stretch of open country follows as you wind south, east, west and northwest, eventually leaving Shaggy Mane for the narrow Ravine Trail on your right. This takes you into a picturesque little valley where, just across a small creek, you come to a fork. Right takes you past a viewpoint over the marsh; left on the more recently constructed branch, which emerges in a meadow near the heritage Annand/Rowlatt Farmstead, with the one-time Lochiel Schoolhouse a little beyond. Leaving the farm, the trail heads north across the open field to a picnic area and the park's 8th Avenue Visitor Centre.

From here to your starting point, you may drop into the valley and take the west leg of the short Little River Loop Trail, its scenic meadow particularly attractive in its fall colours. Or you may stay above, on the rim of the valley, using Shaggy Mane Trail round the western perimeter before dropping to your starting point, thus completing your walk over the gently rolling countryside just north of Canada's border with the United States.

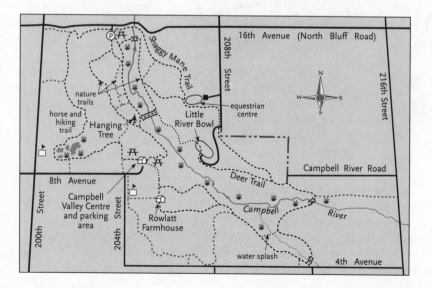

71 ALDERGROVE LAKE REGIONAL PARK

short circuit:	Round trip 4 km (2.5 mi)	Allow 1 hour
long circuit:	Round trip 7 km (4.3 mi)	Allow 2 hours
	Trails	Good all year

Pepin Brook and marsh.

Do not be misled by the presence of the word "lake" in the title. The body of water so designated is, in fact, no more than a large outdoor swimming pool. Still, GVRD Regional Parks Department is working to make the park fit its name by creating a more realistic lake with nature walks in its eastern purlieu where formerly was an unsightly quarry.

To reach this regional park from Highway 1, turn off at Exit 73 onto Highway 13 and drive south to 8th Avenue on which you go left. Then, just after 272nd Street, a right turn sees you descending into the valley, perhaps taking a few minutes to look at the information board about midway to your parking spot on the far side of the creek, where the trailhead for the Pepin Brook Trail is also found.

Shortly after getting under way on the pleasantly winding trail, you pass two trails to the right that connect with the bridle trail running higher up and farther to the south. Ignore these if you prefer the shorter walk and descend gently into the valley on the left to cross the long arching bridge over the brook and the adjacent marsh, an area oftentimes waterlogged thanks to the activity of beavers. As you start to rise again, you find that the route is more open now with one fairly narrow ridge, the legacy of glaciation. Finally approaching the park road at the information board, you turn south along the margin of a meadow, then east on the trail down the hill to another meadow, across the road from the picnic site. Now you may simply follow the road back to your start or, to exploit the park to its fullest, circle behind the picnic shelter crossing the pedestrian bridge to the west and traversing the "lake" area before returning to your transportation.

For the longer circuit, leave the Pepin Brook Trail at the second fork, rising to join the Rock'n Horse Trail, a multi-purpose route that heads south, leaving the comfort of the trees to emerge on the verge of the one-time gravel pit, an area you may soon be able to explore. But for now keep right, skirting the hollow and facing south, with berry fields on the other hand. Gradually you work round to the east, into a treed valley and out again, eventually arriving at a viewpoint with trees behind and broad fields in front stretching south and east, with Mount Baker and the other great peaks of the Cascade Range as backdrop.

Resuming your walk, you turn north into the trees on a trail that undulates along, passing en route an enormous boulder, another instance of glacial deposition, and coming out onto LeFeuvre Road opposite the Valley Gravel operation. Thirty metres along the road, you are able to escape back onto the pedestrian trail, travelling west above the marshy valley and descending finally to join the Pepin Brook Trail at its bridge. Now you may go left for a quick return or right as described previously for the short circuit.

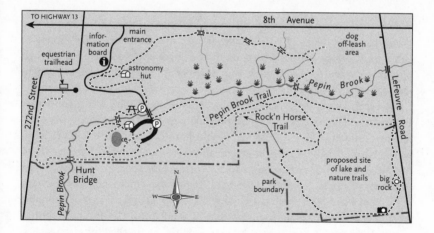

72 MATSQUI TRAIL

One-way trip 10.4 km (6.5 mi)   Allow 2.5 hours

Dykes and roads   Good all year

Mission Bridge with Mission City beyond.

If you wish, you may stretch this into a return trip that will take you the better part of a day; there are, however, intermediate points with access to the river at which you may turn around once you feel you have had enough of this stretch of the Centennial Trail north of Abbotsford. If you can organize two cars, you may also turn this into a very pleasant one-way outing.

To reach the walk's western end in this regional park along the Fraser River, leave Highway 1 at the Mount Lehman Road interchange (Exit 83) and drive north to Harris Road. Turn right here and travel east 3 km (1.9 mi) to Glenmore Road, where you go left and cross the railway to the trailhead on the dyke. From here, you head upstream and, soon after passing that reminder of the less savoury aspects of human existence, the James Sewage Treatment Plant, you reach the Gladwin Road access point, another possible start, 1.6 km (1 mi) from the beginning. Then 2.2 km (1.4 mi) more brings you to the Mission Bridge and the park facilities in its shadow, also reached directly from Highway 11 via Harris Road and Riverside Street.

The next short stretch takes you beneath the highway bridge and over the CP Railway crossing, used at one time by the road as well to provide access to Mission from the south. On the dyke again, you come to Kelleher Road.

Now the route begins bending from northeast to southeast, at the same time drawing back from the main current sufficiently far to permit cottonwood trees to grow, with even one or two houses on the river side of the embankment close to Walters Road.

Another possible turnaround is at Beharrell Road, where dyke and river begin to come together again 4.5 km (2.8 mi) from the park's centre. A short walk to the top of the bank gives you a view of Westminster Abbey, the Benedictine foundation that dominates the countryside west of Mission.

If you intend to go all the way along the trail, you must still cover 2.5 km (1.6 mi) to reach Page Road, close to a quarry under the battlements of Sumas Mountain, having passed the small Page Lake on your right and an undeveloped recreation site between the dyke and the river on your left.

From here, you have nothing for it but to turn about for the journey downriver to whichever of the points you started from. The distance from Glenmore to Page Road suggests the advisability of a car ferry to make the whole trail a one-way trip, not unlike a portage, reference to which may be a reminder that Matsqui itself means "portage," making the single-direction trip even more appropriate.

The recent addition of some 4 km (2.5 mi) westwards makes such a one-way trip still more attractive. Thanks to GVRD's obtaining permission from the Matsqui First Nation to cross its reserve, you may now start at Olund Park, 2.7 km (1.7 mi) west of Glenmore on Harris Road, for a very different experience from the open dyke just described. This extension meanders up and down through woodland and pasture with the occasional glimpse of the Fraser River below before descending to river level just before the Glenmore trailhead. Alone or as part of a Matsqui Trail outing this walk is likely to be a popular one, and its being part of the Fraser Valley Regional Trail as well as the Trans Canada Trail will almost certainly add to its attraction.

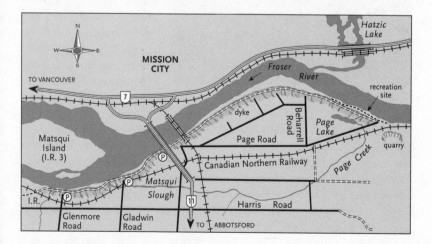

73 SEVEN SISTERS TRAIL

low level:	Round trip 4.8 km (3 mi)	Allow 1.5 hours
high level:	Round trip 10 km (6.2 mi)	Allow 4 hours
	Elevation gain 290 m (950 ft)	High point 325 m (1070 ft)
	Trails	Best April to November

On the Seven Sisters Trail.

Whether you are staying in one of Cultus Lake's many campsites or simply visiting the area for the day, you may find this walk's variations to your liking. To reach the popular provincial park via Yarrow, leave Highway 1 at Exit 104; alternatively, go off at Exit 119A for Sardis. Either way you eventually find yourself driving the Columbia Valley Highway past Cultus Lake village to the Entrance Bay day-use area, where you may park.

Now on foot, turn west, passing through the screen of trees and over Windfall Creek to the Jade Bay boat launch. Here you go left, cross the highway and continue uphill to just past campsite #7, where your trail ascends out of the valley before levelling off in second-growth forest, the mixture suggesting the early days of logging, when the tree cover was left to restore itself. Through this, the trail rises and falls gently until a large Douglas-fir and a flight of steps announce your arrival at the grove of the Seven Sisters, survivors of the original forest.

For a short stroll, you may return from this spot, but continuing to Clear Creek campground gives you the chance to view a solitary giant at close quarters. On your way, you pass the ends of two trails on your left coming down from the bench above, and you may note these for future reference. Once in the campground, turn left and ascend the access road, crossing Clear Creek, staying left at a fork, and finally reaching a five-way junction with a washroom between the two middle roads.

Take the one just below the washplace, and you soon reach the trail, which is joined by another from the right that comes up from the main road. The tree, when you reach it, is truly worth the effort, if only because of the details provided of its past, from its birth in the thirteenth century, long before this land was known to Europeans. After this, if you return by the same route, you will have had a walk of 4.8 km (3 mi).

If you are fit, experienced and have some time at your disposal, another possibility presents itself, though it does involve a rise of nearly 300 m (1000 ft) and extends your round-trip distance considerably. This time, having made your way back through the campground onto the Seven Sisters Trail, turn uphill at the first fork on what was presumably a logging road, go left at the T-junction onto the high-level horse trail and, after about 15 minutes rising steadily, note yet another track joining from the left. This, of course, is the other trail you passed on your outward trip; it provides a possible return and a walk of 6 km (3.7 mi).

Should you continue to climb, your route eventually levels off as you reach the upper waters of Windfall Creek and realize the appropriateness of its name. After this, it is virtually downhill all the way until you reach what was obviously an old logging road now reverting nicely to nature. Here you turn left and downhill until you come out upon Edmeston Road, a little above the highway at Lakeside Lodge. From here, a short turn back left brings you once more to the beach and, eventually, your car.

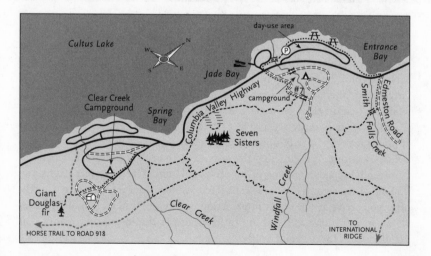

74 TEAPOT HILL

Round trip 5 km (3.1 mi)　　Allow 2 hours
Elevation gain 250 m (820 ft)　High point 290 m (950 ft)
Trails and roads　　　　　　Good most of the year

View along Columbia Valley towards the International Boundary.

To discover why this sporting little bump is so quaintly named, you must park at the low end of Road 918 in Cultus Lake Provincial Park, a short distance beyond the entrance to Clear Creek campground and just short of the entrance to the Honeymoon Bay group campgrounds, parking space being available just off the Columbia Valley Highway.

The trail rises quite steeply at first to join the service road, which then settles down to a steady uphill grade. Before you have gone far, however, a B.C. Parks notice has supplied the answer to the riddle, and henceforth you climb enlightened. Next you may note a trail joining from the left after some 800 m, with a sign to the horse trail. This could be your return route. Shortly after you arrive at your next intersection, where the trail to Teapot Hill goes right, an information board indicating some of the interesting plants you should watch for on your walk.

The trail, rerouted in the past few years, no longer has a long flight of steps to daunt you, and you make your ascent along the side of a ridge instead of up its snout. Still, you eventually reach ridge level at a station with a view over Cultus Lake and across it to the ridge of Vedder Mountain. Thereafter the trail to the main summit proceeds uninterrupted, but before going on you may want to inspect an instance of violence in nature where a large Douglas-fir has been struck by a lightning bolt, the scar running all the way down its trunk, while, if you look upwards, you can see the forest giant's scorched crest and upper limbs.

At your destination, you find that B.C. Parks has decided that the drop-off is sufficiently steep to warrant the use of restraining wires, the side towards the lake being virtually sheer, and from here you have views that would do credit to a more lofty eminence. Immediately below you are the cabins and playing fields of the Columbia Bible Camp, whose campers created the southern, now abandoned, route to your miniature mountain; while farther off is the little residential settlement of Lindell Beach, with the Maple Bay picnic area and campground close to the south end of Cultus Lake. Farther south still lies the International Boundary while, as before, the ridges of Vedder Mountain block the view to the north.

Your return is by the same route as far as the intersection with Road 918. Here you may choose a somewhat longer and more energetic return than by the main trail. For this, jog right on Road 918 and then almost immediately go left on the horse trail. On this you meander through the forest, surmounting its steep little undulations until after some 30 minutes you arrive at a fork. Leave the bridle trail here and go left, descending once more to Road 918, where a right turn brings you back to your parking just east of the Honeymoon Bay group campgrounds, a peculiar use, one would think, given the name of the location.

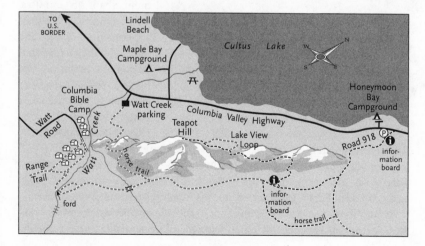

75 COQUIHALLA HISTORIC TRAILS

Round trip 8 km (5 mi)   Allow 3 hours
Elevation gain 185 m (600 ft)   High point 335 m (1100 ft)
Trails and roads   Good most of the year

Southernmost trestle and river below.

One of Hope's attractions is the historic Kettle Valley Railway and the Othello-Quintette Tunnels, that succession of bridges and passages by which the Coquihalla Canyon was made passable for rail traffic. Here you may marvel at the pertinacity of these railroad builders who produced one of the most expensive pieces of trackage not only in Canada, but in the world.

The 2-km (1.2-mi) stroll through the tunnels and back will take you no more than 45 minutes, only enough to whet your appetite for more; and more you may experience by combining this piece of history with an earlier attempt to link the coast with the interior—the Hope–Nicola Valley Cattle Trail, constructed in 1875 using in part a trade route carved out in 1860.

For your approach, drive along 6th Avenue in Hope, turn east on Kawkawa Lake Road and stay with it to a major fork, where you go right on Othello Road, then cut back right again on Tunnel Road to reach the parking lot.

Now follow the old railbed, taking time to learn the history of the railway and its amazing construction through the Coquihalla gorge from the information boards along the way. After the last tunnel, walk westwards until just beyond a yellow gate you reach a rough track heading uphill to join the cattle trail, railway construction having obliterated it at line level.

On the cattle road you rise steadily, travelling through fine open forest with occasional sounds of the new Coquihalla Highway on the river's opposite bank an audible reminder of this valley's continuing importance as a link between coast and interior. Two open viewpoints, in particular, provide the chance to rest briefly as you make height, though the quality of the trail is astonishing considering that it has been in place since 1860.

Finally you reach the pass, a small plaque on a tree marking the spot, and from here your trail descends until you arrive at a T-junction with a sign indicating the Hope–Nicola Valley trail. Go right to reach a small clearing, where you go right again, following orange tapes as you wind down steeply through encroaching greenery to an old road, on which you go left. On this latter you meet yet one more old road and on this you go right, descending gently to where Tunnel Road goes off right, 0.7 km (0.4 mi) from the parking area.

It is unfortunate that the build-up of ice causes B.C. Parks to close the tunnels in winter, from about mid-November until April; all is not lost, however, for a walk on the historic railway and trail is possible in all seasons. To do this leave Kawkawa Lake Road a short distance beyond the Coquihalla River bridge and go right on Kettle Valley Road to a parking space before a gate. Now walk upstream on the old right-of-way to join the cattle trail just before the yellow barrier. A return trip to the pass will give a walk of about 6 km (3.7 mi), for which you should allow about 2 hours.

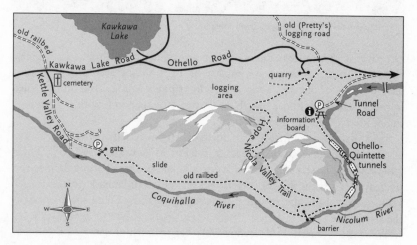

76 CHATHAM REACH

from Alouette bridge: Round trip 10 km (6.2 mi)   Allow 3 hours
from end of Harris Road: Round trip 4 km (2.5 mi)   Allow 1 hour
                           Dykes   Good all year

View upstream to ridges enclosing Widgeon Slough.

Pitt River with its succession of dykes offers many fine outings, and this one, with its superb upriver views, must rank high on any aesthetic scale. You have a choice of distance as well: a short trip of 4 km (2.5 mi) and another of more than double that length, the latter providing you with a stretch of the Alouette River for good measure.

For the shorter excursion, turn north off Highway 7 (Lougheed Highway) on Dewdney Trunk Road just east of the Pitt River bridge. Go left at the T-junction onto Harris Road and drive to the end of that thoroughfare at the river dyke, crossing the Alouette River en route. To embark on the longer walk, stop at the bridge over the Alouette, the better parking space being on the south side.

From the Alouette bridge your walk begins with crossing to the north bank, prior to setting off westwards downstream. As you proceed, assorted small farms lie below you on your right; then, as you approach Pitt River, a variety of boathouses and pleasure craft sit on the water to your left. Having arrived at the confluence of the tributary and the main stream, you begin your northward march along the Pitt, its tidal waters providing passage for tugs and small boats, its wide shoreline marshes home to a multitude of wildlife. Waterfowl of many kinds are present as well as herons and raptors; spring is a wonderful time, with nesting birds going about their business on every hand. At any time of the year, however, the prospect ahead would be hard to beat: the wide expanse of the Pitt River making its great bend that encloses Addington Marsh and, beyond that, the ridges and knolls surrounding Widgeon Slough with, as background to it all, the snow-capped mountains at the head of Pitt Lake. After a walk of some 35 minutes, you come to the starting point of the shorter walk and acquire a feeling of smugness in the thought of the extra exercise you are getting as well.

Proceeding, you observe that a narrow band of rough ground with trees and shrubs now separates the dyke from the various agricultural enterprises and homes on your right. Finally, you come to an information board announcing that this narrow strip of land has been left in its natural state for wildlife habitat—small recompense, it seems, for the many hectares lost to human endeavours. Then, just beyond, a gate bars further progress and you must turn around.

After your upstream views, you may find the return a little anticlimactic, the sight of new urban developments on the slopes west of the river no match for nature's work. Still, the countryside has its own quiet beauty, and city bustle seems far off as, after a visit to that part of the river that commemorates William Pitt, Earl of Chatham, you retrace your steps to whichever starting point you selected.

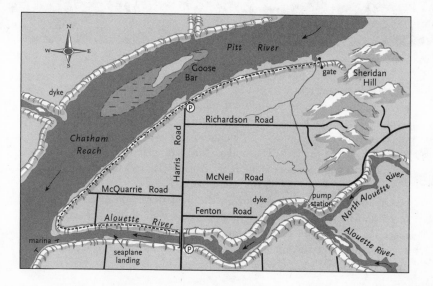

77 ALOUETTE RIVER DYKES

Round trip 14.5 km (9 mi)   Allow 4.5 hours
Dykes   Good all year

At the confluence.

Situated in the heartland of Pitt Meadows, this walk has much to offer: low-level, easy walking and magnificent mountain scenery amid the peace and serenity of a countryside far removed from cities and highways. To reach the start, turn left off Highway 7 (Lougheed Highway) onto Dewdney Trunk Road just east of the Pitt River bridge. Turn left again at the T-junction onto Harris Road and continue along it for 2.5 km (1.6 mi) to a bridge over the Alouette River. Park here on the south bank.

On foot, you head upstream on the busiest section of dyke, carrying recreationists of all sorts and conditions as well as the occasional farm machine, for the land south of here is highly developed agriculturally. After a short distance, you come to the confluence of the North Alouette and the main stream, both arms wide and slow-moving as they traverse the lowlands. Now your dyke turns southeast and even due south on occasion, following the windings of the river until finally, at a bridge, you meet the road you have been paralleling for the last short while.

Cross this bridge and, turning left onto the grassy dyke along the north side of the river, embark on the most peaceful, most delightful part of the trip, in the triangle enclosed between the two branches of the Alouette, some of the original marsh remaining though attempts at draining and cultivating are afoot. After about 30 minutes you are back at the meeting of the waters and turn northeast, with the peaks and ridges of Golden Ears in full view. On this stretch the dyke runs straight, leaving a wide margin of marsh between you and the meanderings of the North Alouette. Quite soon you change direction again and, closing the gap, head eastwards towards Neaves Road, once more with the river on one side and a drainage canal on the other. Now you look clear to Mount Baker, agricultural development having levelled the cottonwood trees, sometime nesting place for the local herons. At the road, cross on its bridge and turn left, dodging around a small slough and some remaining cottonwoods before resuming your march along the grassy north bank, looking ahead now to Sheridan Hill, whose base you eventually reach before you swing away on the next stage of your walk.

Back on a gravelled dyke, make for the confluence of the two Alouettes, where you turn west towards the crossing of Harris Road and the end of your excursion, reflecting that the whole course has been Y shaped, with more or less equal distances between bridges; and that it has revealed to you two faces of Pitt Meadows: the original marsh with its abundance of wildlife, and the more recently reclaimed lands with their produce destined to meet human needs.

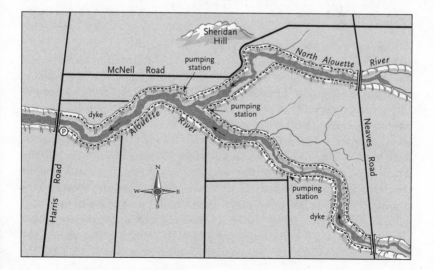

78 PITT WILDLIFE MANAGEMENT AREA

| long circuit: | Round trip 12 km (7.5 mi) | Allow 4 hours |
| | Dykes | Good most of the year |

Boardwalk east from Snake Rock Dyke.

This tract of polder south of Pitt Lake has become even richer in possibilities than before with the creation of a north-south forest walk along its eastern boundary from just south of the lake to a termination level with Koerner Road. This section, a distance of 5.6 km (3.5 mi), rises to as much as 160 m (500 ft) in the process. Not only that, it is furnished with viewing pavilions like miniature Rhine castles that give you views to west and north, supplementing the bird-watching towers on the dykes themselves, which, connected as they are, allow you to enjoy walks of varied length.

For these, there are two major starting points, both reached by going east on Dewdney Trunk Road and north on Harris Road as for the walk to Chatham Reach (Walk 76). Fork right off Harris on McNeil, which takes you east around the south end of Sheridan Hill. Thereafter you go left again on Rannie Road. For a southern access point, park just north of the wide power line that crosses the whole valley and walk 1.7 km (1.1 mi) along Koerner Road to the beginning of the Snake Rock Dyke, looking towards the bluff on which is perched the most southerly of the viewpoints. Towards it you set your face for a walk of about 15 minutes, noting in passing another dyke coming in from the left, your return if you decide on a circular outing.

Near the eastern edge of the marsh, you must choose: complete a dyke circuit by way of left turns for a round trip of 4 km (2.5 mi) or continue by a footbridge and boardwalk to the valley's steep eastern wall, entering the screen of trees and either turning north on the forest track or making for the steep trail to a viewpoint.

To reach the northern access point, continue on Rannie Road to its end at the lake. From here the Pitt Lake Dyke stretches east but, less obvious, another dyke, tree-clad, begins here also, diverging from the other, the two providing a round trip of 5.6 km (3.5 mi) when connected by the north-south Swan Dyke. A more energetic variant of this takes you a little farther east and uses the northern segment of the forest trail with its climb of 160 m (500 ft), especially steep from south to north.

One long circuit starts on Pitt Lake Dyke, then turns south to meet Nature Dyke, on which you might also begin for a walk shorter by 1.9 km (1.2 mi). From this common point you continue south on Mountain Dyke to Homilk'um Dyke, which takes you westwards past an observation tower and brings you to a T-junction, where you turn right once again. Now on Crane Dyke, make your way to Rannie Road. Turn left (south) for a short distance to a track leading onto the Pitt River Dyke, where a right turn takes you back to the lake outlet and your car.

On the walks just described, as well as the many opportunities to observe nature, especially birdlife, the enclosing mountains provide a magnificent backdrop to the views north, east and west. If you are lucky to have a clear day, therefore, you may find it rewarding to choose your route with this idea in mind: do the forest walk from north to south with an outlook up Widgeon Creek from the pavilions and return north on open dyke, the peaks around Pitt Lake before your eyes. You should be prepared, though, for the odd windfall or washout on the forest trail, lack of regular maintenance being a perennial problem.

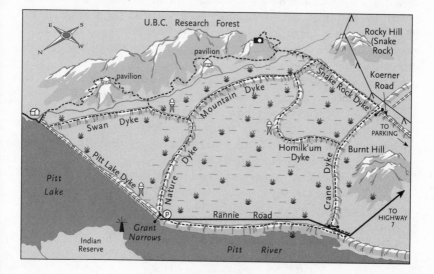

79 UBC MALCOLM KNAPP RESEARCH FOREST

blue trail to knoll:	Round trip 8 km (5 mi)	Allow 3.5 hours
	Elevation gain 298 m (975 ft)	High point 335 m (1100 ft)
	Roads and trails	Good most of the year

Mills Bridge.

To honour one of its outstanding personalities, the University of British Columbia dedicated to Malcolm Knapp its research forest in Maple Ridge.

To reach the forest from Highway 7 (Lougheed Highway) in Haney, follow the signs for Golden Ears Provincial Park, staying with 232nd Street when the park road turns right after the bridge over the South Alouette River. Thereafter, a fork right on Silver Valley Road brings you to the parking area. To the left is the office, where, for a dollar, you may obtain an excellent self-guiding booklet and map.

Armed with this brochure, you may enjoy the demonstration forest on your own. (Please: no dogs or bikes.) The easy red trail takes up to an hour, the green a little longer; the yellow provides the most detailed information about various aspects of forestry and requires about 2 hours for its 3.2 km (2 mi), while the blue is primarily a hiking trail, doubling the length of the yellow and giving the greatest variety of scenery.

One possibility, once you have sampled the basic routes, is to follow the blue trail, adding a side trip to a knoll with a view and ending with a detour onto the green trail for your return by the North Alouette River.

Except for the green, all trails start by going left past the office, crossing the arboretum and an old road, then entering the forest. The blue is the first to diverge, heading off left and losing altitude as it heads down an open slope to cross Spring Creek and continues left to a forest road (G), which it crosses again and again as it winds through a managed plantation. After its seventh crossing comes a patch of scrub and then a T-junction where an old trail comes up Blaney Creek, whose waters are now audible below. Go right here, rising to cross yet another road (M), and continue your northward course for a short distance before you reach a fork just as you start to turn east.

Now you deviate left and up a track to meet a road on which you go right, circling a small knoll whose summit and shelter cabin you finally attain from the north side. Here you are rewarded with views northwards to Golden Ears and southwards to the whole sweep of the Fraser Valley, from Mount Baker to the Strait of Georgia.

Back on the blue trail you turn southeast, reenter forest, cross two roads and finally link up with the yellow trail again beside a small pond. From here the shortest route to the green trail is left a little past the pond on Road A12, then down to the river on a trail to the Mills Bridge, a graduation gift from forestry students. You may either follow the river down its east bank or fork left, ascending to meet Road A and descending on it to the bridge over the falls, being rejoined by the river trail a little before.

On the west side go left on the green trail, keeping left at the first fork then going right to emerge on main road F not far from your starting point. Here you may cross the road to wander through the arboretum and its fine collection before taking leave of this teaching forest.

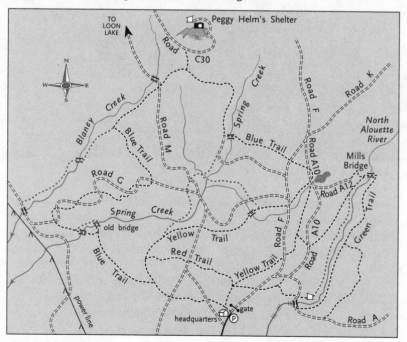

80 MIKE LAKE

long circuit:	Round trip 5.6 km (3.5 mi)	Allow 2 hours
	Elevation gain 180 m (600 ft)	High point 430 m (1400 ft)
	Roads and trails	Best March to November

Fishing in Mike Lake.

Contrasting with the spectacular mountain scenery in much of the rest of Golden Ears Provincial Park are the surroundings of this unobtrusive body of water with its tall conifers, its only contact with the high country to the north being its parking lot where hikers and climbers begin their trips to Alouette Mountain or Blanshard Peak. Even if you have no such ambitions, you do have a choice of two trails, one a short round of the lake of 2 km (1.2 mi), the other a longer circuit mostly within the encircling forest.

To reach the start of these walks, follow the Golden Ears park signs north from Haney, and from the park entrance drive a farther 4.5 km (2.8 mi) along the main access road, then turn left at the park headquarters sign. Go left again after a short distance and travel on a dirt road for about 1.6 km (1 mi) to the parking area by the lake, some 200 m beyond the point where Incline Trail goes off to the right. Just west of the parking lot a locked gate bars the road to vehicles, thereby ensuring peace for your walk along it.

The more gentle ascent in each case is clockwise, so, having passed the locked gate, head west. Shortly before a notice that you are in the UBC research forest, Lakeside Trail goes off right. If you follow it, you soon realize why this was the preferred direction, as it dips to lake level in a series of switchbacks preparatory to crossing a marshy tract on a boardwalk. If you continue on the road, stay right at a fork and right again at the next junction, which has a locked gate to the left.

Next turn right at a point where you glimpse Mount Blanshard, your only mountain view. Now you are heading back east, rising a little on the one-time railway grade, until you come to the park sign for Alouette Mountain and you recognize your return route, Incline Trail, dropping right downhill. This trail also owes its existence to logging days, when it was used as a route to skyline logs down to the lake from the railroad above.

On this stretch you speedily lose the height gained so gently earlier, descending the steep Incline Trail and ignoring Eric Dunning Trail to your left. Finally, just before the bridge spanning the lake outlet, Lakeside Trail joins from your right, having stayed with low ground round the lake's north side. If you have followed the longer circuit to the junction yet still have lots of energy, you may cut back right on the lake trail instead of gently crossing the outlet and walking back along the road to your starting point. By so doing, however, you add 2 km (1.2 mi) to your trip and give yourself the short but sharp ascent from lake to road close to the end of your walk.

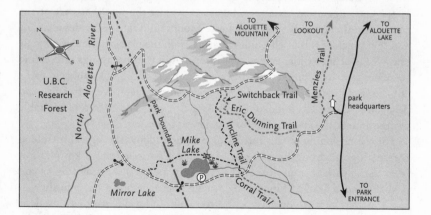

81 ALOUETTE NATURE LOOP

Round trip 6 km (3.7 mi)	Allow 2.5 hours
Elevation gain 170 m (560 ft)	High point 320 m (1050 ft)
Trails	Best March to November

Looking across Alouette Lake to Mount Crickmer.

What title do you give a walk that embraces sections of no fewer than five trails in Golden Ears Provincial Park: Spirea, Bog, Lookout, Menzies and Loop? Our suggestion, as above, takes account of the fact that part of the route is on the lower slopes of Alouette Mountain, that it provides a circuit and that much of it is a self-guiding nature trail, the placards increasing your knowledge of forest lore as you walk along. Add to those things interesting stretches of marsh complete with sphagnum moss and skunk cabbage, a seventy-year-old forest of hemlock that restored the tree cover after fire had devastated the valley, a lookout over Alouette Lake and even a picnic table by its shore at the end of your outing, if you so desire.

For the beginning of this intriguing mixture, follow the signs for Golden Ears park north from the east end of Haney. Continue for 7.2 km (4.5 mi) beyond the park entrance to a right turn into a day-use area, noting as you pass the Spirea Trail parking lot about a kilometre before, a possible alternative starting point if you wish a shorter walk. In lot #2, park as closely as possible to the south end; your route, signed "Spirea Nature Trail," is on the opposite side of the access road and takes you into the woods. Almost immediately you drop left to cross a small creek on a bridge. (If you go straight ahead on the bridle trail you will have to ford the stream.) After crossing, you must traverse an access road to the Alouette Dam before reentering the trees and beginning to rise in nice open forest, the bright green of the moss in the understorey attesting to generous precipitation in the valley.

After some 20 minutes, you come to a fork where the trail from the Spirea parking lot joins and now you are on Bog Trail, upgraded and renamed Spirea Universal Access Trail. Here, on boardwalks, you cross what would otherwise be very muddy ground. Shortly thereafter, as the path begins to curve right, go left at the sign "Lookout Trail," cross the horse trail for the umpteenth time, then the main access road and start rising again in forest. This trail is joined by Menzies Trail coming from your left. Soon after, a clearing to your right provides the view over the lake and towards Mount Crickmer, which you may enjoy from a seat on a little bluff.

Continuing, seek out a bridle trail coming uphill from the right for your descent; it will bring you back to the main road a short distance before the Spirea parking lot. Cross the road and go left on the horse trail, then left again on the pedestrian path. This takes you between road and bog along the final part of the nature walk until, within sight of the parking area, you swing away right onto its first part to rejoin your outward route east of the boardwalk. Now you go left and retrace your steps downhill to your starting point.

Back at your car, you can drop down to the beach picnic area to refresh yourself; you may find all its tables occupied, though, on a fine summer weekend, for it is a popular area with Greater Vancouver residents.

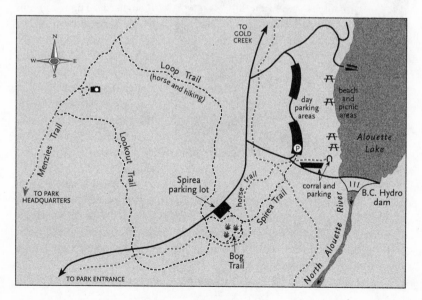

82 GOLD CREEK TRAILS

Gold Creek Lookout:	Round trip 8 km (5 mi)	Allow 3.5 hours
	Elevation gain 150 m (500 ft)	High point 320 m (1050 ft)
Viewpoint Beach:	Round trip 8 km (5 mi)	Allow 3.5 hours
	Elevation gain 180 m (600 ft)	High point 350 m (1150 ft)
	Trails	Good most of the year

Waterfall on Viewpoint Trail.

Removal years ago of its popular Burma Bridge means that walks can be along only one side of Gold Creek at a time. Even so, there are many options if you are staying in Golden Ears Provincial Park and looking for a nice late-afternoon appetite-rouser; and many of the trails, alone or combined, are suitable for the day visitor eager for some exercise.

Having followed park signs from Highway 7 (Lougheed Highway) in Maple Ridge, drive from the entrance along the main access road for 11.6 km (7.2 mi) to a fork. Go left then left again for the West Canyon parking lot, or left then right for the Gold Creek day-use area if you wish to sample the eastside trails.

The West Canyon Trail follows an old railway grade with, for the observant, some interesting relics of the 1920s logging era along the way. On it, you proceed north for about 10 minutes until, after crossing a creek, you see leading uphill to the left a path signed "Viewpoint Trail," a sporting little trail and pleasant, but alas, its views obscured by a growing forest.

Continuing, your route rises gently northwards bordered by mixed deciduous and coniferous trees until, having crossed two major creeks and the impressive erosion associated with them, you reach the railway's end at a fork. Going right, you descend by a rough track to Gold Creek and a viewing spot just below its Lower Falls; on the left branch you head up steeply on the Golden Ears Trail to a lookout over the upper Gold Creek valley. Either viewpoint makes a satisfying destination for your excursion up the West Canyon.

The best views, however, are to be enjoyed from the east side, where you may follow the Lower Falls Trail running more or less parallel to the creek. Eventually, after nearly an hour, you arrive at the spray-enshrouded and mighty Lower Falls, awe-inspiring in their power.

But although the Lower Falls Trail is undoubtedly the most popular of the east-side walks, it is short—only a 5.4-km (3-mi) round trip—so you may wish to try the multi-purpose East Canyon Trail to Viewpoint Beach. For the latter, start on Corral Trail, which not surprisingly goes off from the corral just north of the parking lots. Very soon this meets the main East Canyon Trail and you go left, rising gently and, in spring, fording innumerable streamlets until, after some 30 minutes, you pass a huge washout and come to an old gate, a reminder that your route was once a logging road. Next the trail crests at a spot with a glimpse of Blanshard Peak through the trees before it descends to river level then, at a fork just beyond a horse camp, left takes you to Viewpoint Beach, a truly spectacular destination. Here you may pause to enjoy the magnificent view of the aptly named Edge Peak and the mountain that gave the park its name.

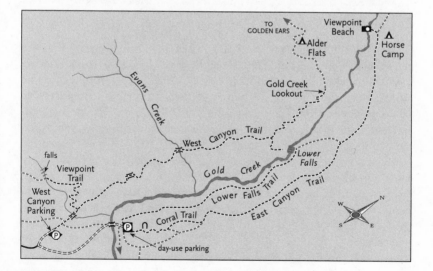

175

83 KANAKA CREEK

Riverfront Trail:	Round trip 3 km (1.9 mi)	Allow 1 hour
Canyon Loop:	Round trip 3.5 km (2.2 mi)	Allow 1.5 hours
	Trails	Good all year

North Fork, Kanaka Creek.

Kanaka Creek Regional Park, extending in a narrow band upstream from the creek's mouth just east of Haney to north of the Dewdney Trunk Road on the lower slopes of Blue Mountain, is still in the making. Although a trail system along the whole of the park is yet only a plan, the more accessible sections, notably the Fraser Riverfront, Cliff Falls and Bell-Irving Fish Hatchery, are already well provided with pathways, affording you experience of its many faces, from canyons and cliffs to meadows and marsh.

For the Fraser Riverfront entrance on River Road, turn right off Highway 7 (Lougheed Highway) just east of its junction with the Haney Bypass. From the parking lot you set off through trees, very soon coming to a viewpoint over the creek, here wide and slow as it winds towards its demise in the Fraser River. Next you reach a T-junction beside the Fraser itself, the left branch taking you upstream and out of the park, following the riverbank to a small-craft harbour at Kanaka Landing. Staying right within the park, however, brings you to a high-arching bridge where a plaque informs you that the Kanaka (Hawaiians) were once employed by the Hudson's Bay Company at Fort Langley across the Fraser, hence the creek's name. Now you make a circuit of the marshy peninsula created by the stream's final meander, passing meadows, lush berry bushes and impressive cottonwood trees en route back to the bridge. From here you return as you came, with, perhaps, one last look down the Fraser from the neighbouring viewpoint.

To reach the other regions of the park, for the time being you need your car; turn right onto Lougheed Highway and drive to the Albion traffic light, where you go left on 240th Street, driving north to cross Kanaka Creek near the Fish Fence, another park feature. Stay with 240th a little farther, then go right onto 112th Avenue, following signs for the hatchery as you wind your way to 256th Street and the entrance to the parking lot on its right side.

On foot, cross 256th Street, where at a yellow gate you embark on Canyon Trail, which gradually rises above creek level amidst mostly deciduous trees, with maples to make fall resplendent and cottonwoods to scent the spring air. Quite soon you come to a fork where, if you go right towards the North Fork Loop, you drop to cross a footbridge over the canyon, then rise again to another fork, where left takes you into a wide clearing and picnic area situated between the main stream and its north fork. Across the North Fork bridge to the west you may visit viewpoints overlooking the rapids and falls tumbling over cliffs and waterworn rocks before you return to the meadow and beyond it the crossing where the Canyon Trail departs, affording a grandstand view of the main gorge. Then, ignoring all deviations from the trail as you travel upstream, you are soon back at the hatchery, your excursion over.

If you wish to go directly to this middle reach of the Kanaka, you may approach from the Dewdney Trunk Road by turning south on 252nd Street, following signs for Cliff Park or, alternatively, by going south at Websters Corners on 256th Street to the Bell-Irving Fish Hatchery.

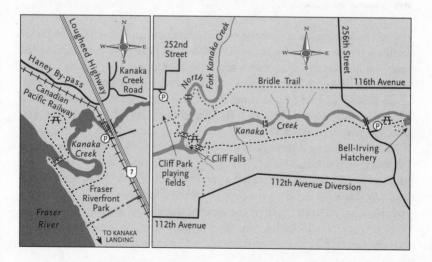

84 ROLLEY LAKE AND FALLS

including falls loop: Round trip 5 km (3.1 mi) Allow 2 hours
Trails Good all year

Viewing spot on Rolley Lake.

If you are looking for a destination for a country spin, one close to picnic facilities by the shore of a placid lake, then this provincial park may be the spot you are seeking. You have a gentle walk, too, not only round the lake but with a detour to some falls as well if you wish more exercise.

To reach this spot as you come from the west, use the Dewdney Trunk Road, less busy than Highway 7 (Lougheed Highway). East of Haney you pass the quaintly named Websters Corners, then some 10 km (6 mi) beyond it (noting in passing Wilson Road on your right, should you wish to return by Highway 7), you come to Bell Road going off left. On this you travel north until, at its end, you must turn left again to enter the park. Its developed area is on the lake's south side, with the part reserved for day use near its western end. Here, by an open beach, is the sign for the start of the lake trail.

If you set off clockwise, you soon cross a lengthy boardwalk over an extensive stretch of marshy ground, created by various inlet streams that are virtually hidden in lush vegetation, the whole making an interesting ecological study as you travel along, gradually trending east towards higher and drier conditions, with a screen of second-growth trees between you and the lake. Next comes a crossing of the lake's outlet, with the lake trail staying right. For the falls on Rolley Creek, you stay left, to find yourself, rather disconcertingly, in the park campground.

There is no need to worry, however. By going left, then left again, you find yourself on the right track, Rolley Falls Trail, on which you soon come to a fork and a sign announcing that you are entering Mission Municipal Forest. Keep left for the falls, and after descending a little, you are soon gazing into the waters of the upper falls from a bridge. For the more spectacular lower falls you must cross and zigzag down to a fine viewpoint overlooking the cascade. From here you may return whence you came; however, you may continue to descend, crossing a tributary creek, to reach the Florence Lake Forest Road, about 3 km (1.9 mi) from its junction with the Dewdney Trunk Road just west of Stave Falls Dam—an alternative starting point for your walk.

Now you must recross Rolley Creek on the road bridge and start the ascent of the steep bank to the south, looking upstream for views of this lower part of the rushing creek. Then you reach the margin of the ravine and join an old logging road whose easier gradient takes you back to meet your outward route, where you go left to the campground. Here, your best procedure is to go right twice, retracing your steps to the fork by the outlet, if you wish to avoid the embarrassment of wandering through campsites.

Finally you go back left along the lake's south shore to the picnic tables and your vehicle, pondering, perhaps, the fate that brought James and Fanny Rolley to these shores more than a century ago, remote, one would imagine, from any other dwelling in those long-ago days.

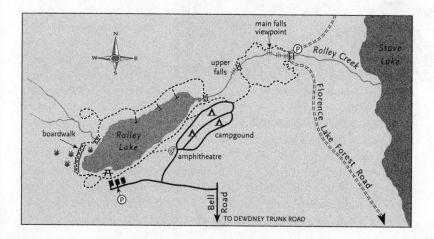

85 HAYWARD LAKE

Railway Trail:	Round trip 12 km (7.4 mi)	Allow 3.5 hours
Hayward Reservoir	Round trip 17 km (10.5 mi)	Allow 5.5 hours
circuit:	Trails and roads	Good all year

Reflections in Hairsine Inlet.

The one-time railway track between Stave Falls and Ruskin gave us a walk along the west side of Hayward Lake, one of the stretches of water created by the Western Canada Power Company but now operated by B.C. Hydro, its successor. More recently, in the forest along the lake's east side, B.C. Hydro has built Reservoir Trail, which, combined with the Railway Trail, makes possible a circumambulation full of interest and variety.

A good place to start this outing is from Hayward Lake Recreation Area, reached by driving east from Maple Ridge on the Dewdney Trunk Road and turning south on the approach road just west of Stave Falls Dam. Here, additional to the long circuit, is a short nature loop, Beaver Pond Trail, which gives you a chance to see the work of beavers, their skill in dam building rivalling that of their human counterparts.

As you walk south on Railway Trail, you must deviate from the right-of-way where the railway line was carried over small bays and creek mouths on trestles, two detours in particular taking you up and over, footbridges and walkways supplying the crossings in lieu of the derelict railway bridges. As well, alternative trails diverging from the shoreline path enliven your walk before you arrive at a parking area off Wilson Road. A few minutes more and your trail emerges at Ruskin Dam, some 6 km (3.7 mi) from the start and a possible turnaround, the more arduous part of the circuit being still ahead.

If you decide to continue, cross on the dam and go left to the trailhead information board beyond which you enter the trees, shortly arriving at a viewpoint over the lake. Then you descend to traverse a floating bridge across the long Hairsine Inlet and proceed to regain the height you just lost, surrounded by tall second-growth forest and a healthy understorey of ferns and moss. Thus you pursue your upsy-downsy route, down to a canoe landing and up again, into Mission Municipal Forest and out again, over countless creeks, eventually to arrive at a junction with a track dropping left to a vantage point for Steelhead Falls.

After this interlude your trail crosses Steelhead Creek itself and traverses a long walkway over Brown Creek just before another fork, right going this time to a parking lot on the Dewdney Trunk Road. But you stay left with the Reservoir Trail, ascending a little to cross a power line and come out on the road shortly after. Fortunately, you soon leave the busy thoroughfare and descend on a steep zigzagging track through the forest to meet the road once more not far east of a dam. This time there's no escape. To complete the circuit you must walk west (left) on the road, crossing two dams, the Blind Slough and Stave Falls Dams, en route to the access road into the recreation area and thus back to your vehicle.

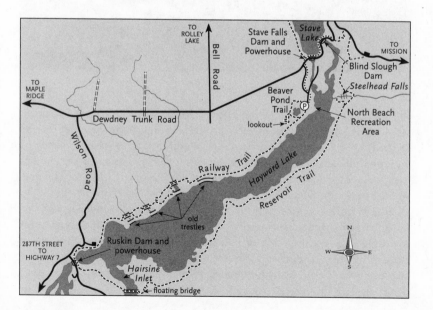

86 HOOVER LAKE FOREST TRAIL

to lake:	Round trip 7.5 km (4.7 mi)	Allow 3 hours
	Elevation gain 225 m (740 ft)	High point 500 m (1640 ft)
including viewpoints:	Round trip 11.5 km (7.1 mi)	Allow 4.5 hours
	Elevation gain 470 m (1540 ft)	High point 670 m (2200 ft)
	Roads and trails	Best April to November

Hoover Lake.

If you have already experienced Hayward Lake (Walk 85) from lake level, you may be interested in seeing it from above, from the viewpoint at the end of the Hoover Lake forest road, with, as bonus, a visit to Hoover Lake itself en route. The trailhead and parking spot are situated a mere 2.5 km (1.5 mi) east of Stave Falls Dam on the north side of the Dewdney Trunk Road, opposite the municipal landfill.

On the trail, which, in its initial stages, is a sometimes active logging road in the Mission Municipal Forest, you rise steadily northwards through what is mainly second-growth forest, industrial roads going off left from time to time to operations west of Hoover Creek. After the third such road, you arrive at a fork with a sign announcing that the lake is only 700 m away down the dark little track to the left. As you proceed you notice signs of past logging—large old stumps and the remains of a railway heading straight for the lake—while your route works from one side to the other with boardwalk to assist over the wet spots. At the lake, remote and peaceful, another stretch of boardwalk leads to the left through a variety of marsh plants to the little headland beyond, a spot for fishing or maybe just for contemplation.

Back at the forest road, if you choose to continue uphill you will pass a number of viewpoints with prospects to the north, east and south as your route works its way round the mountain to end, not on a summit with panoramic views, but at a wide landing looking down on Hayward Lake and the Fraser Valley beyond. However, on your way along the east side of the slope you are enchanted by the sight of the great cone of Mount Baker across the valley on your left; and on your return you are rewarded with the view to the north of the magnificent peaks commemorating the two friends, Robie Reid and Judge Howay. As you descend, you may also see stretching into the distance the expansive Stave Lake, that huge reservoir serving our voracious appetite for power; and from the great to the little, you may spot Hoover Lake almost at your feet as you swing round the mountain, south-ward bound once more.

If the foregoing seems a little ambitious, the Stave Dam Forest Interpretation Trail only 1.3 km (0.8 mi) west along the Dewdney Trunk Road may be just the thing for you. This delightful walk created for the Mission Municipal Forest rises through mostly second-growth forest to an open bluff with views over the forest and to Hayward Lake—even as far as Vancouver Island and the Gulf Islands when conditions are right. A brochure (available at the Public Works Building, 33835 Dewdney Trunk Road) explains the significance of its ten stops, providing a wealth of information, which makes the hike truly worth the energy expended on the 1.6-km (1-mi) loop with its 150-m (490-ft) elevation gain.

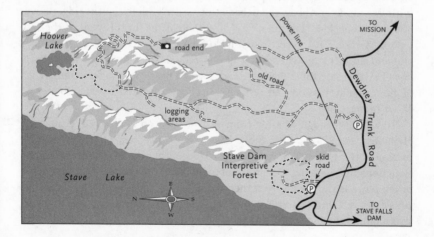

87 MISSION TRAIL

Round trip 5 km (3.1 mi)   Allow 2.5 hours
Elevation gain 150 m (490 ft)   High point 198 m (650 ft)
Trails and paths   Good all year

Westminster Abbey.

Given that the steep central portion of this trail connects St. Mary's School with Westminster Abbey, the Benedictine Order's edifice on the ridge above, you might consider "Pilgrim's Way" a suitable name for this walk at the east end of Mission City, even though it does have flat sections at its beginning and end. In fact, the whole walk has an ecclesiastical flavour, starting as it does in the Fraser River Heritage Park located near the few remaining relics of the original mission and residential school, operated by the Oblates of Mary Immaculate.

Travelling through Mission from east or west on Highway 7 (Lougheed Highway), turn north onto Stave Lake Street, then east on 5th Avenue to park near the restored Norma Kenney House, the first of a series of reconstructions that includes the Grotto of Saint Mary of Lourdes. Your first point of reference is the northeast corner of the belt of trees below the ridge that runs east-west, but to start your walk in a suitably chastened frame of mind, you might walk due east to the pioneer cemetery.

Thereafter, traverse the foundation stones of the former school to pick up your proper trail over to the north, pass into the belt of trees on the right and continue across the meadow beyond, with the present school buildings in view ahead. Just before the school fence, turn left through the bushes into the trees and, ignoring all minor tracks to the left, stay with the main trail to a major fork. Here, going right would take you into the school grounds, so keep left, then left again almost at once as you begin to rise steeply on your *via dolorosa*, the abbey bells perhaps ringing out as you climb, great maples on either side, a splendid sight in the fall. Ignoring all left forks as you head up to the ridge, you emerge finally in the open at the east end of a wide field, crowned not with crosses but with soccer goalposts.

Next you join a gravel road going right, the abbey tower visible a short distance left. Very shortly comes your reward: a bluff view over the Fraser Valley to Sumas Mountain in the foreground with mighty Mount Baker rearing its snow-clad head aloft to the right, while over to your left the Cheam peaks vie for your attention.

Your best return is by the same route, but before you descend you should stay right on the surfaced path to visit the abbey and seminary, the hilltop location worthy of a religious order whose members have traditionally sought the high places. Mount St. Benedict, a Fraser Valley peak, commemorates their love of the mountains.

Back at the eastern verge of the park, you may turn half right onto a wide gravel track that you soon desert for a footpath signed "To the Grotto" and, rising to a meadow crowned by that picturesque shrine, a fitting finale to this outing.

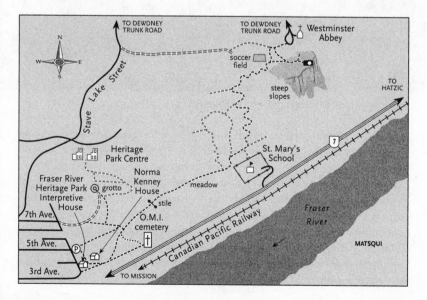

88 WEAVER LAKE

Round trip 6.4 km (4 mi)   Allow 3 hours
Trails   Best April to November

Weaver Lake viewed from above on Hemlock Valley Road.

This picturesque lake, with an already popular B.C. Forest Service recreation site near its outlet creek, has an encircling trail, Denham's Trail, to add another outdoor activity to fishing and boating, the main pursuits of its camping visitors. Turning north from Highway 7 (Lougheed Highway) at Sasquatch Inn in Harrison Mills, the road crosses the Chehalis River, then stays right at the Hemlock Valley fork after 8 km (5 mi). You next pass two salmonid-enhancement locations, the second near your crossing of Weaver Creek itself. Beyond that point, drive for 1.5 km (0.9 mi), then turn left and begin your climb to the lake, in the process rising steeply on the rough road to reach the wilderness camping spot.

For this walk the better direction is clockwise, beginning just beyond the outlet bridge, if only because this lets you stay close to the water on the first part of your walk. As you proceed, different arms of the lake open up before you, and as you near its west end, you have the sight of a great rock bluff dropping sheer to the water, a daunting indication that you will have to surmount it or return the way you came.

Fishing on Weaver Lake.

Actually, sets of wooden steps help you up, and it is, after all, a gain of less than 50 m (160 ft), but you may be glad nevertheless to rest at the high point to savour the view before descending to lake level again to continue your walk. On this stretch, the route leaves the shore and the character of the forest changes, the preponderance of conifers giving way to such deciduous trees as vine maple and alder, plus shade-loving flowers like coral root. Unfortunately, this habitat also encourages bushes, so the trail may be a little overgrown from time to time. There is no cause for alarm, however; the frequent orange markers will keep you on track.

Working your way back to the lake, you see a renewed growth of conifers; the ground, however, is still damp underfoot, necessitating the use of boardwalks here and there, and this part of your trip is not so inspiring as its first segment. Eventually you leave the main lake altogether for a small lagoon, preparatory to stepping out on the road again, with a turn to the right bringing the parking lot into sight once more.

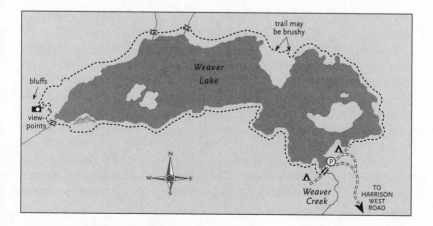

89 CAMPBELL LAKE TRAIL

to helipad:	Round trip 7 km (4.3 mi)	Allow 4.5 hours
to lake:	Round trip 10 km (6.2 mi)	Allow 6 hours
	Elevation gain 610 m (2000 ft)	High point 625 m (2050 ft)
	Trails and roads	Good most of the year

Lunch at Campbell Lake.

Here is a trail to test your mettle: Harrison Hot Springs' challenge to Vancouver's Grouse Grind, close to the village by whose chamber of commerce it was created, though it is now maintained by the B.C. Forest Service. To reach its beginning, drive north on Highway 9 (Hot Springs Road) 5.7 km (3.5 mi) from its junction with Highway 7 (Lougheed Highway), then turn left into the small parking space opposite Balsam Avenue and about 300 m short of the information centre.

For your start, after you have absorbed the statistical information on the trailhead signboard, head into the village water-supply area, rising almost immediately to a reservoir, at which point you jog briefly right, the trail being marked for "Campbell Lake." Thereafter it rises steadily in long swings on the route of an old road, shaded by deciduous trees mainly and overgrown here and there by low shrubs and flowers until you reach your first major viewpoint at Tower 92 on the power line right-of-way, a viewpoint only slightly improved upon by an open bluff on the edge of the forest beyond. From both of these vantage points the view across the valley to the Cheam Range and Lucky Four Group is particularly fine.

Once in the tall timber the trail zigzags upwards assisted occasionally by steps, in various stages of repair, past huge boulders and over awkward gaps, craftily bridged by sturdy logs; and now and again a thoughtful trailbuilder has placed a log seat on which you may rest and admire this very attractive forest with its fine trees, mossy rocks and logs, and varied ferns and flowers. Finally, after about 2 hours from the start, you emerge at an area cleared for a helipad, where you may enjoy extensive views of Harrison Lake and the mountains girdling it and its islands. And to the north, opposite one of these islands, Long Island, you may just distinguish the little knob on which perches the heritage Harrison Lookout, a relic of the not-so-distant past.

This makes a fine destination and for most will be completely satisfying, but for those who find the lure of the lake irresistible, some 1.5 km (0.9 mi) of trail still lies ahead, so you should allow an extra hour at least if you decide to proceed.

From here the trail returns to the forest, dropping gently along the north side of the ridge, crossing a long log bridge and eventually joining a grass-covered road across an old rock slide and through alder and maple to the little mountain lake. Disappointingly enough, you may find a camper in residence, a rough logging road from Mount Woodside making the lake accessible by 4WD vehicles.

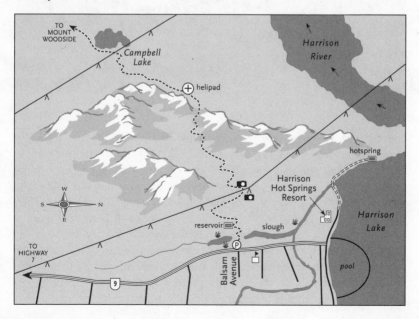

90 SASQUATCH PROVINCIAL PARK

to Hicks Lake:	Round trip 6.5 km (4 mi)	Allow 3 hours
	Trails	Good most of the year

Beaver lodge.

Popular with campers, this provincial park also provides a fine single-day outing round one of its lakes, even if its name, Hicks, lacks the true romantic flavour. And you may extend the lake circuit by adding a marsh loop, complete with beaver lodge, for good measure. Access is easy too: follow the park signs from Highway 9 (Hot Springs Road) along Lillooet Road, then turn north along Harrison Lake's east side on Rockwell Drive to a marked right turn where a left would take you to the Green Point day-use area.

In the park, you first pass Trout Lake, then, at a T-junction, you fork right for Hicks, cross the lake's outlet creek, then turn left at signs for the day-use area and a boat launch. On this you proceed to the farthest parking lot, beyond which the road is barred by a locked gate, where begins your circuit of the lake. Travelling clockwise, you first pass the entrance to the group campground, after which the road deteriorates nicely to trail status, with a neat example of a debris torrent exhibiting the power of water at one point.

At the south end of the lake as you turn towards the west, a short detour down to the lakeside brings you to an attractive sandy beach. Then, resuming your walk, you come to a park boundary marker. Here you leave your friendly road (it leads towards Agassiz) for an even more attractive trail, heading north along the west side of the lake and emerging into the open at a small bay just below some campsites. Here, despite the lack of a sign (at present), your route continues round a peninsula close to the shore, mainly in trees, but with viewpoints here and there. Finally you come to another open bay, the lake outlet and its fish ladder a little beyond.

From here, for a quick return to your starting point, you may cross the bridge over the dam, working first right towards the shore then veering back left to emerge beside the parking lot. More interesting, however, is to stay on the west side of the creek walking north to your original approach road, with the beaver marsh straight ahead. Cross the road and drop down to the marsh trail, going clockwise round it to save the lodge-viewing platform to the last, with possible sighting of some of its occupants as the climax to your trip.

Actually, you may sight more wildlife if, after your visit to Hicks Lake, you go right at the T-junction for a trip to its smaller neighbour, Deer Lake. Here, from a parking lot close to Lakeside campground, you may stroll along the shore for a short distance with the chance of seeing mountain goats on the crags to the north, another instance of the variety offered the visitor to Sasquatch Provincial Park.

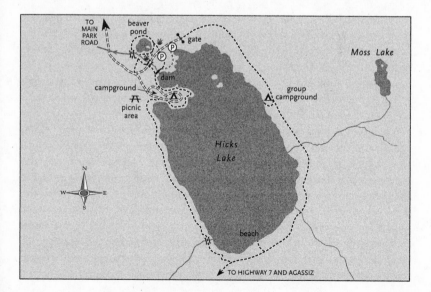

91 KILLARNEY LAKE

Round trip 8 km (5 mi)   Allow 2.5 hours
Trails   Good most of the year

Looking across the lagoon from Memorial Garden.

Since this gemlike stretch of water is on Bowen Island, you must reach it from the mainland by B.C. Ferries from Horseshoe Bay, a short trip but satisfying in itself, with the mountains of Howe Sound for company. Parking near the ferry terminal may be difficult, particularly in summer, so if you have plenty of time you may travel by bus #250 along West Vancouver's scenic Marine Drive or by the express #257 after having checked the ferry schedule (phone 1-888-223-3779).

On disembarking at Snug Cove, walk towards the one-time Union Steamship Company store for information about Crippen Regional Park, in which your walk lies. Go right on Cardena Drive, then left on a wooded trail that passes a memorial garden, which also provides a fine view over Deep Bay to the Howe Sound mountains. Continuing, you pass above a tidy little stream, complete with fish ladders and a viewing platform, and arrive at Miller Road, which you cross onto Hatchery Trail. This leads you through mixed forest to a wide meadow and an intersection, with the hatchery to the left. Go right, however, past the Bihora riding range and cross the meadows to meet a major trail, where you proceed left for a short distance to another fork, this time going right to eventually come out on a little country lane, Magee Road.

On this you go a few metres to the left before turning right onto the Killarney Lake Loop Trail to begin your walk along the lake. Though you are mainly in forest the ground drops away to the left, giving glimpses of the lake with the Mount Gardner massif behind. Then, finally, after a detour to a particularly clear viewpoint, you reach marshy ground at the far end of the lake crossed by an attractive boardwalk.

Now on the lake's west side, you turn south, regaled by the sight of water plants and birds. By lake's end a road and your track are virtually side by side; however, your route soon turns off left towards a picnic area by the dam that reveals the lake's artificiality. On Magee Road again, turn left and cross the outlet, then after a few metres go right on a track that starts up the roadside bank and eventually rejoins the main trail back to Miller Road. Here you turn right to find your outward trail on the left just beyond the Killarney Creek bridge.

If, as sometimes happens, you have time to put in between ferries, you may, should you still feel energetic, walk south across the picnic area from the ferry terminal and ascend the track on the wooded slope to Dorman Point, with more superb views of the Howe Sound mountains. The round trip is only about 1.5 km, roughly a mile, but the steepness of the last part of the climb suggests that you should allow at least 40 minutes for comfort on your round trip.

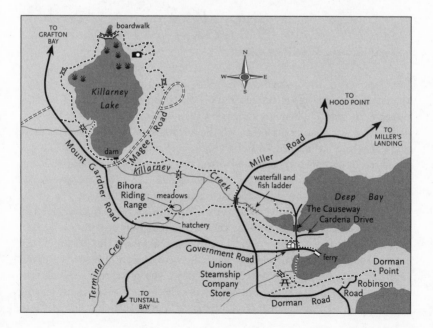

92 PORTEAU BLUFFS

to viewpoint:	Round trip 6 km (3.7 mi)	Allow 3.5 hours
	Elevation gain 365 m (1200 ft)	High point 380 m (1250 ft)
	Trails	
to Phyllis Lake:	Round trip 14 km (8.7 mi)	Allow 5.5 hours
	Elevation gain 488 m (1600 ft)	High point 500 m (1640 ft)
	Trails and roads	Good most of the year

View of Mount Sedgwick from Phyllis Creek Road.

Development of the lower Furry Creek valley and its temporary closure to the public a decade ago effectively cut off the time-honoured approach to the upper Furry and Phyllis Creek areas by the old access road. Fortunately an alternative was soon created through the forest above Porteau and a far more attractive route it has proved to be.

To reach this approach, drive to Porteau Cove Provincial Park, almost 25 km (15.5 mi) north of Horseshoe Bay on Highway 99 (Sea to Sky Highway). On foot cross the highway and walk back about 100 m on the east side to the end of the concrete retaining wall. Here a taped route goes off into the bush, crosses a power line right-of-way, then ascends rapidly to join an old B.C. Rail access road just north of a creek. Turn left and follow this road to nearly its end, where a well-marked route goes off, rising steeply at first, then undulating along in the forest with now and again a glimpse through the trees of the mountains across Howe Sound. Finally the route swings right, leaving the tall trees to cross a small creek and enter a previously logged area with young conifers and bushes pressing in on either side. In a few moments, however, you emerge on an old logging road near the top of an incline with, nearby, a vantage point looking over the Furry Creek developments to Howe Sound and beyond it to Mount Sedgwick's great eastern ridge pointing directly to its summit and yet farther off the impressive peaks of the Tantalus Range.

This makes a fine destination for a short day. However, it may be also the prelude to more ambitious hikes: to Beth Lake at 1050 m (3500 ft) and Capilano Mountain towering above it at 1680 m (5510 ft), within reach of only the fittest; and the more easily attainable Marion and Phyllis Lakes. If you decide to go on, you must descend a little to join the Phyllis Creek road, where you go right and start ascending again to a fork where the B.C. Hydro lines are almost directly overhead.

Here the Beth Lake route goes off left, so you keep right, paralleling the power line and crossing the creek en route as you traverse an area regenerating after being logged several decades ago. Staying with the main route you come to Marion Lake, a possible destination, though its companion, Phyllis, is only some 400 m farther at the end of public access, the valley beyond the divide being within the Greater Vancouver Watershed District.

From here the south shoulder of Capilano Mountain rises on your left hand, and straight in front are the headwaters of the river whose name also commemorates the North Vancouver Natives—the people of Kiap. And Marion and Phyllis? Who knows whose daughters or sweethearts they immortalize?

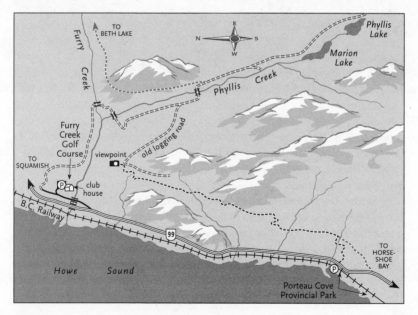

93 SHANNON FALLS

to Olesen Creek bridge:	Round trip 2 km (1.2 mi)	Allow 1 hour
	Trails	Good most of the year
to high bluff:	Round trip 5 km (3.1 mi)	Allow 4 hours
	Elevation gain 473 m (1550 ft)	High point 510 m (1670 ft)
	Trails	Best April to November

Looking across Howe Sound from the high bluff.

It is pretty safe to say that everyone who has travelled Highway 99 to Squamish is aware of these falls where Shannon Creek plunges down a nearly vertical cliff before resuming its more placid course to Howe Sound. But what can you do once you have paid your respects to the gods of the waters from the viewing platform? Well, having admired the overshot water-wheel on the way up, you may look at a few more artifacts by staying right on leaving the platform, then turning right again on the road that goes north from the picnic area.

Nor is that all; continuing north, you find yourself on a trail created by the Federation of Mountain Clubs to Olesen Creek, with perhaps a trip to the top of the falls thrown in. At first your route stays relatively level, as you keep right at one fork and enter the valley of Olesen Creek, but then comes a change as the grade becomes steep indeed, and you mount on steps that might have been designed for giants, gaining altogether some 75 m (250 ft).

At last, relief. A bridge across the creek gives you a breathing space and a view across Howe Sound. Just beyond the screen of trees ahead is the great flight of wooden steps that has replaced the lower Stawamus Chief trail, eroded through overuse. Here, then, you must decide: turn around and retrace your steps or ascend for 185 m (600 ft) on the Chief Trail to a fork that will take you right to recross Olesen Creek on its upper bridge, then travel for some 20 minutes to another viewpoint. Shannon Creek, at the top of the falls, is about 30 minutes beyond that at an elevation of almost 405 m (1330 ft), another possible destination.

If, however, you still have a little energy left, you may proceed, the route now very steep, past the cascades on your right to a bluff with an unobstructed view over Howe Sound and its enclosing mountains as a reward for climbing the extra 100 m (330 ft). This is a satisfying destination at which to linger before returning as you came.

Note: The route you have been following from the top of Shannon Falls was created by the indefatigable Halvor Lunden and beyond this point incorporates stretches of logging roads to link the Chief Trail with Petgill Lake to the south. Farther on, therefore, it may prove a little hard to follow the various connections unless you are experienced in backcountry hiking. As well, it is considerably more demanding in length and altitude gain, requiring as much time again as you have already invested, so you should be properly equipped, with a full day at your disposal, if you decide to push on.

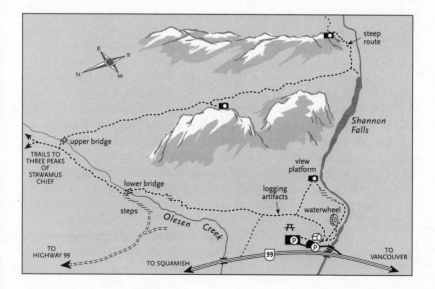

94 SQUAMISH ESTUARY

Round trip 7 km (4.3 mi)   Allow 2.5 hours
Trails, railway track and roads   Good all year

View across the marsh to Stawamus Squaw.

How many of us speeding up Highway 99 on our way to the more obvious attractions of Cheakamus Canyon and Whistler ever consider a visit to the Squamish estuary? Yet here, though beleaguered by industrial development, is a destination in whose estuarine sloughs, meadows and woodland are resources to sustain myriad wild creatures and delight the naturalist.

To increase our appreciation, the Squamish Estuary Conservation Society has produced a brochure that may be found in the Howe Sound Inn (Brew Pub) lobby at the junction of Cleveland Avenue and Vancouver Street. Each of the society's trails may be walked individually, but you may easily combine several to obtain a more comprehensive overview of the whole area. A good place to start on one such combination is at the end of Vancouver Street, which you reach by leaving Highway 99 (Sea to Sky Highway) at the main entry to Squamish and following Cleveland Avenue to its junction with Vancouver Street, where you go right to a parking spot adjacent to a map board.

On foot you are faced immediately with a decision: left is a short walk by a slough ending abruptly on 3rd Avenue; so go right and upstream along the slough, which you soon cross, going left at the approach to the sewage plant and continuing across a railway, a B.C. Rail spur to the docks. Straight ahead you embark on Meadow Loop, which as its name implies is quite open, with spectacular mountain views. Most of the route is on dykes dating as far back as the end of the nineteenth century, when Chinese workers drained the area to grow hay. Today, a dryland log-sorting area is the one obtrusive human activity you notice before you turn south along the Central Channel. Here you may spot a heron waiting patiently in the shallows or, depending on the season, ducks and other waterbirds; and as you proceed you may also note a large old spruce before you swing away eastwards towards the railway once more.

Now turn north along the spur for some minutes to a faint trail leading left onto another heritage dyke. This starts you west on the Forest Loop, on which you may soon turn right on a route through the heart of the woodland or remain on the dyke, which ends at a gravel road. If you choose the latter, for a longer circuit, go right along the road for about 100 m, then left into the trees alongside the Central Channel, this trail named the Swan Walk for the numerous viewpoints where in season you may observe trumpeters on their wintering grounds.

To complete your circuit and return to the Forest Loop, leave the waterway at your second approach to the road and backtrack a few metres to the south, where your route goes left into the trees. Soon there comes a fork, where the two prongs of the Forest Loop meet. Go left again, heading for another three hundred–year–old spruce tree en route to the rail spur. A left turn north along the tracks takes you to a trail on the east side that veers south onto a grassy dyke top, running behind the residential streets of Squamish all the way back to the sewage plant and your return route to the map board.

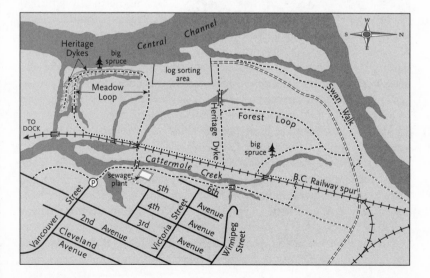

FOUR LAKES TRAIL

Round trip 6 km (3.7 mi)
Trails and roads

Allow 2 hours
Best April to November

Mount Garibaldi reflected in Stump Lake.

As in other areas administered by B.C. Parks, Alice Lake Provincial Park has a well-developed system of hiking trails. There are short ones like those round Alice Lake and Stump Lake and the longer Four Lakes Trail, which includes the paths already mentioned and adds to them the connecting links of a circuit involving Fawn Lake and Edith Lake, even though the latter is not, strictly speaking, in the park.

So well known is Alice Lake park that it is scarcely necessary to say that you reach it by leaving Highway 99 (Sea to Sky Highway) some 12 km (7.5 mi) north of the turnoff for Squamish town centre. At the park entrance keep left and drive uphill to the small parking area just east of the sani-station instead of making straight for the lake. Here, north of the road and opposite the turnoff for South Beach and the eastern campgrounds, you have on your left the sign for Stump Lake Trail, the start of your walk.

At first you are in thick bush, but this thins out when you reach the fork where the arms of the Stump Lake circuit separate, leaving you free to choose whichever you wish. The right branch gives views over DeBeck Hill and towards the Tantalus Range; from the left you see Mount Garibaldi and Alice Ridge; each gives glimpses of the lake and its clusters of water lilies. At the far end, beyond a little island, the trails join, and here you turn away from the lake.

Back in deep forest, you become aware of the increased rush of water and soon you find yourself just above the Cheekye River, which flows down from

Mount Garibaldi, its valley separating Brohm Ridge and Alice Ridge. On this stretch the influence of the stream is manifest in the type of vegetation: lush skunk cabbage and other moisture-loving plants, quite a bit different from elsewhere—the difference soon obvious as you begin to climb eastwards, passing an escape route back to Alice Lake on the right, then rising to the trail's high point as you near Fawn Lake. Surrounded by young forest, Fawn Lake is a little off the trail to the right; where the spur road goes off to it, the foot trail you have been on develops into a gravel road, a status it maintains until you reach lake number three, Edith Lake.

On the way you come to a major intersection, your route crossing the main approach to Alice (Cheekye) Ridge, an approach that antedated creation of the park and remains to give access to the forest lands above. Then, at a fork just preceding the lake, you go right along its west side until you come to a signposted junction. Straight ahead, the route leads to Thunderbird Ridge in the Garibaldi Highlands subdivision, but you go right and uphill as a prelude to your descent to Alice Lake, trail and watercourse arriving together at its south end by a picnic and swimming area. From here you may use either shore to return to your transport. Each is pleasant, but perhaps the one on the east side is the prettier, having views of Debeck Hill across the water; it is also a little shorter. However, if you choose the longer west and north sides, you may add a little nature study as well by walking down one side of the outlet creek and up the other on the Swamp Lantern Interpretive Trail at the northwest corner of the lake.

At the northeast corner you must return to pavement again, but only for a short distance as you walk up through the campsites to the intersection with the park headquarters road where your car is parked.

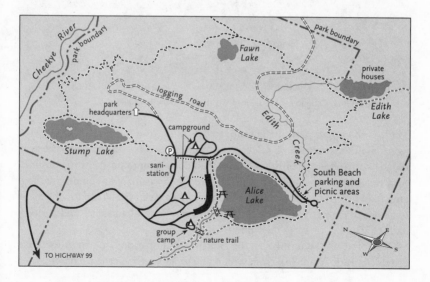

96 DEBECK HILL

Round trip 4 km (2.5 mi)   Allow 2 hours
Elevation gain 270 m (890 ft)   High point 460 m (1500 ft)
Roads   Best April to November

View northeast from summit: Mount Garibaldi (right) and Brohm Ridge (left).

Though the upper part of the route to this miniature mountain has suffered from the construction of television repeater towers, this trip is still very much worthwhile, if only for the tremendous panorama from its summit. And not all is lost along the way, either; the lower part of the original logging road you use is very much as it always was, even to the mellowing signs of past activity: rusted cable, an old power winch abandoned and forlorn, and what is left of a sawdust pile.

The start of your hike is the South Beach parking lot in Alice Lake Provincial Park (Walk 95), from which you walk south via the turnaround for cars and make your way over, under or around the barrier at the end. Just beyond and on your right, the one-time logging road angles back uphill to an old quarry and a change of direction to the southwest, the route nicely shaded by the regrowth of mixed deciduous and coniferous trees.

After some 20 minutes and another elbow bend, you find yourself travelling below some impressive bluffs above on your left. It is on this stretch that you come on signs of bygone logging and pass the old donkey engine near the site of an old sawmill. Beyond here, you swing back left and continue in a southerly direction to the next sharp turn, which takes you back right again. From here a walk of another 200 m or so takes you to the summit, where, having tuned out the TV monstrosities, you can forget the works of man and enjoy the beauties of nature: the great peaks and glaciers of the Tantalus Range on the west side of the Squamish River valley and the impressive summit of Mount Garibaldi above you on the east. And the humbler scene has its charms as well: the park, densely treed, below you on the right; Cheakamus Valley stretching north, with Cloudburst Mountain to the left of it; and, in the southwest, the flat delta lands around Squamish at the head of Howe Sound, with the sound itself and its enclosing mountains receding into the distance beyond.

Should you wish a longer walk or the road access to South Beach be closed, as is usual in the off-season, you may start from the main day-use area and add a walk round the lake to your outing, allowing yourself an extra hour for the pleasure.

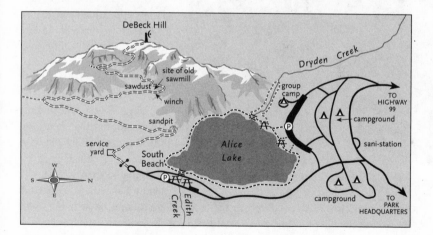

EVANS LAKE FOREST

97

to Hut Lakes:	Round trip 13 km (8 mi)	Allow 5 hours
	Elevation gain 395 m (1300 ft)	High point 610 m (2000 ft)
	Roads	
ridge circuit:	Round trip 8 km (5 mi)	Allow 4 hours
	Elevation gain 290 m (950 ft)	High point 445 m (1450 ft)
	Trails and roads	Good April to November

Alpha Mountain seen across Levette Lake.

An old logging road gives you access to Levette Lake and Hut (Hud) Lakes, though the last named do involve a longish walk with considerable change in elevation. You may, therefore, consider concentrating on the circular trail system in the south part of the area, given that all of these outings begin at the same spot, the fork where the gated road to the left goes into the private Evans Lake Forest Education Centre.

On your approach, having gone west from Highway 99 (Sea to Sky Highway) for Cheekye opposite the Alice Lake turnoff, drive to the crossing of the Cheakamus River, go right at once on the Paradise Valley road for 2.1 km (1.3 mi), then, at a crossroads, turn left on the Evans Lake road. This road rises steeply for 1.3 km (0.8 mi) to the fork, where there is parking for a few cars, with the old road going on and the start of the loop trail on your right.

With one or all of the lakes as your objective, continue on the old road, by now quite steep and rough in places. After about 45 minutes, you come to two successive private roads to the left, then a third providing a viewpoint over Levette Lake, with the majestic peaks of the Tantalus Range as a background. To reach Hut Lakes, stay right at the third fork, rising steadily on the very eroded, but well-shaded old road. Once over the col, you pass a reedy little pond on your left, then your trail swings west before descending to the lakes' basin, losing height you must regain on your return.

Your interesting alternative, the trail system over the ridges on either side of the road, is mainly in sparse forest, thin enough to allow you views over the Cheakamus Valley south to Sky Pilot Mountain as well as to the Tantalus across the valley of the Squamish. For this, take the Copperbush Trail uphill to the right from your parking by the fork, the orange triangles a tribute to the forest camp staff and students. You may omit the detour to Silver Summit if you intend to do the complete circuit, but having gone left at that junction, you may want to stop briefly at an interesting pool before continuing up over a bluff top with nearly panoramic views, descending the sometimes rocky, bushy trail and crossing a bridge to meet the Levette Lake road, with the option of returning along it if you do not wish to carry on with the loop.

To continue, go right, cross the creek again and walk uphill to where the road recrosses yet once more. Immediately beyond on the left, Skyline Trail, its route marked with red triangles, cuts back sharply, using an old logging road at first but leaving it for a trail on the left after about 15 minutes. This heads along a ridge crest with a succession of striking mountain views until it drops, partway on a log stairway, into a little valley before rising again to the next ridge, then descending once more to join another old road now called the Fraser-Burrard Trail. Stay with this when you come to a fork, a former trail to the right being closed to public use. Your present route now makes its way uneventfully to meet the Levette Lake road, where a right turn and a quick march soon return you to your vehicle.

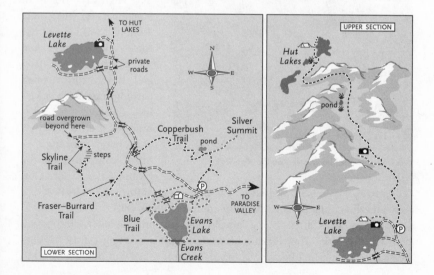

98 BROHM LAKE INTERPRETIVE FOREST

Round trip 8 km (5 mi) or less	Allow 2.5 hours
Elevation gain 150 m (500 ft)	High point 350 m (1150 ft)
Trails	Best May to October

West Vancouver Senior Ramblers on the High Trail.

In recent years the Squamish Forest District has been developing an interpretive trail system for hikers and bikers in the wooded area south of Brohm Lake, and now the pattern of loops, connectors and viewpoints is complete for us to enjoy. With maps and distances indicated at major intersections, nothing remains but to choose the variant with most appeal.

To find the trailhead, drive Highway 99 (Sea to Sky Highway) north of Squamish for just over 2 km (1.2 mi) beyond the Alice Lake turnoff, then move into the left lane and watch for a small parking area with a yellow gate prominent behind. (If traffic is heavy, you may continue to make your turn at the Brohm Lake parking lot, 2.2 km/1.4 mi farther on.) Just past the gate is an information kiosk with a map and directions to help you fully appreciate your walk.

A few minutes farther along this old road (the original Highway 99), you come to the Alder Trail forking off to the right and rising gently to meet Bridge Trail, so called because going right on it takes you down to Brohm

Lake, where the narrows have been bridged. If you head that way, an undulating trail along the southwest side of the lake brings you in short order to a connector climbing back to the main system. The subsequent junction with High Trail could also be reached with rather less effort by going left from Alder on Bridge Trail, then right on High as it continues past a small pond, over a boardwalk, through a rocky stretch and down to the fork. Now the route swings abruptly to the left and crosses more bridging before another option presents itself: a steep trail, assisted by even steeper steps, to a "fire lookout" complete with little shelter. From here on a fine day the majestic peaks of the Tantalus Range make an unforgettable spectacle.

Back on High Trail you work round the knoll and emerge on a south-facing slope with another splendid view of the Tantalus peaks seen over a tree-thinning demonstration plot, then you begin the steady zigzag descent into the valley, where your trail merges with an old forest road. Again you are faced with a decision: whether to take the direct route to the parking lot, passing on the way the other ends of High Trail and Cheakamus Loop before rejoining and turning left on the old Highway 99 in a hollow below the present thoroughfare; or whether to follow the Cheakamus Loop, which climbs first to viewpoints looking northwest towards Cloudburst Mountain and south to the Tantalus before eventually levelling off and merging into an old logging road that winds its way down through the gap between two hillocks to join the main forest road, where a right turn sends you homeward bound.

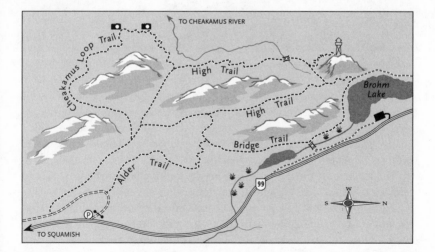

99 BROHM LAKE

Brohm Lake and Powerline Trails:	Round trip 5.7 km (3.5 mi) Trails	Allow 2.5 hours Best May to November

A popular spot for diving on Brohm Lake.

If ever a walk revealed the folly of using distance alone as a guide, it is this one on a B.C. Forest Service trail. The apparent discrepancy between distance and time soon disappears, however, as you rise and descend, rollercoaster fashion, the thrill increased on the east side of the lake by the steep drop to the water below.

The usual start for the walk is from the parking lot on the west side of Highway 99 (Sea to Sky Highway), about 4.5 km (2.8 mi) north of the Alice Lake junction. From this spot you may ease into the walk by going south on a gentle trail paralleling the highway, crossing the bridge over the reedy narrows and turning north again at the fork where Bridge Trail (Walk 98) goes left. Now you begin your upsy-downsy way along the lake, passing en route a second trail into the interpretive forest before arriving at a junction with the Thompson Trail, which leads down to the Tenderfoot Fish Hatchery. Leaving that for later consideration, continue 100 m to another fork. Here you must decide whether to opt for the short return by the lake, which, however, involves ascending a long flight of steps to a dizzying height above the water, or to choose the longer route starting up Brohm Creek on the left.

Going left, the trail, at first a peaceful, shady, mossy old logging road, follows the creek north for a pleasant kilometre or so before swinging right across the creek and towards the highway. Just before the road the route turns south on Powerline Trail, again rising and falling over a series of little ridges with splendid views of the Tantalus Range over to the right front and the Sky Pilot group farther off down the valley to the left. Finally, descending a little you come to the top of that long stairway where the Lake Trail joins from the right. Here you turn left on the roller coaster to a final fork, where you may choose either arm of the Rock Bluff Loop, left dropping directly to the parking lot, right taking a more circuitous route by the lake's edge.

And the Thompson Trail? It provides a somewhat more challenging start to either circuit and, combined with their ups and downs, will provide you with a real workout.

To reach its trailhead, you leave Highway 99 at the Alice Lake crossroads and go left to Cheekye, where you cross the Cheakamus River and immediately turn right on the Paradise Valley road. Stay with this road for 4.2 km (2.6 mi), recrossing the river and coming to a T-junction just across the railway at Midnight Way. Here you go right for about 200 m to park at the Tenderfoot Fish Hatchery.

On foot, make your way along the track beside the railway, then about 350 m beyond the hatchery premises, go left towards the creek, then right to a bridge. The trail is not long, only 1.75 km (1 mi), but it climbs 230 m (750 ft), working over and round mossy rocks and up steps to crest finally at a gentle divide only a few minutes from Brohm Lake.

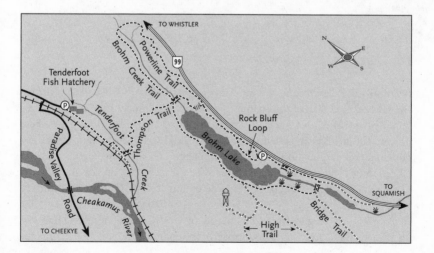

100 BRANDYWINE/CALCHEAK

Round trip 8 km (5 mi)   Allow 3 hours
Trails   Best May to October

Suspension bridge over Callaghan Creek.

Brandywine Falls Provincial Park exists primarily to provide a viewpoint for the falls on the creek of that name; it has, however, much more to offer: Lava Lake, Swim Lake, even Daisy if you do not mind struggling back up the best part of 100 m (330 ft). Even so, the most striking trail, one that leaves the park and takes you north to the confluence of Callaghan Creek and the Cheakamus River (hence the name) was the creation of the B.C. Forest Service; in fact, its northern end is a recreation area for which that ministry is responsible.

From the parking lot about 37 km (23 mi) north of Squamish on Highway 99 (Sea to Sky Highway), you cross Brandywine Creek on the main falls trail, ignoring the track going uphill left just beyond the bridge. That leads to Lava Lake and a wide cross-country ski trail, interesting for its lava surface, broken into cobblestone-like shapes. You, however, continue towards the B.C. Rail tracks, noting the Swim Lake/CalCheak sign just before you cross the line for the falls viewpoint, with the Daisy Lake trail going off left immediately after you are over the tracks.

For the CalCheak walk, return to the sign, walk north a few paces, then go left towards Swim Lake, your trail diverging right just before you reach it. Now you go north, rising to a ridge from which you look down on the lake, with, farther on, other smaller bodies of water right and left. Much of your route consists of lava underfoot, with a healthy growth of forest covering the ridges of shattered columnar basalt, over and between which the trail winds. Then, having crossed the railway tracks some time earlier, you emerge briefly from trees again at the whistle stop of McGuire, its name on a post now the only visible sign of the one-time station.

Back in the forest you soon hear the river, and from now on your way is along the Cheakamus River to the pedestrian suspension bridge that takes you over its tributary, Callaghan Creek, to the simple recreation site just beyond. This can be reached from Highway 99 if you are coming from the south by going right a short distance past McGuire and 4.0 km (2.5 mi) north of the Brandywine Falls park turnoff and driving 1.6 km (1 mi) on an old logging road.

Your return is by the same route all the way, unless you wish to take the road right and uphill at McGuire for a walk back along the route that doubles as a cross-country ski trail in winter. This trail starts on the power line but soon seeks the shade of the trees, lodgepole pine forest mostly, with the occasional marshy area around the numerous little ponds along the way. Your route this time is wholly to the west of the railway, bringing you back to Brandywine Creek just north of the parking lot.

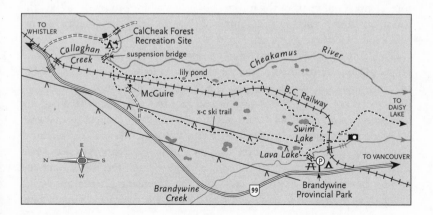

101 CRATER RIM LOOP

Round trip 8 km (5 mi)	Allow 4 hours
Elevation gain 325 m (1060 ft)	High point 870 m (2860 ft)
Trails and roads	Best June to October

Suspension Bridge 2000.

This hike is in the Whistler Interpretive Forest, the second of three demonstration forests in the Squamish Forest District, created in a previously logged-over area to introduce outdoor recreationists to a young regenerating forest being managed for multiple resource use. Here, for the walker, there are many possibilities—some exclusive to pedestrians, others to be shared with bikers—the guide to the forest presenting a daunting array of choices, far more than suffice for one day's outing. The following description, therefore, samples only part of the forest's potential: a bit of riverside, a lake, the rim of an extinct volcano and a forested ridge to whet the appetite for further explorations on your own.

The approach road (signposted) turns off Highway 99 (Sea to Sky Highway) just north of the railway crossing at Function Junction, 48 km (30 mi) north of Squamish and 2.5 km (1.5 mi) south of Whistler. Immediately on your left is the main entrance to the forest, with a parking area and the start of the first of your trails, the Riverside Trail, at its east end.

Enhanced by nature information along the way, the trail rises almost right away over a minor ridge, descends again to cross Eastside Main (Cheakamus Lake Road), and traverses another strip of forest before briefly joining the Westside Main to pass over the turbulent Cheakamus River. Thereafter, the trail winds up and down along the riverbank, approaching the road from time to time to facilitate kayak "put-ins," until, just over 2 km (1.2 mi) from the start, it comes to a junction, with left crossing high above the torrent on Suspension Bridge 2000 and linking with the east-side trails. Going straight ahead you begin to climb to meet the mainline again at the Logger's Lake trailhead and parking place. (If you drive to this spot, you may concentrate on the shorter 2-hour circuit of Crater Rim and Logger's Lake, or continue on Riverside Trail south to connect with other trails, such as the Basalt Valley or Riparian.)

From here you walk up an old logging road for a few minutes to the beginning of the Crater Rim Trail with its sign and statistics, indicating a 100-m (328-ft) rise in the 3.2-km (2-mi) round trip, and you go left, gaining much of that altitude in the short ascent to the rim. Then the trail undulates along through sparse forest with glimpses inward to the lake and outward to the Cheakamus Valley until you reach a fork where Ridge Trail goes left to join Basalt Valley Spur. You keep right, however, and just beyond the high point you come to a wooden bench with a splendid view of Black Tusk, a good place to pause. Shortly thereafter, as the trail curves round with the rim, you reach another viewpoint, this time westwards towards Mounts Fee and Cayley, before you proceed to lose height quickly on a steep little track down to a rock slide, across which a path has been partially smoothed. Beyond here the route runs through some alder to join first one old road then another, on which you go left to where the Ridge Trail heads off north into the trees (right goes back to Logger's Lake). As you work along this combined hiking/biking trail, do not be seduced by an attractive-looking pedestrian route going off left to dead-end above a quarry but instead descend to the next junction. There, for the shorter route back to your transportation, keep left and descend to the mainline, along which a few metres brings you back to Riverside Trail and a retracing of your outward steps.

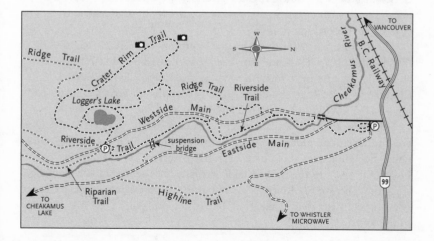

102 CHEAKAMUS LAKE

to west end:	Round trip 6 km (3.7 mi)	Allow 3 hours
	Trails	Best late June to October

View south towards Cheakamus Glacier.

This fine body of water, just 3 km (1.9 mi) inside the western boundary of Garibaldi Provincial Park, provides a variety of picturesque spots along its north shore, with views across the lake to the McBride Range and the glaciers of the park's high country.

The approach is as for the Whistler Interpretive Forest, through which it travels (Walk 101). This time, however, pass the parking area at the entrance and go left at the next fork on what is variously called Eastside Main or Cheakamus Lake Road and climb steadily towards the road's end at a parking area 8.5 km (5.3 mi) from the highway.

From here the trail heads east, crossing two small creeks before bringing you to the park boundary. Now you continue in tall timber, an indication of what this whole area must have been like before so much of it was logged. Progress is easy, for the trail remains virtually level as it gradually converges with the Cheakamus River. After about 30 minutes, you come to a sign pointing right for Helm Lake Trail, one of the routes into the high country to the south.

Beyond here, your trail continues through the forest with its healthy growth of devil's club, especially where the route is close to the riverbank. Gradually you notice the current slackening, the water becomes a deeper green, and vistas of the lake begin to open out ahead until you find yourself at its western end.

Though any spot along the lakeshore may serve as a destination, the wilderness campsite at the mouth of Singing Creek provides a point of reference. In any case, the alternation of treed areas with avalanche-created open spaces gives nice contrasts along the trail, the clear forest floor being interspersed with stretches of lush grass and flowers where the sun exerts its influence. There are places, however, where a rocky face should be negotiated with care. Wherever you do stop, you are rewarded with views; in addition, fishing is a possibility if you have come prepared. It is peaceful, too, since powerboats are not permitted, though thoughtless bikers may be somewhat intrusive on occasion.

The return poses no problems either. It is pleasant to wander along the trail through the forest until the trees thin out at the park boundary, when, across the river, an interesting lava flow and other volcanic rubble begin to show themselves. Now might be the time to investigate some of the intriguing loops you noted en route to the trailhead. On the west side of the road, viewpoints of interest on the Plantation and Craterview Loops may be reached comfortably by car, as can the Valleyview and Crater Lookouts. Thus, on one outing you may combine a walking trip into a provincial park with an educational foray through a demonstration forest.

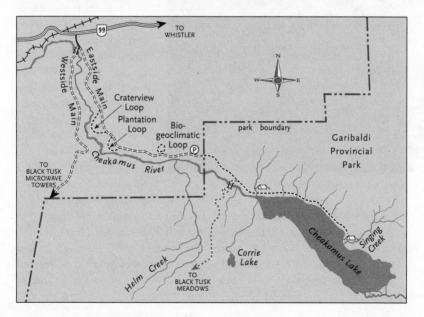

103 SHADOW LAKE INTERPRETIVE FOREST

| Round trip 6.5 km (4 mi) | Allow 2 hours |
| Trails and roads | Best June to October |

Reflections in Shadow Lake.

The most distant from Vancouver, this, the third of Squamish Forest District's three demonstration forests, lies some 17 km (10.5 mi) north of Whistler Village. As you drive north, Highway 99 crosses the railway 10 km (6.2 mi) beyond the end of Green Lake and shortly thereafter on your right is the parking lot, marked with a large sign and complete with information kiosk.

Immediately south of the parking area is a bijou forestry loop of 400 m for those who simply want to stretch their legs and break the tedium of a long drive; those who want more substance must cross the highway to the main trailhead. From here, you may choose any one of several routes varying in length and focus, or you may roll them all into one to experience everything this forest has to offer.

For the latter, you may start by going north from the main trailhead, following the signs for the High Forestry Trail, which passes through an area planted in 1970 after being clear-cut earlier, so you may study the effects of the various management prescriptions practised as you go along. Shortly after an exit to the highway on the right and gradually descending, the trail changes direction from north to south, then comes to a fork. Here you may continue straight ahead or double back briefly through an area regenerating naturally after selective cutting before turning south again along the Soo River flats to join the direct route. Now you are travelling on the Low Forestry Trail, an old logging road maturing nicely to trail status.

Continue straight ahead towards Shadow Lake at the next fork and ignore a second track coming in on the left from the highway. Then, when the lake loop splits, go left, clockwise, along the east side through some fairly tall conifers, natural regeneration after a forest fire in the 1920s. At the south end of the lake, left again will start you on the Green River Crossing Trail, which takes you out in reverse direction to traverse the railway, beyond which a trail leads up a bank across the way and onwards to a parking spot by the Soo River Forest Service Road. From here a short walk brings you to the top of a mossy rock bluff with limited views of the forest and the valley to the north. However, since you must return by the same route to resume the lake circuit, you may opt to forgo this 1.6-km (1-mi) round trip to the viewpoint and continue northwest along the water's edge to the next junction, where a short loop trail following an oxbow bend of the river winds through a grove of old-growth Western red cedar and past a one-time trapper's cabin.

Back on the lake trail, you cross the outlet creek and soon come to the end of the circuit, going left to retrace your route along the old logging road, the second trail to the right thereafter returning you to highway and transportation.

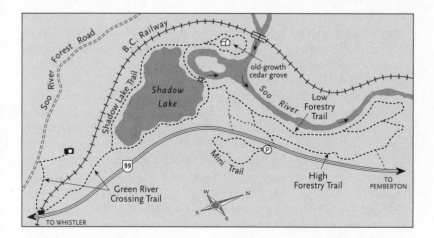

104 SOAMES HILL REGIONAL PARK

Round trip 5 km (3.1 mi) | Allow 2.5 hours
Elevation gain 185 m (600 ft) | High point 260 m (850 ft)
Trails | Good most of the year

View south over Gibsons.

As you approach Langdale by B.C. Ferries, you may notice a neat conical hill a little to the left. Known locally as "The Knob," Soames Hill is now in a regional park so that its approaches receive at least minimal attention, as do the steep flights of steps to its various splendid viewpoints. The park, however, embraces more than the hill, and you may enjoy a forest walk instead of, or in addition to, your ascent of the knob.

As a visitor to the Sunshine Coast, you reach the main entrance to the park by going left from the ferry exit, then half right onto North Road, on which you drive 2.5 km (1.6 mi) to a left turn on Chamberlin Road, followed quickly by another left on Bridgeman Road. Where Bridgeman ends you see signs for Soames Hill Regional Park accompanied by a map and statistics of the trails.

Heading into the forest on the main trail with yellow markers, ignore the first trail to the left (it takes you out of the park again) and take the second, marked green, mounting a flight of steps to a junction where a sign points right for Viewpoint 4, with left taking you to the other three. After enjoying the view over Gibsons at #4 and returning to the fork, you soon reach the next intersection. Here you stay left and uphill to reach one more viewpoint, with the other two, somewhat higher still, allowing you to gaze across Howe Sound and its islands.

On your return to the green trail, go left for the longer, more energetic return to the yellow where, at the junction, the forlorn posts for an information board remind of an earlier approach now privatized. Here you turn right on the yellow trail, with a choice to be made in a few metres: whether to make a quick return on the yellow, which rises slightly before levelling off on its way to the park entrance; or to linger in the lower reaches of the park.

If you choose the latter, the blue/yellow trail on the left drops steeply to emerge on the highway at Soames Road, so prefer the blue/white that circles to the south and west, through mainly second-growth forest, with decaying stumps here and there, relics of the original trees, and one huge surviving Douglas-fir blackened by an ancient fire. After passing a cut-off to the fir signed with white, the blue/white eventually brings you to a junction with the blue trail. Go right, rising to regain lost altitude and coming quite soon to a fork where you continue on the blue trail until, meeting the main yellow trail, you go left towards your vehicle, passing en route the steep trail you ascended earlier to the knob, and comparing in your mind the two very different faces of Soames Hill Regional Park.

A final option is a pedestrian approach from the ferry. Turn south on the highway and drop to the seafront at Hopkins Landing as soon as possible, then ascend again by the last easement before Soames Point. This takes you to Point Road, then continues between the houses numbered 1061 and 1069 as an inconspicuous trail up to the main road about 1 km (0.6 mi) north of the blue/yellow trailhead on Soames Road.

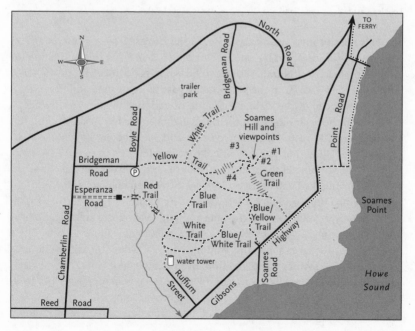

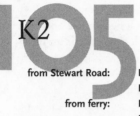

K2

from Stewart Road:	Round trip 8 km (5 mi)	Allow 4.5 hours
	Elevation gain 442 m (1450 ft)	High point 640 m (2100 ft)
from ferry:	Round trip 14 km (8.7 mi)	Allow 6 hours
	Elevation gain 634 m (2080 ft)	Roads and trails
	Trails	Best June to October

Looking east over Bowen Island and Horseshoe Bay to Mount Baker.

No, this doesn't involve an expedition to the Himalayas—a short voyage on a ferry will suffice if you live in the Vancouver area. K2 is the local name for Knob Number Two; Number One or Old Knob is Soames Hill (Walk 104). Although the views from the second may cost more in time and effort than those from the first, the walk itself is full of variety and very worthwhile.

To reach the beginning from the traffic lights at the ferry exit, drive uphill on Highway 101 to the next intersection and go right on Stewart Road to park at the T-junction just beyond the power line. From here, walk right to find the beginning of the trail in thick bush on the left at the top of a small rise. Once embarked you find a multitude of coloured markers, the white and orange (Walk 106) heading off left after a few minutes. Ignoring all distractions, however, you cleave to the blue and pink as you rise steadily, eventually arriving on the verge of the Langdale Creek ravine above a pretty little waterfall. A few paces above this vantage point, avoiding the first hazardous plunge into the ravine, you must drop into the gully and cross the creek at a quiet spot above the falls before climbing the steep bank opposite to a fork, where the blue trail, signed YMCA, heads right and east, while you keep left with the pink, en route for the summit. Next you pass two more forks going right; negotiate a very eroded stretch of old road; and come to a pleasant, mossy section in second-growth forest where you must follow the markers closely as they lead you from one old road to another. Then you descend briefly to cross another creek, beyond which a rough track traverses the west side of the knob on an easy ascent, until, close to the summit, you reach a fork and turn right for the top. From your vantage point on the knoll you look out south over Soames Hill as far as Vancouver Island and east over Langdale to Bowen Island and Horseshoe Bay, with Mount Baker dominant in the far distance.

You return as you came until you reach the fork above the Langdale Falls, where you must decide whether to continue as you came or to seek variety by going left on the more circuitous route signed "YMCA." Opting for the latter, you proceed downhill past a T-junction on the trail through alder forest to the power line, on which you turn right, after noting the trail coming in on the left from Wharf Road. Next you march along the right-of-way until your trail, now marked with white, veers back into the trees to cross Langdale Creek and climb the steep west bank in long switchbacks. Keep right at the top and soon you meet your outward route and go left, retracing your steps to Stewart Road.

This trip would also suit walk-on ferry passengers who don't object to walking a little on the road, some 1.5 km (1 mi) from the boat to the end of pavement on Wharf Road, the first road on the left along the Port Mellon Highway. Continue on the deteriorating road to a fork just before a small quarry and keep right on the water-eroded old road as it rises to meet the power line. Go left on this to the fork with the pink marking tapes.

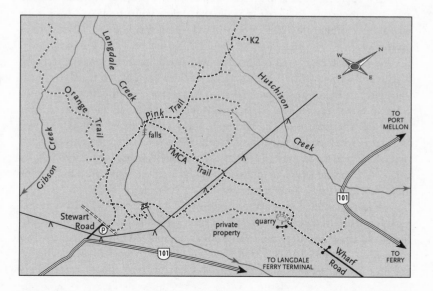

106 SOUTH ELPHINSTONE HERITAGE TRAILS

Round trip 5 km (3.1 mi)	Allow 3.5 hours
Elevation gain 454 m (1490 ft)	High point 680 m (2230 ft)
Roads and trails	Best June to October

Logging artifact on Tramway Trail.

Here is a sporting outing, with, for a bonus, the historical overtones of the area's cedar-cutting industry: a walk that takes you up by one trail with return by another; a walk, too, that may be longer or shorter. The choice is up to you.

One possible beginning is from Gilmour Road, reached from the ferry by following Highway 101 and, where it coincides with North Road, by turning right onto Cemetery Road, then going right again on Gilmour Road to where it is intersected by a power line. Having parked, you should head west up the right-of-way to Keith Road, the continuation of Cemetery. On it, you go right before turning left below Boothill Ranch R.V. Park on a quiet track that brings you to the gate to Mount Elphinstone Pioneer Cemetery. Walk up the road to the cemetery to find your trail bearing the sign "Mt. Elphinstone Trail" starting uphill from just to the left.

Variously named Cemetery or Tramway Trail and marked with red diamonds, this route rises quite steeply at first, with a large wheel, relic of past forest industry, inviting your attention after about 20 minutes. A little farther on, as the slope levels, a trail with white markers goes right, paralleling the route of a one-time flume, but you stay left, arriving almost immediately at Chaster Creek. Here you may observe the remains of an old dam and, in the bushes, an aged donkey engine, relics of the "First Camp," dating back to the early part of the century. Across and above the creek, a bike trail, 102 B.C. North, wanders off left, while your route takes you alongside the moss-covered ruins of a tramway, signs of which accompany you from time to time until you break out on an old B & K logging road, renamed West Ridge Trail, on which you turn right. Eventually, after scrambling across a seemingly endless series of ditches, you come to another instance of past exploitation of the mountain: the route to the site of an abandoned cablevision tower. (With the desire, the energy and lots of time, you might ascend the extra, steep 270 m (900 ft) to the former site for magnificent views over Gibsons and the islands at the mouth of Howe Sound.)

In any event, this is your return route, Cablevision Trail, identified by yellow markers. However, you may go a little farther, almost to the end of the old road, where the Shaker Trail, this time marked in orange, winds its way downhill to the site of a former Japanese camp on Gibson Creek. At this point the yellow and orange trails are quite close, and this is your opportunity, if you have descended thus far on Shaker Trail, to make your way back to Cablevision Trail via the white route that heads off right above the crossing of the creek. (If you opt to remain with the orange route, you will come down to the power line at Stewart Road, leaving you with another half-hour's walk on the right-of-way to retrieve your vehicle.)

Back with the yellow markers you continue downhill, your trail zigzagging back and forth across the route of the old cablevision line until finally you emerge on Gilmour Road opposite a house. Here a turn right brings the power line into view again, ending your expedition back into history.

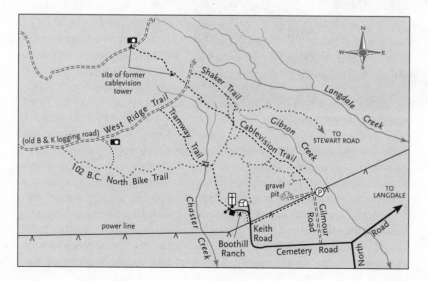

107 TRIANGLE LAKE

Round trip 7.8 km (4.8 mi)　　Allow 3 hours
Trails and roads　　　　　　　Good all year

Ascending a rocky section of trail.

It's not often on the Sechelt Peninsula that you find a trail that doesn't owe its existence to an old logging or skid road, but in the Triangle Lake Trail we have such a one, a foot trail built in 1995 into the ecologically interesting and sensitive peat bog area around the lake. If you wish to make a circular outing, however, your return takes the customary route along an old road.

To start, drive Highway 101 northwest about 7 km (4.3 mi) from the traffic lights at Sechelt and go left on the Redrooffs Road for 1.8 km (1.1 mi). The trailhead is marked by three yellow posts on the right, just past the turnoff to Sargeant Bay Provincial Park.

On foot you come immediately to the first of many maps with trail and distance information; go right on the footpath towards Colvin Creek, left being the bike route to Trout Lake. Soon you cross the creek and wind upstream in second-growth cedar, with a healthy undergrowth of ferns and moss amongst the stumps and fallen logs. Next you come to a second fork with left heading out to the Trout Lake Trail, so again stay right beside the creek, eventually leaving it to ascend a rocky section, then dropping into a dell on its right with some notable Douglas-firs amongst the cedar. Shortly thereafter a short spur to the left leads out to a sunny bluff with a view of a cutover area being reclothed by young trees, through which you may pass on your return trip if you opt for the circuit. Back on the trail, you meet and go right briefly on an old road before climbing up and over a dry spine, ideal habitat for some arbutus trees.

At the next junction you are provided with the information that you have come 3.2 km (2 mi) from Sargeant Bay and have to go only 0.5 km to reach the lake. With this joyful news you proceed on your way to arrive, not beside the lake as you anticipated, but at a small lookout above it with no access to the water and its surrounding peat bog. Still, from your vantage point you may observe water lilies and other colourful marsh plants as well as an eagle or two if you are lucky—recompense for any disappointment.

You may return as you came. For variety, however, at the first junction after leaving Triangle Lake, head for the Trout Lake Trail turning left and south on the old road, which travels mainly through alder and young conifers. After some 20 minutes go left, then left again following signs for Sargeant Bay, eventually passing from young forest into an area of old timber, with yet another fork left, another right and finally the meeting with your outward route. If this sounds a little confusing, be reassured: the Sargeant Bay Society that initiated the project has provided trail signs liberally along both biking and hiking routes.

With its approach road so close, you may want to top off your day with a visit to Sargeant Bay, where besides a charming bay and shoreline there is a marsh bordering the small Colvin Lake on the landward side, lots of birdlife and a possible beaver dam in competition with the fish ladders at the outlet from the lake.

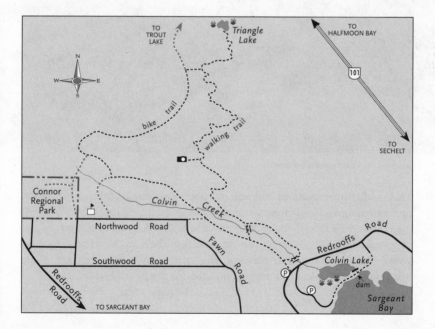

108 MOUNT DANIEL

Round trip 5 km (3.1 mi)
Elevation gain 375 m (1230 ft)
Marked route

Allow 2.5 hours
High point 420 m (1375 ft)
Best May to October

Admiring the view from Mount Daniel.

This miniature mountain, supposedly once associated with the initiation rites of young Sechelt Native women, provides an interesting adventure outing, with a superb view over Pender Harbour, its islets, bays and peninsulas to round off the experience. Mount Daniel is the double summit seen on your left front as you drive north on Highway 101 towards the Garden Bay Road junction, 5.8 km (3.6 mi) beyond the Madeira Park turnoff. Go left as for Garden Bay and drive 3.2 km (2 mi) to the high point, where an old road goes off left.

Though your track has provided access to a garbage dump in the not-too-distant past, the objects in it are becoming nicely grassed over, their location, perhaps, a midden for some future archaeologist to study the quaint artifacts of twentieth-century humans. Stay left twice, changing direction the second time and reaching a point where the road was blocked by old tree roots and the like. On the left side of this obstruction the trail, well-trodden now, takes off through a thicket of alder.

Keep a watchful eye on the track as you gradually work round to the right, with a luxuriant growth of ferns on either side of your route. Steadily you rise; the fern changes to salal, and higher still you may have to negotiate a few deadfalls. After about an hour's walking, you reach a bluff where the last vestiges of the one-time logging road end; a taped trail, however, continues south, and this brings you to the main summit in another 10 minutes or so. But—there is little view.

For this, you must look for tapes that lead you down and round to open rock where the above lack is amply remedied; Garden Bay is right at your feet and Beaver Island stretches to the southwest. Here is a spot for contemplation, especially on a warm summer evening, with the westering sun etching the Vancouver Island mountains across the strait. It is a natural temple that you will be loath to leave.

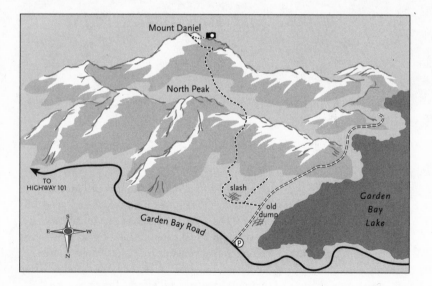

109 SKOOKUMCHUCK NARROWS

Round trip 8 km (5 mi)
Trails

Allow 3 hours
Good all year

Tidal race off North Point.

Anyone who visits the Sechelt Peninsula and fails to pay respects to this natural wonder is missing an unforgettable experience; and it is free in return for the expenditure of the small amount of energy required to walk on good, virtually level trails. The shoreline by the great tidal race is provincial parkland, too, so there are no attempts at commercial exploitation of a scene of great beauty. Check tide tables beforehand to ensure that the waters are either strongly ebbing or flowing, or, better still, plan to be there for an hour before and after a tide change, so that you have the full effect of the spectacle.

To reach the beginning of the trail, turn right off Highway 101 at the Egmont signpost, a little short of the Powell River ferry terminal at Earls Cove. Drive 5.4 km (3.4 mi) on this roller coaster of a road, passing two lakes, North and Waugh, before coming to the parking spot just before a country store. After studying the information board at the trailhead, follow the road down to cross a small creek before climbing uphill past a bakery and some houses that share the right-of-way. Soon, however, signs of human settlement disappear and you are alone with the forest, a healthy second growth, its floor carpeted with salal, red-flowering currant and a variety of ferns.

After 20 minutes or so you see water through the trees, but as you come closer, you recognize it for the surface of another lake, not the inlet that you are seeking. Still among trees, the trail follows its southern shoreline, then leaves it behind. Next, some 2.8 km (1.7 mi) from the start of your walk, you come to the first dividing of the ways; the left-hand trail leads to toilets, North Point and the Narrows Viewpoint, and its right-hand fork is anonymous as it goes off a little uphill. Nevertheless, following it may be the more rewarding choice.

If you do so, you eventually come to a notice announcing the proximity of the narrows, and soon you emerge on a brow of rock overlooking the great race. Then, as you follow the coast trail back, you have varied opportunities to watch the tide flowing into or out of Sechelt Inlet, noting its great whirlpools and eddies as well as the tremendous rush of white water. The two points, Roland and North, give grandstand views of the spectacle from the inlet to its mountain background, but the great attraction is the unresisting flow of water over the submarine rock ledges. And should you be there at low tide as well, the exposed rocky shoreline displays a wealth of intertidal life as bonus.

When time comes to return, you can only retrace your steps, first to the junction and thence back to the trailhead, humbled perhaps by the sheer power and beauty of these natural forces; or perhaps silently pondering the origin of the names. It would be inspiring if the person who named Egmont did so with the chords of Beethoven's great overture ringing in his ears as an aural counterpoint to the visible grandeur of the scene. In contrast, *skookumchuck* is the Chinook term for powerful water, though it is interesting that *skookum* in Salishan originally meant demon, a not unlikely connotation.

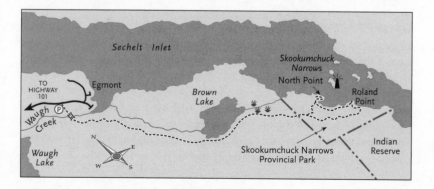

OTHER DESTINATIONS

The destinations listed here, with a brief note on their respective approaches, provide short walks that may be combined with other activities on family outings.

VANCOUVER

COAL HARBOUR SEAWALK: You may now make your way along the harbour front all the way from Devonian Harbour Park just south of the Stanley Park Causeway as far as Canada Place.

CAMOSUN BOG: Part of Pacific Spirit Regional Park, with access from Camosun Street and 19th Avenue. Information and brochures may be obtained from the park office on West 16th Avenue.

FRASER RIVER PARK: From S.W. Marine Drive turn south on Angus Drive to study human and natural history.

MUSQUEAM PARK: Park on Crown Street just south of S.W. Marine Drive. Trails through the park connect with horse trails to and along the Fraser River.

QUEEN ELIZABETH PARK: Go east from Cambie Street on 30th Avenue for this, the highest point in Vancouver.

VANDUSEN BOTANICAL GARDEN: Parking is located on the west side of Oak Street at 37th Avenue (admission charge).

EAST OF VANCOUVER

BURNABY URBAN TRAIL: One of the more attractive parts of the trail runs from Cliff Avenue at Hastings Street to Squint Lake Park off Greystone Drive.

ROBERT BURNABY PARK: This gem of a park is approached from either Kingsway or Canada Way, by driving northeast on 16th Avenue then left on 1st Street. Next go right on 20th Avenue, then immediately left on Hill Avenue and finally left past the tennis courts.

QUEEN'S PARK: The "grande dame" of parks in New Westminster has its entrance off First Street at Third Avenue. You may also turn west off McBride Boulevard going south.

GLENBROOK RAVINE PARK: Across McBride Boulevard from Queen's Park, this park is on the site of the former B.C. Penitentiary. Continue south on McBride then go left on Columbia Street, left on Richmond Street and left again on Jamieson Court.

BARNET MARINE PARK: The park sign is on the north side of Highway 7A (Barnet Highway) in Burnaby. A shoreline trail is being developed along this part of Burrard Inlet.

RIVERVIEW FOREST: This mini-wilderness forest may be reached from Mundy Lake Park at its exit east of Lost Lake or from roadside parking on Mariner Way where a large sign marks its entrance. Leave Highway 1 on Gaglardi Way (Exit 37), turn right on Lougheed, then left on Austin Avenue to its end at Mariner Way, where you go left and uphill.

In Fraser River Park. (p. 230)

Skunk cabbage.

MAQUABEAK PARK: Turn off Highway 1 at Exit 44, just west of the Port Mann Bridge. Follow the signs for United Boulevard South, from which you go left on Burbridge Street, following signs for the park under the bridge. A trail runs upstream as far as the mouth of the Coquitlam River.

WEST VANCOUVER

AMBLESIDE PARK: Providing for diverse activities, this seaside park is reached by going south off Marine Drive on 13th Street.

CAULFEILD TRAIL: From just west of Cypress Creek in West Vancouver turn south from Marine Drive onto Stearman Avenue, then go briefly west on Ross Crescent to parking on the left. The walk extends 1.3 km (0.8 mi) west on beach and rocks to Caulfeild Cove.

CENTENNIAL SEAWALK: This popular waterfront esplanade has numerous access points south from Marine Drive between 13th and 25th Streets.

DOUGLAS WOODWARD PARK: Turn north off Highway 1/99 (Upper Levels Highway) at 15th Street (Exit 11), go right on Cross Creek Road, left on Tyrol Road, briefly right again on 15th, then left to parking at the end of Camelot Road.

VILLAGE WALKS: A map showing the routes and distances of three walks is located in Memorial Park at the intersection of Marine Drive and 19th Street. The West Vancouver Municipal Map, also showing the routes, is available from the Municipal Hall at 750 17th Street.

NORTH VANCOUVER

GROUSEWOODS: Drive or bus to Cleveland Park on the east side of Nancy Greene Way, cross the park diagonally to emerge on Cliffridge Avenue, go left and left again on Esperanza Drive to its end, where the trails begin.

PRINCESS PARK: From Lonsdale Avenue in North Vancouver, drive east on Osborne Road and north on Princess Avenue to the parking lot. Walks radiate from here through the park, along a power line and along Hastings Creek.

UPPER HASTINGS CREEK: This interesting valley in North Vancouver is reached by leaving Highway 1/99 (Upper Levels Highway) at Exit 19, driving east on Lynn Valley Road, with a left on Fromme Road and left again on Wendel Street taking you to Chaucer Avenue, where the creek is on the north side. Its trails may link with those in Princess Park.

HARBOURVIEW PARK: This little park on the east side of Lynn Creek in North Vancouver is reached by turning south off Main Street on Mountain Highway, going right on Dominion Street, right again on Harbour Avenue, then left to park close to the creek.

WINDRIDGE PARK: Mount Seymour Parkway, reached from Exit 22 off Highway 1/99 (Upper Levels Highway), provides the approach. Go off it to the right on Lytton Street to park near the Ron Andrews Recreation Centre.

MAPLEWOOD FLATS CONSERVATION AREA: Follow the Dollarton Highway for 2 km (1.2 mi) east of the Ironworkers Memorial (Second Narrows) Bridge and go right to parking at the Pacific Environmental Science Centre. Paths are wheelchair accessible, with free guided walks available summer evenings and weekends (phone 604-924-2581).

INDIAN RIVER NEIGHBOURHOOD TRAILS: Arriving by car, turn up Mount Seymour Road and park at the lot just north of Hamber Place; by bus, start on a lane going north off Mount Seymour Parkway just east of the fire station.

SOUTH OF VANCOUVER (RICHMOND)

IONA BEACH REGIONAL PARK: Turn off Highway 99 immediately south of the Oak Street Bridge onto Sea Island Way, cross the swing bridge and turn right on Grauer Road, right again on McDonald, and left on Ferguson. Besides bird watching and picnicking, there is a 4-km (2.5-mi) jetty that you may walk or cycle.

SOUTH OF VANCOUVER (DELTA)

BURNS BOG: This raised peat bog is the remnant of a lake formed during the retreat of the ice at the end of the last glacial era. Part of the bog, preserved as the Delta Nature Reserve, may be approached most easily from Vancouver by driving south on Highway 91 and going right at the first exit after the Alex Fraser Bridge for Nordel Way/River Road. Keeping right for River Road, go right again on Nordel Court and head for the far side of the Great Pacific Forum parking lot.

GEORGE C. REIFEL MIGRATORY BIRD SANCTUARY: Turn right off Highway 99 onto Highway 17 (Exit 28) south of the George Massey Tunnel, then go right again on Highway 10 (Ladner Trunk Road), which becomes 48th Avenue. Jog half left onto 47A Avenue at a traffic light, then left again onto River Road. Continue west and turn right to cross a single-lane bridge onto Westham Island and follow the signs to the parking area. For information about admission fees and hours, call 604-946-6980.

LADNER HARBOUR PARK: Just south of the George Massey Tunnel, turn off Highway 99 at Exit 29 for Ladner. Follow River Road west, then turn north at the bridge across the slough.

SOUTH OF VANCOUVER (SURREY)

BEAR CREEK PARK: Parking is off 88th Avenue and 140th Street east of Highway 99A (King George Highway) in Surrey. This park has many trails, picnic areas and a children's playground.

ELGIN HERITAGE PARK: To visit this ecologically rich marsh and historically significant park on the lower Nicomekl River, take Highway 99A (King George Highway) south, turn west onto Crescent Road, then go right just past 140th Street to the park.

GREEN TIMBERS PARK: The entrance leading to some 5 km (3 mi) of trails is on 100th Avenue in North Surrey, between 140th and 148th Streets. The park lies north of the heritage Green Timbers Urban Forest, as yet undeveloped.

HI-KNOLL PARK: Noted for its wildflowers and its undisturbed forest, this area may be reached by taking Highway 10 east to 192nd Street and going south, then east on Colebrook Road, which splits the park almost in two.

SERPENTINE FEN: Located in the triangle between Highways 99 and 99A (King George Highway), Surrey's wildlife area is most easily approached southwards via the latter road. For the main parking and picnic area turn west on Wade Road (44th Avenue) at the garden shop.

SEMIAHMOO HERITAGE TRAIL: Only fragments remain of this historic trail that provided a route from the Native villages in the south to the salmon-fishing grounds of the Fraser delta. One short segment starts at the Elgin School at the intersection of Crescent Road and 144th Street. Another cuts across the eastern corner of Sunnyside Acres Urban Forest (Walk 67) and may be joined from the crosswalk over 148th Street just south of 28th Avenue.

REDWOOD PARK: From Highway 1 at Exit 53 drive south on 176th Street (Highway 15) and go left (east) on 20th Avenue to the park sign on the right. The park was part of the homestead of a settler whose eccentric sons collected and planted 32 species of trees, native and exotic. Walking trails let you examine these as well as the treehouse, the sons' final home.

FRASER VALLEY SOUTH

FORT LANGLEY: For this national historic park, the birthplace of B.C., turn off Highway 1 at 200th Street (Exit 58) and follow signs.

GLEN VALLEY REGIONAL PARK: In addition to fishing and picnicking here, you will find short trails amongst the cottonwoods at Poplar Bar, which you reach by going north on 264th Street (Country Line Road) from Highway 1 (Exit 73), right on 88th Avenue, then left on 272nd Street to River Road, where you go right to the park.

CENTENNIAL PARK (ABBOTSFORD): Nature trails, fishing, swimming and picnicking are only a few of the activities available in this park on the shore of Mill Lake. Leave Highway 1 at Exit 87 and go north on Clearbrook Road, east on South Fraser Way and south on Gladwin Road to the park.

SUMAS MOUNTAIN: For a walk atop this mountain, leave Highway 1 east of Abbotsford at Exit 95 (Whatcom Road) and drive east along North Parallel Road to Sumas Mountain Road. Now go north for almost 8 km (5 mi) to Batt Road, on which you go right for 1 km (0.6 mi) before doubling back right on an unpaved service road, which winds its way for just over 7 km (4.5 mi) to a parking spot on the left at a trail down to Chadsey Lake. Another kilometre (0.6 mi) brings you to road's end beside a microwave tower convenient for trails to the summit and down to the lake.

Woodpecker holes in cedar.

FRASER VALLEY SOUTH (CHILLIWACK AREA)

ROTARY VEDDER RIVER TRAIL: Now part of the Trans Canada Trail, this multi-purpose trail has fine views of mountain and river and also provides good fishing. It has several access points, but the most popular is from Vedder Road, on which you drive south from Highway 1 at Exit 119A to the parking spot just before the Vedder Bridge.

MOUNT THOM: From the summit of this miniature mountain you have magnificent views of Cultus Lake, the Fraser Valley and the mountains beyond. Drive east from Chilliwack to Exit 123 and go south on Prest Road then left (east) on Bailey Road, which becomes Elk View Road. Next turn right (south) on Ryder Lake Road, which becomes Extrom, then right on Forester Road and right again on Churchill Park Way to the park entrance.

BRIDAL VEIL FALLS: Turn south off Highway 1 at the Agassiz-Rosedale junction (Exit 135) and continue about 1.6 km (1 mi) on the frontage road before going right towards the falls.

CHEAM LAKE WETLANDS REGIONAL PARK: About 5 km (3 mi) of trails and boardwalks have been developed on the site of a one-time mine for agricul-

Columnar basalt seen from CalCheak Trail. (p. 210)

tural marl lime. Leave Highway 1 at Exit 135, go north on Highway 9, right on Yale Road East to Popkum Road North, left as far as Elgey Road, then left again to the park.

CHILLIWACK RIVER ECOLOGICAL RESERVE: Depart Highway 1 at Exit 119A and drive south to Vedder Crossing, then east about 40 km (25 mi) to Chilliwack Lake and another 12 km (7.5 mi) along the lake to parking at Depot Creek.

FRASER VALLEY NORTH

BURNT HILL (BIG PINE MOUNTAIN): Access to this ecological reserve is from the east side of Rannie Road (Walk 78) via a narrow board over a ditch.

STAVE RIVER WETLANDS TRAIL: Turn north from Highway 7 (Lougheed Highway) on 287th Street near Ruskin and drive to Ruskin Dam. Cross it, and watch for the Ruskin recreation site sign on your right. Walk south from the parking area.

NEILSON REGIONAL PARK: From Highway 7 (Lougheed Highway) east of Mission at Hatzic, turn north on Dewdney Trunk Road, go right on McEwen Avenue, then left on Edwards Street East to the park by Hatzic Lake.

CASCADE CREEK FALLS: Turn north from Highway 7 (Lougheed Highway) on Sylvester Road some 6.5 km (4 mi) east of Mission City. Continue for 13.6 km (8.5 mi) to Ridge View Road and go right for about another kilometre.

DAVIS LAKE: For this provincial park, continue north on Sylvester Road (see above) for 2.8 km (1.7 mi) to a wide layby on the left just beyond Murdo Creek. From here a steep trail descends by the McDonald Falls to the lake.

DEWDNEY (HATZIC) DYKE: Drive east on Highway 7 (Lougheed Highway) to McKamie Road, 6.5 km (4 mi) beyond the eastern junction with Highway 11 in Mission. Turn right, cross the railway tracks and go left at the first fork to a gate on the dyke, with parking on the left at the Dewdney Nature Regional Park.

HARRISON AREA

HEMLOCK VALLEY: Turn north off Highway 7 (Lougheed Highway) at the Sasquatch Inn in Harrison Mills. Drive about 7.8 km (5 mi) before going left on the Hemlock Valley approach road. The amenities are generally closed in summer, so take a picnic.

WEAVER CREEK: The salmon spawning grounds are 11.2 km (7 mi) north of the Sasquatch Inn, where you turn off from Highway 7 (Lougheed Highway). Spawning is normally near the end of October.

HARRISON LOOKOUT: Turn off Highway 7 (Lougheed Highway) at Harrison Mills as for Weaver Lake (Walk 88) and drive 37.8 km (23.5 mi), the last 26.6 km (16.5 mi) on gravel, to a fork where the mainline continues ahead and up. Now go right for about 500 m to a parking spot opposite the trailhead sign. A short, steep trail ascends to the now historic B.C. Forest Service lookout with its panoramic views.

KILBY PROVINCIAL PARK: Turn south off Highway 7 (Lougheed Highway) just east of the Harrison River bridge for this park where you may enjoy wildlife, walking or exploring the past at the Kilby General Store.

WHIPPOORWILL POINT: Walk westwards along the esplanade in Harrison Hot Springs to the hot spring building, behind which a rough trail ascends. En route to the point it passes a secluded little beach at Sandy Cove.

HOWE SOUND

KEATS ISLAND: For anyone who enjoys riding ferries this is the ideal outing, but it does require perfect timing, involving as it does two ferries with interlocking schedules: the morning ferry from Horseshoe Bay is met at Langdale by the *Dogwood Princess* (limited space and no vehicles), berthed immediately to the right and ready to depart for New Brighton on Gambier Island en route to Keats Island. Here there are several possible walks as well as swimming and picnicking at Plumper Cove across the island. Be mindful to ascertain ferry times to ensure you make the connections necessary for your return.

PORTEAU COVE: As well as recreational diving you may enjoy a stroll or camp in this provincial park, located almost 25 km (15.5 mi) north of Horseshoe Bay.

MURRIN PROVINCIAL PARK: This small park is 3 km (1.9 mi) north of Britannia Beach. Park on the west side of the road for a pleasant walk along Browning Lake.

SQUAMISH/PEMBERTON

BRACKENDALE DYKES: Bald eagles congregate in this area from late fall to early spring. Drive north from Squamish, turning west off Highway 99 (Sea to Sky Highway) on Mamquam Road, then north on Government to an area opposite the Easter Seal Camp.

CAT LAKE RECREATION AREA: A trail encircles this small lake, which you approach from Highway 99 by going right on the Cheekye River Forest

Service Road, 3.6 km (2.2 mi) north of the Alice Lake turnoff, thereafter following signs for Cat Lake for just over 2 km (1.2 mi).

RAINBOW FALLS: Turn left off Highway 99 as you approach Whistler from the south, go west on Alta Lake Road, crossing the railway and driving along the north sides of Alpha, Nita and Alta Lakes, to park at the crossing over Twentyone Mile Creek. The falls are a short distance upstream from the Rainbow Lake trailhead.

LOST LAKE (WHISTLER): From Highway 99 turn right on Village Gate Boulevard, go left on Blackcomb Way and park in lot #3, from which the trail begins.

VALLEY TRAIL (WHISTLER): This paved walkway, bikeway and winter cross-country ski trail runs across the valley floor from Alpha Lake, past Nita, Alta, Lost and Green Lakes. It has numerous access points, including that via Lost Lake, above.

BLACKCOMB MOUNTAIN: For an unforgettable outing, choose a fine day mid-June to early September and invest in a ticket on the Wizard Express, which rises to 1860 m (6100 ft) from the Blackcomb Daylodge in the Upper Village, which you may reach by a pedestrian trail from parking lot #3. A useful brochure provides descriptions of various trails on top.

WHISTLER MOUNTAIN: Across Fitzsimmons Creek Valley from Blackcomb you may enjoy magnificent mountain scenery by taking the Whistler Express (Gondola) from the south end of the main village to 1837 m (6030 ft). Arm yourself first with the brochure describing trails and other mountain activities.

COUGAR MOUNTAIN ANCIENT CEDARS: Turn left from Highway 99 at the north end of Green Lake and drive 5 km (3.1 mi) to the trailhead, staying right at forks. A 4WD vehicle is recommended.

NAIRN FALLS: A little south of Pemberton and 28 km (17.4 mi) north of Whistler on Highway 99, these falls may be reached by walking upstream along the Green River from the provincial park's day-use parking lot.

SUNSHINE COAST

CHASTER PARK (GOWER POINT): At School Road, the main street of Gibsons becomes Gower Point Road. Follow this scenic road along the coast to the park.

CLIFF GILKER REGIONAL PARK: For a variety of forest walks with two scenic creeks on the right of Highway 101, drive west about 10 km (6 mi) beyond the Sunnycrest Mall in Gibsons.

Beach at Point Grey. (p. 18)

CHAPMAN CREEK: Drive Highway 101 to Davis Bay and turn in to Brookman Park immediately west of the bridge over Chapman Creek. The trail makes its way up the creekside for nearly 3 km (1.9 mi).

CHAPMAN CREEK FALLS: From Highway 101, 1.8 km (1.1 mi) east of the Sechelt traffic light or about 2 km (1.2 mi) west of Davis Bay, turn uphill on Selma Park Road for about 350 m, then go left up a dirt road to meet a power line. Stay west of the reservoir fence along the pipeline road into the bush, driving as far as you feel comfortable.

SECHELT MARSH: Drive north on Wharf Avenue from the traffic light and continue down to a little bridge just before you reach the head of Sechelt Inlet. The trailhead is on the left just beyond the bridge.

PORPOISE BAY PROVINCIAL PARK: Turn right on Wharf Avenue at the Sechelt traffic lights and follow signs for 5 km (3.1 mi) to the park. Just beyond the park entrance, where the road crosses Angus Creek, a nature trail starts on the north side and takes you through maple and Sitka spruce to the estuary. Chum and coho salmon can be seen spawning in the creek in season.

GRAY CREEK FALLS: Turn north from Highway 101 at the traffic light in Sechelt onto Wharf Avenue, then go right again on Sechelt Inlet Road to the Gray Creek bridge, 8.5 km (5.3 mi) from the light. The trail follows the south bank to two sets of falls.

KINNIKINNICK PARK: To reach this delightful little maze, drive up Trail Avenue from Highway 101 (or Dolphin Street) in Sechelt, turn right on Reef Road, then left on Shoal Way. Pass the arena and go right just before the golf course on Fairway Avenue, at the top of which is a trailhead sign and map.

CONNOR PARK: This small regional park may be approached from Redrooffs Road by going east on Frances Avenue, then north on Westwood Road to its intersection with Northwood Road. The trailhead lies just west of Halfmoon Bay Elementary School.

SMUGGLER COVE: A foot trail leads to this beautiful provincial marine park from parking on Brooks Road 5 km (3.1 mi) from Highway 101, which you leave 14.5 km (9 mi) north of the traffic lights in Sechelt.

PENDER HILL: For superlative views of the Pender Harbour area, drive west on Garden Bay Road from Highway 101. Fork right on Irvines Landing Road, right again on Lee Road for about 1 km (0.6 mi), then right once more following the Sunshine Coast Regional Park signs. From the small parking area a well-graded trail rises about 185 m (600 ft) to the open, rocky summit.

RUBY LAKE–KLEIN LAKE: Part of the long-distance Suncoaster Trail, the lower end of this 4-km (2.5-mi) section begins on the opposite side of Highway 101 from the Dan Bosch Regional Park just 600 m north of the Ruby Lake Resort. Rising some 150 m (500 ft) to the top of the bluffs, it provides fine views of the Ruby Lake area before continuing beyond the pass to Klein Lake.

USEFUL BOOKS

Armstrong, John E. *Vancouver Geology*. Vancouver: Geological Association of Canada, 1990.

Bovey, Robin, and Wayne Campbell. *Birds of Vancouver and the Lower Mainland*. 2nd ed. Edmonton: Lone Pine Publishing, 2001.

Bryceland, Jack, and Mary and David Macaree. *103 Hikes in Southwestern British Columbia*. 5th ed. Vancouver: Greystone Books, 2001.

Cannings, Richard, and Sydney Cannings. *British Columbia: A Natural History*. Vancouver: Greystone Books, 1996.

Cousins, Jean. *Nature Walks around Vancouver*. Vancouver: Greystone Books, 1997.

Lyons, Chester P., and Bill Merilees. *Trees, Shrubs, and Flowers to Know in British Columbia and Washington*. Edmonton: Lone Pine Publishing, 1995.

Parish, Roberta, and Sandra Thomson. *Tree Book: Learning to Recognize Trees of British Columbia*. 2nd ed. Victoria: Ministry of Forests, 1994.

Pojar, Jim, and Andy MacKinnon, eds. *Plants of Coastal British Columbia including Washington, Oregon & Alaska*. Vancouver: Lone Pine Publishing, 1994.

Stoltmann, Randy. *Hiking Guide to the Big Trees of Southwestern British Columbia*. 2nd ed. Vancouver: Western Canada Wilderness Committee, 1991.

Vancouver Natural History Society. *Nature West Coast: As Seen in Lighthouse Park*. 2nd ed. Vancouver: Sono Nis Press, 1987.

——. *The Birders Guide to Vancouver and the Lower Mainland*. Edited by Catherine J. Aitchison. Vancouver: Whitecap Books, 2001.

WEB SITES

B.C. Hydro recreation site at Buntzen Lake
    http://www.bchydro.com/recreation/buntzen.html
British Columbia Provincial Parks
    http://wlapwww.gov.bc.ca/bcparks/index.htm
Burnaby Parks, Recreation and Cultural Services Department
    http://www.burnabyparksrec.org
Coquitlam Parks and Environment, City of
    http://www.city.coquitlam.bc.ca/Parks_Environment/Parks1.htm
Cypress Bowl Recreations Trailmap
    http://www.cypressbowl.com/trail.html
Cypress Provincial Park (PDFs of brochure and map)
    http://wlapwww.gov.bc.ca:80/bcparks/explore/parkpgs/cypress.htm
District of North Vancouver links to trails and parks
    http://www.district.north-van.bc.ca
Federation of Mountain Clubs of B.C.
    http://www.mountainclubs.org
Fraser Valley Regional District Parks
    http://www.fvrd.bc.ca/Regional_Parks/regional_parks.htm
Greater Vancouver Regional District bus information
    http://www.translink.bc.ca
Greater Vancouver Regional District Parks
    http://www.gvrd.bc.ca/services/parks/index.html
Trans Canada Trail official Web site
    http://www.tctrail.ca
Surrey Parks, Recreation and Culture, City of
    http://www.city.surrey.bc.ca/ParksRecCulture/Parks%20&%20Outdoors/
    Parks.htm
Vancouver Board of Parks and Recreation
    http://www.city.vancouver.bc.ca/parks
West Vancouver Parks and Community Services
    http://www.westvancouver.net/parks_and_community/
    parks_and_trails.asp

WALKING TIMES

Time	#	Walk name
2	18	Deer Lake
2	95	Four Lakes Trail
2	54	Historic Mushroom Loop II
2	5	Jericho Park/Spanish Banks
2	80	Mike Lake
2*	20	Molson Way (South)
2	35	Point Atkinson (west)
2	9	Renfrew Triangle
2	28	Ridge Park Loop
2	84	Rolley Lake and Falls
2	103	Shadow Lake Interpretive Forest
2	23	Shoreline Trail (Port Moody)
2	8	Stanley Park
2	74	Teapot Hill
2	68	Tynehead Regional Park
2	32	Whytecliff
2.5	81	Alouette Nature Loop
2.5	58	Baden-Powell Trail (Deep Cove)
2.5	25	Belcarra Regional Park (Jug)
2.5	99	Brohm Lake
2.5	98	Brohm Lake Interpretive Forest
2.5	21	Burnaby Fraser Foreshore Park
2.5	12	Capitol Hill
2.5	69	Derby Reach Regional Park
2.5	56	Dog Mountain (direct)
2.5	7	False Creek
2.5	55	Goldie Lake
2.5	91	Killarney Lake
2.5*	72	Matsqui Trail
2.5	31	Minnekhada Regional Park
2.5	87	Mission Trail
2.5	47	Mosquito Creek (to Montroyal)
2.5	108	Mount Daniel
2.5	22	Mundy Park
2.5	57	Mystery Lake (peak)
2.5	2	Pacific Spirit Regional Park (e-w)
2.5	50	Rice Lake (from Lynn Headwaters)
2.5	104	Soames Hill Regional Park
2.5	94	Squamish Estuary
3	46	Baden-Powell Trail (Grouse-orig)
3	37	Black Mountain Loop
3	65	Boundary Bay (north)

Time	#	Walk name
3*	29	PoCo Trail
3	61	Richmond South Dyke Trail
3	24	Sasamat Lake/Woodhaven Swamp
3	90	Sasquatch Provincial Park
3	33	Seaview/Baden-Powell
3	15	SFU/Stoney Creek
3	109	Skookumchuck Narrows
3	107	Triangle Lake
3	51	Two-Canyon Loop
3	1	UBC Gardens
3	88	Weaver Lake
3	30	Woodland Walks (Lower Burke Ridge)
3.5	14	Burnaby Mountainside Trails (long)
3.5	82	Gold Creek Trails (lookout)
3.5	82	Gold Creek Trails (Viewpoint Beach)
3.5	85	Hayward Lake (Railway)
3.5	42	Hollyburn Heritage Trails
3.5	92	Porteau Bluffs (to viewpoint)
3.5	106	South Elphinstone Heritage Trails
3.5	34	Trans Canada Trail/Nelson Creek Loop
3.5	79	UBC Malcolm Knapp Research Forest
4	41	Brothers Creek Trails
4	64	Brunswick Point
4	70	Campbell Valley
4	44	Capilano Canyon (from Ambleside Park)
4	101	Crater Rim Loop
4	6	English Bay
4	97	Evans Lake Forest (ridge circuit)
4	53	Historic Mushroom Loop I
4	78	Pitt Wildlife Management Area
4	73	Seven Sisters Trail (high)
4	93	Shannon Falls (high bluff)
4.5	77	Alouette River Dykes
4.5	39	Baden-Powell Trail (Hollyburn Ridge)
4.5	70	Campbell Lake Trail (to helipad)
4.5	86	Hoover Lake Forest Trail (& views)
4.5	105	K2 (from Stewart Road)
4.5	40	Lower Hollyburn
4.5	4	Point Grey
5	26	Buntzen Lake
5	97	Evans Lake Forest (to Hut Lakes)
5	30	Woodland Walks (Coquitlam)

Time	#	Walk name
5.5	85	Hayward Lake (Reservoir circuit)
5.5	60	Lulu Island Dykes
5.5	92	Porteau Bluffs (to Phyllis Lake)
6	89	Campbell Lake Trail (to lake)
6	105	K2 (from ferry)

* one-way

ROUND-TRIP DISTANCES

Walk Distances (km)

Distance	#	Walk name
2	93	Shannon Falls (Olesen Creek)
3	43	Ballantree
3	83	Kanaka Creek (Riverfront Trail)
3	57	Mystery Lake (lake)
3	50	Rice Lake (from LSCR)
3+	36	Cypress Falls Park
3.2	62	Richmond Nature Park
3.3	48	Upper Lonsdale Trails
3.5	83	Kanaka Creek (Canyon Loop)
3.5	47	Mosquito Creek (to Mahon)
3.9	3	Chancellor Woods (short)
4	71	Aldergrove Lake Regional Park (short)
4	65	Boundary Bay (south)
4	76	Chatham Reach (from Harris)
4	38	Cypress Bowl
4	96	DeBeck Hill
4	35	Point Atkinson (east)
4	67	South Surrey Urban Forests (Crescent)
4	67	South Surrey Urban Forests (Sunny)
4.4	63	Deas Island
4.5	44	Capilano Canyon (from park road)
4.5	59	Indian Arm Parks (long)
4.5	57	Mystery Lake (peak)
4.8	73	Seven Sisters Trail (low)
4.8	68	Tynehead Regional Park
5-	32	Whytecliff
5	46	Baden-Powell Trail (Grouse-current)
5	11	Burnaby Heights/Trans Canada Trail
5	27	Colony Farm Regional Park
5	66	Crescent Beach (north)
5	87	Mission Trail
5	108	Mount Daniel
5	35	Point Atkinson (west)
5	9	Renfrew Triangle

Distance	#	Walk name
5	28	Ridge Park Loop
5	84	Rolley Lake and Falls
5	93	Shannon Falls (high bluff)
5	23	Shoreline Trail (Port Moody)
5	104	Soames Hill Regional Park
5	106	South Elphinstone Heritage Trails
5	74	Teapot Hill
5.1	49	Lynn Headwaters Loop (Trail)
5.2	25	Belcarra Regional Park (Burns)
5.3	58	Baden-Powell Trail (Deep Cove)
5.5	25	Belcarra Regional Park (Jug)
5.5	14	Burnaby Mountainside Trails (short)
5.5	18	Deer Lake
5.5*	20	Molson Way (South)
5.5	2	Pacific Spirit Regional Park (e-w)
5.6	80	Mike Lake
5.7	99	Brohm Lake
6	81	Alouette Nature Loop
6	46	Baden-Powell Trail (Grouse-orig)
6	3	Chancellor Woods (long)
6	102	Cheakamus Lake
6	56	Dog Mountain (direct)
6	95	Four Lakes Trail
6	55	Goldie Lake
6	5	Jericho Park/Spanish Banks
6	92	Porteau Bluffs (to viewpoint)
6+	45	Bowser Trail
6.4	54	Historic Mushroom Loop II
6.4	88	Weaver Lake
6.5	12	Capitol Hill
6.5	31	Minnekhada Regional Park
6.5	90	Sasquatch Provincial Park
6.5	103	Shadow Lake Interpretive Forest
6.7	42	Hollyburn Heritage Trails
6.8	47	Mosquito Creek (to Montroyal)
7	71	Aldergrove Lake Regional Park (long)
7	70	Campbell Lake Trail (to helipad)
7	22	Mundy Park
7	94	Squamish Estuary
7	8	Stanley Park
7.5	37	Black Mountain Loop
7.5	86	Hoover Lake Forest Trail (lake)

Distance	#	Walk name
10.5-	26	Buntzen Lake
11-	41	Brothers Creek Trails
11	16	Burnaby Lake
11.3-	39	Baden-Powell Trail (Hollyburn Ridge)
11.5	86	Hoover Lake Forest Trail (& views)
12-	70	Campbell Valley
12-	40	Lower Hollyburn
12	14	Burnaby Mountainside Trails (long)
12	44	Capilano Canyon (from Ambleside Park)
12	85	Hayward Lake (Railway)
12	78	Pitt Wildlife Management Area
12	61	Richmond South Dyke Trail
13-	6	English Bay
13	97	Evans Lake Forest (to Hut Lakes)
13	4	Point Grey
14-	64	Brunswick Point
14	105	K2 (from ferry)
14	92	Porteau Bluffs (to Phyllis Lake)
14.5	77	Alouette River Dykes
17	85	Hayward Lake (Reservoir circuit)
23	60	Lulu Island Dykes

* one-way distance
+ or longer
- or shorter

INDEX